Between Levinas
and Lacan

Between Levinas and Lacan

Self, other, ethics

Mari Ruti

Bloomsbury Academic
An imprint of Bloomsbury Publishing Inc

B L O O M S B U R Y
NEW YORK • LONDON • NEW DELHI • SYDNEY

Bloomsbury Academic

An imprint of Bloomsbury Publishing Inc

1385 Broadway	50 Bedford Square
New York	London
NY 10018	WC1B 3DP
USA	UK

www.bloomsbury.com

**BLOOMSBURY and the Diana logo are trademarks
of Bloomsbury Publishing Plc**

First published 2015

© Mari Ruti, 2015

Library of Congress Cataloging-in-Publication Data
Ruti, Mari.
Between Levinas and Lacan: self, other, ethics/Mari Ruti. – 1st [edition].
pages cm
Includes bibliographical references and index.
ISBN 978-1-62892-640-8 (hardback: alk. paper) – ISBN 978-1-62892-639-2
(pbk.: alk. paper) 1. Lévinas, Emmanuel. 2. Phenomenology. 3. Other (Philosophy)
4. Ethics. 5. Lacan, Jacques, 1901-1981. 6. Psychoanalysis. I. Title.
B2430.L484R88 2015
194–dc23
2015000845

ISBN: HB: 978-1-6289-2640-8
PB: 978-1-6289-2639-2
ePub: 978-1-6289-2642-2
ePDF: 978-1-6289-2643-9

Typeset by Deanta Global Publishing Services, Chennai, India

CONTENTS

AUTHOR'S NOTE

In this book, I use the lowercase *other* to refer to the intersubjective other (the other person). When the word is capitalized, it refers to the Lacanian big Other (the symbolic order). Many of the authors I quote do not adhere to this distinction, but their usage should be clear from the context. I have opted for the pronoun *it* when referring to the human subject in order to avoid unnecessary gendering. Otherwise, *he* and *she* are used randomly, depending on context and author's whim.

PREFACE

This book charts the ethical terrain between Levinasian phenomenology and Lacanian psychoanalysis. At first glance, these two approaches may seem more or less incompatible, and in many ways they are, particularly in their understanding of the self-other relationship. If Levinas views the other as a site of unconditional ethical accountability, Lacan is interested in the subject's capacity to dissociate itself from the (often coercive) desire of the other—whether the big Other of symbolic law or more particular others who, for the subject, embody this law. That is, if the Levinasian subject is asked to honor the other regardless of how this other conducts him- or herself, the Lacanian subject behaves "ethically" when it rejects the hegemonic—or otherwise wounding—injunctions of the other. For both Levinas and Lacan, the subject's relationship to the other is primary in the sense that the subject, literally, does not exist without the other, but they see the challenge of ethics quite differently: while Levinas laments our failure to adequately meet the ethical demand arising from the other, Lacan laments the consequences of our failure to adequately escape the normative forms this demand frequently takes. By this I do not mean that Lacan vilifies all interpersonal relationships but merely that, for him, our dependence on the other is one of the ways in which disciplinary power infiltrates our psychic lives. This explains why Lacan does not join Levinas in celebrating the inviolability of the other but instead seeks to rupture the unconscious fantasies that render us overly compliant with respect to the other's desire; it explains why Lacanian ethics sometimes sounds like a mockery of everything that Levinas stands for.

Undoubtedly, the Levinasian approach speaks more easily to our everyday notion of ethics in the sense that we are used to thinking that we should respect the other regardless of how confusing or repellent she may seem. This stance in fact—explicitly or implicitly—underpins many of the difference-based ethical paradigms of contemporary theory. And it has generated one of the most powerful ethical visions of the last decade: Judith Butler's ethics of precarity as an ethics that posits shared human vulnerability—our primordial exposure to others—as an ontological foundation for global justice. At the same time, the Lacanian perspective has also gained momentum in recent years, in part due to Slavoj Žižek's tireless efforts to introduce Lacanian theory to a broad readership and in part due to the relatively recent North American "discovery" of the work of Alain Badiou. Žižek has theorized the so-called Lacanian "act"—a destructive or even suicidal act that allows the subject to sever its ties with the surrounding social fabric—as a countercultural intervention with potentially far-reaching ethical and political consequences. Badiou, in turn, has explained how the truth-event (a sudden revelation of a hitherto invisible truth) can compel the subject to revise its entire mode of being despite the potentially high social cost of doing so. In other words, if for Levinas and Butler, ethics is a matter of recognizing the primacy of the other, for Lacan, Žižek, and Badiou, it is a matter of a profound reconfiguration of subjectivity—of the kind of realignment of priorities that makes it impossible for the subject to stay on the path that it has, consciously or unconsciously, chosen for itself (and that others may expect it to follow).

This book outlines the major differences between Levinas and Butler on the one hand and Lacan, Žižek, and Badiou on the other, focusing specifically on the skirmishes between Butler and Žižek. The most acute example of the latter can be found in *Contingency, Hegemony, Universality: Contemporary Dialogues on the Left*—a text that Butler and Žižek coauthored with Ernesto Laclau in 2000.[1] This text starts out, innocently enough, as a collaboration but quickly disintegrates into a heated, ideologically driven confrontation between the three authors. Comparable—albeit more isolated—bursts of frustration can be found elsewhere in the work of Butler and Žižek from the last two decades, and they always circle back to the same questions about the constitution of subjectivity (e.g., Is there such a thing as the Lacanian real?) and the contours of political action (e.g., Is postmodernism capitalist ideology in disguise?). I will be referring to such debates throughout this book. However, ultimately, my objective is to show that, underneath these differences, one can discern, in the work of Butler and Žižek, a common concern with the thorny relationship between the singularity of experience and the universality of ethics. This concern in fact underlies the work of all the major thinkers I have chosen to examine in this book in the sense that they all, in one way or another, recognize that the singularity of lived experience does not necessarily (and perhaps *should* not) lead to ethical relativism but can be reconciled with the quest for universally applicable ethical principles. However, this quest should not be confused with the attempt to revive the universalism of Western metaphysics, for if Levinas, Butler, Lacan, Žižek, and Badiou have one thing in common, it is their rejection of the sovereign Enlightenment subject, which means that the universalism they advocate cannot be based on principles such as rationality or autonomy but must, instead, seek alternative forms of legitimation. For Levinas and Butler, it is the subject's relational ontology that offers such legitimation: insofar as the subject owes its very existence to the other, its responsibility to the other is nonnegotiable and without exception. Žižek and Badiou, in turn, maintain that even though the act or the event always arises from a specific situation, and even though it annihilates the subject's fantasies of rational self-mastery, the illumination it provides strikes the subject with the force of a universal truth (which is precisely why it cannot be ignored).

Universalism has been a sore spot in contemporary progressive thought because post-'68 theory, for excellent reasons, aligns it with metaphysical foundationalism and Western imperialism. Butler, Žižek, and Badiou, in their own ways, all recognize this alignment, yet they also suggest that embracing ethical relativism—as some strands of poststructuralism and multiculturalism tend to do[2]—is not necessarily the best solution to the violence of traditional Western universalism. As a result, they reach beyond the Enlightenment for alternative ethical paradigms that combine a universalist ethos with a deep respect for the irreducible singularity of experience. How, they ask, can we arrive at generalizable principles of ethical conduct in the context of the immense diversity of human experience? How do we decide what is right or wrong without sliding back into the arrogant solipsism of Western exceptionalism? How do we meet the suffering of others without reducing them to objects of our pity? Does ethics arise from the vulnerable face of the other, as it does in

Levinas? Or does it demand that we look past the specificity of the face to impersonal principles of justice? And what do we do with a face that seems altogether evil, that refuses to respect the integrity of other faces? Where do we draw the line of ethical conduct in a world that recognizes few points of commonality between peoples, cultures, and religions?

The chapters that follow consider such questions in greater detail, but it is worth noting right away that, among the thinkers in question, Butler is the one who most struggles with the universalist implications of her ethical model: perhaps due to her strong poststructuralist inclinations—inclinations that Žižek and Badiou do not share—Butler finds it difficult to acknowledge the universalist tenor of her ethics of precarity even though her efforts to deny this tenor result in theoretical aporias that are impossible to resolve. This is why I have chosen to characterize Butler's universalism as "reluctant" and why I repeatedly call her on the conceptual inconsistencies of her theory even though I tend to agree with her views politically. One might say that my disagreements with Butler are frequently less about the substance of her arguments than about her attempt to have her theoretical cake and eat it too, to remain "a good poststructuralist"—a critic who denounces universalism on ideological grounds—at the same time as she devises an ethical model that is arguably *more* universalist than its Enlightenment predecessors. Her ethics of precarity, I will illustrate, cannot work without a grounding in a generalizable ontology of human vulnerability, with the result that her efforts to downplay its universality ring false.

My disagreements with Butler run through the chapters of this book in ways that make it impossible to deny that I have singled her out as the special target of my critique. Though I also call attention to the problematic aspects of the theories of Žižek and Badiou, especially their unwillingness to admit that the specificity of subject position—based on race, ethnicity, gender, sexuality, religion, and so on—continues to matter in today's world of institutionalized social inequalities, it is Butler who receives most critical attention. This is nothing new in my writing, for I have long found Butler's theories of subjectivity, particularly her assertion that we are all psychically attached to our subjection, too disempowering in discounting the ways in which many of us—not just academics but also defiant people around the world—are capable of taking a degree of critical distance from the power structures that oppress us and sometimes even rising against these structures.[3] In short, Butler's relationship to social power has always seemed unnecessarily meek and, unfortunately, her appropriation of Levinasian ethics during the last decade, as well as her recent (and related) "turn to religion," have fanned the masochistic timbre of her theories to new heights, so that her main message, these days, appears to be that unless I am willing to inhabit the position of relentless self-abnegation, I am automatically a pathetic ethical failure. One of my aims in this book is to demonstrate that this position is counterproductive, and perhaps even harmful, for those whose psyches have been terrorized by interpersonal or collective violence—that such individuals have little to gain from a theory that tells them, as Butler tends to do, that their efforts to build a stronger sense of agency are intrinsically unethical. Simply put, I wish to ask why autonomy is such a red flag for Butler despite the fact that most of the world's population is arguably not suffering from an excess of smug confidence. If, as Butler herself repeatedly reminds us, we are precarious and broken, why insist on breaking us more?

I begin my analysis with a critical overview of the Levinasian-Butlerian position, highlighting the strengths and weaknesses of the idea that a postmetaphysical ethics must begin from the other as an entity that undercuts the subject's coherence of being rather than, say, from *a priori* norms of ethical conduct. Chapter 1 traces Levinas's efforts to "break the obstinacy of being"—the arrogance of the sovereign *I*—that, in his view, characterizes the history of Western philosophy all the way up to Heidegger's attempts to link existential authenticity to the subject's anxiety about the prospect of its death. Arguing that it is not the subject's own death, but rather the death of the other, that matters, Levinas builds a relational ethics that posits the subject's responsibility for the other as unconditional and irrevocable. The vulnerability of the other as "face," Levinas argues, "interrupts" the subject's complacency of being, inaugurating an ethical demand that cannot be ignored. At the same time, Levinas draws a clear distinction between ethics (where normative considerations have no place) and justice (which arbitrates between individuals on the basis of *a priori* norms of right and wrong), thereby suggesting that justice curtails our ethical accountability. I propose that his distinction—which recognizes the importance of normative deliberations—is what Butler loses track of in her efforts to translate the Levinasian ethical paradigm into a blueprint for global justice, with the consequence that her theory places no limits on the behavior of the victimizer.

Chapter 2 offers a more detailed reading of Butler's efforts to build an ethics of precarity capable of addressing concerns of global justice. I find Butler's ethics compelling for its capacity to devise a model of universalism—of generalizable human vulnerability—that sidesteps some of the failings of Enlightenment universalism, such as its excessive rationalism. I appreciate Butler's ability to level distinctions between individuals and to reveal the core of woundability that may allow people of vastly different backgrounds and life experiences to empathize with each other's suffering, and consequently perhaps to do something about this suffering. Yet I also question Butler's conviction that grief serves as a basis for ethical and political accountability, for it seems to me that grief could just as well have the opposite effect of paralyzing action. Even more insidiously, the emphasis on grief could make relatively privileged Western subjects feel like they are accomplishing something—working for social justice—when in fact nothing is changing in the world; the notion that there is something inherently "decent" about grief could make it too easy for Westerners to feel so good about their "virtuous" capacity to mourn the losses of the rest of the world that they (conveniently) cease to feel any urgency about doing anything else.

Chapter 3 introduces the Lacanian counterpoint to the Levinasian-Butlerian model, explaining why Žižek and Badiou refuse to view precarity as a feasible foundation for ethics. Essentially, Žižek and Badiou believe that when we choose to define the human being as a victim, we foreclose the possibility of the kinds of courageous acts (or events) that disturb the status quo of the hegemonic cultural order and that, potentially at least, allow new social configurations, including more just collective arrangements, to come into being. Žižek and Badiou themselves advocate a more radical approach, arguing that it is only when the subject risks its ordinary way of being (including, perhaps, its grief) that it becomes a "real" subject—a subject with agency and thus the capacity for ethical and political action. In more explicitly psychoanalytic terms, because Žižek and Badiou define the Lacanian "real" as an internal limit to the proper functioning of the symbolic order—as a site of the kind of unruly jouissance that the symbolic desperately seeks, but ultimately fails, to metabolize—they regard the subject's capacity to tap into this real as a source of both personal and collective rebelliousness.

Chapter 4 pursues this line of reasoning by bringing Lacan into conversation with Herbert Marcuse and recent feminist and queer theory. The main question of this chapter is how it is that some subjects become defiant enough to stage acts of personal or collective resistance. I argue that, on a basic level, defiance often arises from a curiosity about alternative ways of living—from what some would label "deviant" desires—and that psychoanalysis, at least as Lacan envisioned it, is one way to cultivate such curiosity. Ultimately, I wish to show that when feminist and queer theory chooses to embrace a more revolutionary spirit than the one offered by Butlerian notions of performativity, resignification, and reiteration, it is highly compatible with Lacanian theory. This is a reality that both Butler and Žižek have tried to deny, albeit for opposing reasons: Butler (for bad reasons) dislikes Lacan too much to be willing to acknowledge his value for feminist and queer theory, whereas Žižek (for equally bad reasons) dislikes feminist and queer theory too much to be willing to acknowledge any kinship between its central concerns and his beloved Lacan. I hope to illustrate that such theoretical wedges are as unnecessary as they are misleading.

Chapter 5 revisits the major themes of the book by focusing on what I see as the major shortcoming of both the Levinasian-Butlerian model and the loosely Lacanian model of Žižek and Badiou, namely their attempt to devise an ethics wholly devoid of any normative content. Because both of these approaches reject the legacies of the Enlightenment more or less wholesale, they also— by default, as it were—reject the parameters of normative ethics, including the possibility of *a priori* norms.[4] Though I understand the reasons for this rejection, I show that it leads to the kinds of ethical impasses that are difficult to defend. In the Levinasian-Butlerian model, it gives rise to the assumption that the other is sacred— and therefore beyond reproach—regardless of how appallingly she behaves; in the Lacanian model, it gives rise to the assumption that any action is justifiable as long as it expresses the "truth" of the subject's inner directive (what Lacan characterizes as the truth of the subject's desire). To address this problem, I introduce key ideas about normative ethics developed by Habermasian feminists Seyla Benhabib, Nancy Fraser, and Amy Allen. Perhaps most important among these is the notion that the Habermasian discourse model allows for the possibility of *a priori* principles that are normatively legitimate and binding without being metaphysically grounded. Such principles are fashioned through an ongoing democratic process, which means that they are intrinsically provisional—valid only until they are displaced by a revised set of norms—yet, for the time being, they are capable of guiding decisions regarding right and wrong. Butler, Žižek, and Badiou have all been scornful of Habermasian ethics because of its rationalist biases, but it is easy enough to show that the feminists who have taken Habermas seriously have worked quite hard—and successfully—to correct these biases, and that they have, moreover, managed to grapple productively with the question of how we might be able to address normative concerns without resorting to a fixed definition of what justice is supposed to entail.

For me, reading Habermasian feminists in preparation for writing this book was an intellectual game changer because they brought to the task a "real-life" component—even a "levelheadedness," for lack of a better word—that I have found missing in my own field of progressive critical theory (broadly understood). Readers who are familiar with some of my previous work know that I have been annoyed at some of the conceptual excesses of my field, wondering what it is that we are doing (besides building our careers) when we come up with one theory after another that *sounds* intensely transformative but that has limited viability outside the pages of an academic tome. In a way, I have always been "a bad poststructuralist" in the sense that I believe that there are things "outside the text," and that our texts—whenever relevant (which is not always)—should somehow address this outside. I do not mean to suggest that I believe in "reality" as an entity that can be distinguished from the discursive, conceptual, and ideological categories that we use to make sense of it; the "world," for me, is always a socially constructed world. Still, I have found myself repeatedly butting heads with critics who appear more interested in locating the next radical edge—the point of highest rhetorical impact—in critical theory than in following the movement of thought to places that they could actually back up by their real-life choices.

I realize that this way of putting things risks implying that theory, for me, is not a part of "real life." This, however, is not what I mean, for I believe that theory—or theorizing—can be a "real-life" intervention, that there is often something intrinsically "alive" about theory. The task of theory, for me, is to reveal previously unrecognized possibilities (for life, desire, action, thought, the imagination, and so on)—possibilities that are not always realizable in the "real" world but that cause us to see differently, and perhaps, as a result, allow us to make different kinds of decisions about how we approach the task of living. In Wendy Brown's words, "As a meaning-making enterprise, theory depicts a world that does not quite exist, that is not quite the world we inhabit. But this is theory's incomparable value, not its failure."[5] As a theorist, I can hardly contest Brown's conclusion that theory's "most important *political* offering is this opening of a breathing space between the world of common meanings and the world of alternative ones, a space of potential renewal for thought, desire, and action" (*EW* 81).

I could not agree more. Yet I have also learned that there is, for me, a line—an admittedly blurry one—that sometimes emerges in specific contexts and tells me that "now theory has stepped over the ledge," that "now theory is merely regurgitating what everyone in the field already takes for granted," that "now theory has become dogmatic," that "now theory is merely interested in its own voice," or that "now theory has become self-indulgent, devoid of any 'real-life' power." Though I concur with Brown that theory is never "wrong" per se, but merely more or less illuminating, more or less provocative, more or less persuasive (*EW* 81), I am increasingly impatient with the kind of theorizing that feels more like an empty exercise in writerly acrobatics than an exercise in thought. My judgment about this can be unpredictable in the sense that sometimes opaque, challenging texts—like those of Lacan—feel like a genuine exercise in thought, whereas other convoluted texts make me suspect that they are using their density opportunistically, as a way of hiding the relative simplicity of their ideas. In addition, writing this book taught me that I have a lot more tolerance for writerly acrobatics in contexts other than ethics—that there is something about the "real-life" weightiness regarding how we conceptualize ethics, including what is fair and what is not, whose pain counts and whose does not, and who gets blamed and who does not, that makes me particularly wary of theoretical approaches that seem too disconnected from the "real" world of suffering.

Against this backdrop, reading Habermasian feminists came as an inspiration in the sense that I was introduced to arguments that felt exciting without being one-sided, over the top, or shrouded in discursive mystifications designed to make ideas sound more difficult than they actually are. *Measured* is the term that jumps to mind, and though there are those in my field who would translate this into *timid, boring, and conformist*, I kept translating it into *smart—very smart indeed*. What is more, reading Benhabib, Fraser, and Allen made me realize that, if I am going to be honest about it, I have more appreciation for basic Enlightenment values of equality, justice, reciprocal respect, and democratic process than my training in poststructuralist theory and Lacanian psychoanalysis might suggest. Indeed, I came to recognize that I am not alone in this, that when it comes to ethics specifically, progressive critics (Butler included) sometimes fall back on the very Enlightenment values they criticize. This in itself is not a problem, for it is entirely possible to be critical of values that one also on some level esteems. The problem, rather, is the stubborn denial of this esteem in posthumanist theory, for this denial keeps us stuck in predictable patterns of thought when it would be more interesting to create conversations across ideological boundaries. I concede that staging a conversation between Lacan and Habermas might not get us too far. But staging one between Lacanians—among whom I sometimes count myself—and Habermasian *feminists* could have wide-ranging theoretical repercussions, not the least because these feminists have their own way of being critical of Enlightenment philosophy. It is because I wanted to start such a conversation that I ended up concluding this book with the kinds of normative considerations that are rarely a part of posthumanist theory. I do not offer any resolutions, any grand reconciliations; I merely crack open the door in the hope that others will walk through it.

Acknowledgments

I am deeply thankful to the following individuals for making this book possible: my all-around amazing editor at Bloomsbury Press, Haaris Naqvi; my talented and meticulous research assistants Julia Cooper and Philip Sayers; my colleagues Amy Allen, Stefan Bird-Pollan, Anupama Mohan, Noriko Murai, Gail Newman, Ross Truscott, and Sang Wu for inviting me to present from this book at their respective institutions; Maurits van Bever Donker for his astute response to my paper on Butler at the University of the

Western Cape; Sara Salih for her unfailing acumen; the students in my 2013–14 graduate seminars; and the generous peer reviewers who expressed the kind of faith in my work that I myself do not always have. I am also grateful to the Canadian Social Science and Humanities Research Council for its support for this project. An overview of the book's arguments was published in *Angelaki: Journal of the Theoretical Humanities*. An abridged version of Chapter 4 was published in *The Journal for the Psychoanalysis of Culture and Society*. Finally, thanks to Spencer Mackoff for restoring my faith in young Lacanian-Žižekians. Losing that faith in 2012 shattered a great deal (see Chapter 3), so getting some of it back has meant more than I can say.

1

Breaking the obstinacy of being: Levinas's ethics of the face

Ethics, concern for the being of the other-than-oneself, non-indifference toward the death of the other, and hence, the possibility of dying for the other—a chance for holiness—would be the expansion of that ontological contraction that is expressed by the verb to be, dis-inter-estedness breaking the obstinacy of being, opening the order of the human, of grace, and of sacrifice.

EMMANUEL LEVINAS[1]

1

It is, these days, a theoretical commonplace that there is no self without the other—that the self owes its very existence to those who have facilitated its coming-into-being and who sustain its ongoing attempts to claim a foothold in the world. Human ontology, in other words, is inherently social so that it makes no sense to talk about the self as an autonomous entity who unilaterally acts on the world. Rather, the self—the human subject—is formed and maintained through its bonds to others, bonds that, among other things, make it susceptible to suffering. This has tremendous repercussions for ethics, for if subjectivity is inherently relational—if the presence of the other is constitutive of subjectivity as such—there is no way to envision the subject outside of ethics; the subject is implicated in an ethical relationship to the other from the get-go, before it has developed the capacity to make normative distinctions between right and wrong. This way of envisioning subjectivity is one reason that Levinasian phenomenology has played such a crucial role in recent ethical theory, for Levinas sought to understand precisely what it means to proceed from ethics to ontology rather than the other way around. He sought to grasp how ethics is something that the subject engages in through its very act of taking up space in the world, through its very act of inhaling oxygen that is, consequently, not available to someone else.

For Levinas, every breath I take is a breath that the other cannot take. I am, in a fundamental sense, always already guilty in that my existence, almost by definition, diminishes the other's chances of survival; the simple fact of my being—my capacity to be—represents an infringement of someone else's being. This is why Levinas argues that my "place in the sun" is nothing but "a usurpation of places that belong to the other man who has already been oppressed or starved by me" (*EN* 130). On this view, the Pascalian notion of "a place in the sun" is the prototype of violence, "of occupying the place of another, and thus, concretely, of exiling him, of consigning him to the miserable condition in some 'third' or 'fourth' world, of killing him" (*EN* 149). Though it is easy to find moments of Eurocentrism, xenophobia, and racism in Levinas, in this instance he connects the violence of (ontological) being to the violence of Western imperialism specifically, suggesting that there is a link between the flourishing of the Western subject and the nonflourishing of the non-Western one. That is, an awareness of biopolitical and necropolitical forces seems intrinsic to Levinasian ethics even if this awareness often remains implicit. On the most concrete level, this ethics is premised on "a concern for the other man, a care for his food, drink, clothing, health, and shelter" (*EN* 212).

This concern for, and primacy of, the other leads to an unconditional, irrevocable, and asymmetrical ethical accountability that makes me answerable to the other regardless of how the other behaves. Later in this chapter, and throughout this book, I will address the problematic aspects of this vision. But at this early point in the argument, let me merely emphasize that this unqualified responsibility arises precisely from the fact that, for Levinas, there is no self without the other: because of the essentially relational nature of subjectivity, the other animates my being in ways that make it impossible for me to dissociate myself from the other. Or, to use a verb that Levinas often uses, the other "interrupts" my consciousness and self-consistency, leaving an imprint that is both inaugurative and ineradicable. This imprint brings me into existence as a subject and there is nothing I can do to rid myself of the ethical burden it places upon me; my social formation means that I cannot, under any circumstances, refuse, renounce, or trade away my responsibility for the other, nor can I expect the other to reciprocate it. I am, as Levinas puts it, a "chosen hostage": I have been selected for an eternal bondage to the other ("For all eternity, one man is answerable for an other"), yet I welcome my bondage as the precondition of my being (*EN* 227).

Levinasian ethics notoriously crystallizes on the other as face. Although Levinas maintains that the face should not be understood in a narrow way—that the face "is not the color of the eyes, the shape of the nose, the ruddiness of the cheeks, etc." (*EN* 232)— there is obviously something about the face that, for him, most viscerally conveys the vulnerability, defenselessness, woundability, and mortality of the other. As Levinas indicates, the face represents "extreme exposure—before all human intending—as to a shot at 'point blank' range" (*EN* 145). Such an exposed face "summons me, demands me, claims me: as if the invisible death faced by the face of the other—pure otherness, separated somehow from all unity—were 'my business'" (*EN* 145). The other "regards" me not only in the sense that he looks at me but also in the sense that his well-being is, immediately and primordially, my responsibility. If I turn away from the other in indifference, I become an accomplice in, and answerable for, his death. Again, Levinas emphasizes that the face should not be taken literally, noting that if I am standing in line outside of Lubyanka, Moscow, waiting for news of a friend or relative arrested for "political crimes," the naked neck of the person in front of me can evoke my responsibility for him or her just as effectively as a face would (*EN* 232). Yet there is still something about the face that conveys the absolute singularity of the other, reminding me that the other is utterly irreducible to myself; the other as face is completely exposed yet also enigmatic, beyond my grasp, which is why he or she cannot but derail ("interrupt") my ontological complacency.

The Levinasian notion of the other as a site of irreducible alterity has had a tremendous impact on posthumanist theorizing about interpersonal ethics. From the attempts of Luce Irigaray and Jacques Derrida to conceptualize a form of relationality that does not strive to assimilate the other to the self to Eric Santner's attempts to conceptualize ways of embracing the contorted opacity (or "creatureliness") of the other,[2] contemporary thinkers have been fascinated by the idea that the other intrinsically eludes our comprehension. Levinas certainly lends himself to such a reading, for he envisions the face as what cannot be "possessed" by our conceptual grids. As he expresses the matter, "The face, for its part, is inviolable; those eyes, which are absolutely without protection, the most naked part of the human body, none the less offer an absolute resistance to possession."[3] This resistance to possession defies fusion between self and other, preserving "the discontinuity of relationship"; it ensures that the other remains utterly transcendent, utterly foreign, in the sense that I cannot reduce him to what is familiar to me: while the other as face appeals to me, rendering me responsible, he simultaneously "breaks with the world that can be common to us."[4] It is for this reason that ethics, for Levinas, is an invocation "prior to commonality," "a relation with a being who, in a certain sense, is not in relation to me—or, if you like, who is in relation with me only inasmuch as he is entirely in relation to himself" (EN 33). "In its epiphany," Levinas specifies, the sensible part of the other "turns into total resistance to the grasp" (TI 197).

The other's resistance to my grasp can, unfortunately, cause me to want to violate the other. As Levinas explains, it is a "resistance in which the temptation to murder is inscribed": "The Other is the only being that one can be tempted to kill. This temptation of murder and this impossibility of murder constitute the very vision of the face. To see a face is already to hear 'You shall not kill,' and to hear 'You shall not kill' is to hear 'Social justice'" (DF 8–9). The face therefore presents both the temptation and the impossibility of murder. Because the face reveals what is weak, bare, and destitute in the other, it raises the possibility of the other's death, and therefore of

what Levinas describes as "an incitement to murder, the temptation
to go to the extreme, to completely neglect the other" (*EN* 104).
But it also functions as an absolute prohibition against murder; the
face may provoke my aggressive impulses, but it also calls me to an
unqualified responsibility to *not* act on that aggression. As Levinas
argues, if the face opens the prospect of a "total negation," to be
in relation to the face is, precisely, "to be unable to kill" (*EN* 10).
Ethics, in this sense, does not eradicate violence but rather entails
a relentless struggle to fend off the temptation of aggression. As
Judith Butler remarks in a different context, nonviolence "involves
an aggressive vigilance over aggression's tendency to emerge as
violence."[5]

2

Levinas thus privileges relationality over ontology, particularly over
consciousness as a structure of "being," which is exactly why he—to
refer back to the quotation with which I opened this chapter—
seeks to break "the obstinacy of being," to explode the "ontological
contraction that is expressed by the verb to be," so as to move
beyond the sovereign, self-contained *I* to the realm of what he
calls "the order of the human, of grace, and of sacrifice" (*EN* 202).
Levinas repeatedly contrasts his vision with that of Heidegger: if
Heidegger is primarily interested in *Dasein*'s undertaking of being—
in a relatively self-centered venture that does not leave much room
for the idea that "giving, feeding the hungry and clothing the naked
is the meaning of being" (*EN* 116)—Levinas locates meaning solely
in the subject's relationship to the other. He in fact draws a distinction
between "being" as a site of ontological exertion on the one hand
and "the human" as a modality of intersubjective generosity on the
other, specifying that ethics is where "the human" erupts into the
economy of being in ways that disrupt the age-old plot of ontology
(*EN* xiii); "humanity," in short, ruptures "being." In this manner,
ethics—what Levinas famously characterizes as "otherwise than
being"—shatters the subject's preoccupation with itself, its struggle
for survival, its solipsistic obsession with its "perseverance," and
replaces these by a devotion to the other: "When human existence
interrupts and goes beyond its effort to be—its Spinozan *conatus
essendi*—there is a vocation of an existing-for-the-other stronger

than the threat of death: the fellow human being's existential adventure matters to the *I* more than its own, posing from the start the *I* as responsible for the being of the other" (*EN* xii–xiii).

The properly human, for Levinas, therefore begins when I transcend my ontology and begin to exist for the other. In this sense, ethics brings about a kind of crisis, upheaval, or suspension of being, which jolts me out of my absorption in my own life. Furthermore, Levinasian ethics demands that I prefer "injustice undergone to injustice committed" (*EN* 132), which is why I cannot, under any circumstances, injure the other. Quite the contrary, I should be willing to sacrifice myself for the other, to die in the other's place or—when this is not possible (say, because the other is going to die anyway)— to make sure that the other does not die alone. Of course, I cannot actually die for the other in any ultimate sense for the simple reason that the other will always eventually die; I cannot make the other immortal. But there are situations where I can postpone the other's death, where I can, for instance, redirect the aggressor's murderous rage from the other to myself. And, at the very least, I can make sure that I do not remain indifferent to the other's death, that I do not callously turn away from the other's need at the moment of his or her death.

In this context, Levinas postulates that there is something self-serving about Heidegger's attempt to locate the possibility of existential authenticity in *Dasein*'s relationship to its own death. Referring to Heidegger's notion of "being-toward-death," Levinas complains: "The uniqueness of the human *I*, which nothing should alienate, is here thought in terms of death: that everyone dies for himself. An inalienable identity in dying!" (*EN* 226). In this manner, Levinas faults Heidegger for not recognizing that it is not my own death, but the death of the other, that should concern me. Along closely related lines, Levinas criticizes Heidegger for conceptualizing authenticity "in terms of the 'mine,' of everything personal, in terms of *Jemeinigkeit*, an original contraction of the me in mineness . . . in terms of a *belonging to self* and *for self* in their inalienable self-belonging" (*EN* 225–6). In other words, Heideggerian authenticity is problematic for Levinas because it "must remain pure of all influence undergone, without admixture, without owing anything to anyone, outside of everything that would compromise the noninterchangeability, the uniqueness of that *I* of 'mineness'" (*EN* 226).

It may well be theoretically inconsistent for Levinas to attack the uniqueness of the *I* while at the same time insisting on the uniqueness of the other (on his "total resistance to the grasp"), for this implies that the *I* never occupies the place of impenetrable otherness. Yet Levinas's accusation that Heideggerian authenticity aspires toward the kind of pristine purity of being that cannot tolerate "admixture" of any kind also carries a particular poignancy in the post-Holocaust world within which Levinas sought to stage his ethical intervention. For obvious political reasons, such solipsistic authenticity—which dissolves the subject's connection to others—is what Levinas wishes to reject; arguing that the authenticity of the *I* is not predicated on the self's virile "mineness" but rather on its willingness to sacrifice itself for the other, Levinas effectively undermines Heidegger's *Dasein* as an entity that seeks to reject all "influence undergone."

Though Levinas's critique here is aimed at Heidegger specifically, ultimately it extends to the entire Western metaphysical tradition, of which Heidegger could be argued to be the last—already somewhat rebellious—representative. I say "rebellious" because Heidegger's analysis of the ways in which *Dasein* finds itself "thrown" into a preexisting world, imbricated in the concrete texture of its surroundings, and surrounded by objects and living entities that it should not seek to subjugate, already goes some distance in discrediting the sovereign subject of the metaphysical tradition. Levinas, however, is not convinced by Heidegger's efforts to break with this tradition, for he reads Heidegger as an inheritor of metaphysical paradigms that defend the self's independence, its robust autonomy, by denying the self's debt to the other, by holding tight onto its "mineness" in the face of any and all contamination by the other. And, as did many other European thinkers of his generation, Levinas concludes that this ethos of "every man for himself," this instinct for "pure being before or without ethics," is "a metaphor for the cruelty of the cruel in the struggle for life and the egotism of wars" (*EN* 202). Levinas thus sees a direct link between the self-governing subject of Western metaphysics and the devastating violence of National Socialism. And, logically, once this link has been established, the only way to prevent similar violence in the future is to find a new model for subjectivity. This is exactly what Levinas's "being-for-the-other," the ethical subject who has been "chosen" for self-sacrifice, is designed to furnish: "It is in the personal relationship, from me to the other, that the ethical 'event,' charity and mercy, generosity and obedience, lead beyond or rise above being" (*EN* 202).

3

It is in part because of his resistance to the metaphysical tradition that Levinas stresses that the ethical relationship to the other is not one of thinking. Thinking, according to him, seeks to triumph over all otherness, to synthesize or summarize it so as to confine it within thought's conceptual system of abstraction. In this sense, thought aims at precisely the kind of possession of the other that Levinasian ethics is meant to counter. As Levinas elaborates, "Thought, *qua* learning [*apprendre*], requires a taking [*prendre*], a seizure, a *grip* on what is learned, and a possession. The 'seizing' of learning is not purely metaphorical. . . . The being that appears to the knowing subject not only instructs it, but ipso facto *gives* itself to it. Perception already grasps" (*EN* 125–6). To this grasping, greedy attitude toward the other Levinas opposes a reciprocal, "interhuman" discourse which does not aim to reduce the other to a set of concepts, for when the other is mediated by concepts, he is forced into a mold that is alien to him. If metaphysical attempts to understand the other ask him to capitulate to a foreign horizon of intelligibility, the Levinasian face-to-face represents "a relation with a depth," "a gap in the horizon" (*EN* 10). Or, to express the matter slightly differently, if inert things let themselves be taken by surprise by understanding, the face in its immediacy cannot be surprised in this manner; if things allow themselves to be distilled into concepts, the face cannot be comprehended in terms of a conceptual apparatus external to itself. That is, as a being whose meaning cannot be captured (tamed, conquered, domesticated) by concepts, the other as face defies generality (the genus): "He does not enter entirely into the opening of being in which I already stand as in the field of my freedom. It is not in terms of being in general that he comes toward me" (*EN* 9–10). In this way, the other safeguards his singularity. Though I may strive to understand him in terms of his history or habits, what "escapes understanding in him is himself" (*EN* 9).

In Chapter 3, we will discover that Slavoj Žižek has accused Levinas of gentrifying the other as face, of downplaying the other's strangeness, but it seems to me that Levinas is well aware of this strangeness, for he repeatedly reminds us that ethics is a matter of relating to what resists easy relationality, what does not open itself to our curiosity or interpretative efforts. Indeed, Levinas explicitly recognizes the other's strangeness when he writes: "The interhuman is also in the recourse that people have to one another for help, before the astonishing alterity of the other has been banalized or dimmed down to a simple exchange of courtesies that has become established as an 'interpersonal commerce' of customs" (*EN* 101). Levinas here admits that we tend to suppress the other's "astonishing alterity" (strangeness) beneath the façade of social niceties that make collective life possible. However, ethics (the "interhuman") intervenes *prior* to this moment of suppression, when the other's strangeness has not yet been "banalized or dimmed down." In this sense, far from gentrifying the other, as Žižek insists, Levinasian ethics strives to preserve his or her uncanny alterity.

A comparison with Heidegger might once again be of use. While Heideggerian ethics asks me to recognize the independent reality of the other—to let the other "be"—Levinasian ethics demands that I meet the nonnegotiable alterity of the other with "sympathy or love, ways of being that are different from impassive contemplation" (*EN* 5). Though the Heideggerian ethos of allowing the other to disclose himself in his own terms, without interference from the perceptual apparatus of the perceiving subject, acknowledges that the other is not merely an object ready-at-hand, an object with use-value, it stops short of sympathy and love; it stops short of admitting that the relationship to the other is intrinsically intersubjective (and thus inherently ethical). Likewise, it fails to admit that the other as face represents what Levinas calls "a *surplus* of significance" (*EN* 131)—a surplus that, precisely, makes it impossible for me to reduce him to a nexus of generalizable attributes that offer me the easy comfort of familiarity because I share these same attributes. This surplus of significance, Levinas proposes, is what demands that I go beyond Heideggerian contemplation by speaking to the other, by addressing him as a living presence for whom I am responsible. In this sense, to the extent that I manage to "understand" the other, "I simultaneously tell him my understanding" (*EN* 7). Relationality, in other words, is inherent to understanding.

More specifically, what sets the ethical relationship apart from mere rational (abstract) understanding is that in "every attitude toward the human being there is a greeting—even if it is the refusal of a greeting" (EN 7). I may refuse to address the other in a greeting, or the other may refuse to acknowledge my greeting, but even in these actions, there is already an encounter, a meeting of some kind. What distinguishes my relationship to the other from my relationship to inert objects is that in the former there is always a call and response, an address and reply, a greeting and reaction (even if this reaction is merely a refusal of the greeting). Sociality, in short, takes precedence over rational understanding. And, as I have underscored, for Levinas, one of the problems with Western metaphysics is that it refuses this sociality, that it uses reason to assassinate alterity. In such reason, "conceptual synthesis and synopsis are stronger than the dispersion and incompatibility of what gives itself as an other" (EN 126). In opposition to such a model—which overcomes the other's resistance by "a cunning trick of the hunter, who catches what is strong and irreducible in a being through its weaknesses"—Levinas envisions reason as an exercise of intersubjectivity in which "things are 'talked over,' in which the resistance of beings *qua* beings is not broken, but pacified" (EN 8).

It is worth noting here that although Levinas admits that there is a certain madness to the degree of nonreciprocal responsibility and self-sacrifice that his ethics calls for, he does not see it as a matter of discarding reason per se but merely of softening reason's tendency to colonize the other: "the beginning of a new rationality beyond being" (EN 228). I call attention to this in part because I would like to counter the contemporary tendency to associate the deconstruction of the Western metaphysical subject—to which Levinas clearly contributes—with the demise of rationality in all of its forms. Later in this book, I will give the irrational a prominent place. But ultimately I would like to make my way to a conception of subjectivity that is at once irrational and (sort of) rational, out of joint and (sort of) "together," self-alienated and (sort of) in touch with itself, driven by unconscious motivations and (sort of) self-reflexive. Levinas does not pick up all these threads, but his emphasis on the fact that the move away from the *conatus essendi* of Western metaphysics does not necessarily imply the loss of rationality but merely its drastic reconfiguration opens a path for rethinking rationality. For Levinas, such a rethinking entails recognizing the entanglement of reason in relationality, in the ethical link between self and other. As he remarks, ethics reaches beyond ontology toward a different type of wisdom, "but without rejecting the peace of reason" (*EN* xi).

4

To recap: because of the insurmountable otherness of the other—of the "surplus of significance" that clings to the other—I cannot ever fully negate him or her. I can annul the being of things by possessing them, but the only way I can annul the other is by murdering him. This is exactly why the other is "the sole being I can wish to kill" (*TI* 198). Yet, as we have learned, ethics dictates that I refrain from killing the other regardless of how he has conducted himself. This is how Levinas arrives at the very difficult idea that even the executioner, even the brute, has a face: "Jean-Toussaint Desanti asked a young Japanese who was commenting on my works during a thesis defense if an SS man has what I mean by a face. A very disturbing question which calls, in my opinion, for an affirmative answer. An affirmative answer that is painful each time" (*EN* 231). The basic asymmetry of intersubjectivity—the fact that I am irrevocably responsible for the other—therefore asks that I honor the face of the other even when the other appears entirely evil. Yet Levinas simultaneously qualifies this disquieting conclusion by distinguishing between the realm of ethics as a face-to-face encounter and the realm of justice as a matter of arbitrating between different faces. "When I speak of Justice," he specifies, "I separate myself from the idea of nonresistance to evil . . . the 'executioner' is the one who threatens my neighbor and, in this sense, calls for violence and no longer has a Face" (*EN* 105). Levinas thus recognizes the necessity of violence when my neighbor is endangered by the executioner. But he seems to reserve the right to a violent response to an institution, such as the juridical system: "There is a certain measure of violence necessary in terms of justice; but if one speaks of justice, it is necessary to allow judges, it is necessary to allow institutions and the state; to live in a world of citizens, and not only in the order of the Face to Face" (*EN* 105). Speaking more concretely, Levinas states, "During the Barbie trial, I could say: Honor to the West! Even with regard to those whose 'cruelty' has never stood trial, justice continues to be exercised. The defendant, deemed innocent, has the right to a defense, to consideration. It is admirable that justice worked that way, despite the apocalyptic atmosphere" (*EN* 231).

What remains unclear here is whether I have the right to act violently in order to defend the other (my neighbor) when he is being threatened by the executioner or whether I must leave this to the justice system. However, Levinas confirms that the "problematic of the executioner" is a matter of justice rather than of ethics, adding that justice alleviates the burden of my ethical accountability: "If there were no order of Justice, there would be no limit to my responsibility" (*EN* 105). That is, justice makes ethics bearable by curtailing its terrain. As Levinas exclaims, if the other as face "were my only interlocutor, I would have had nothing but obligations!" (*EN* 104). Fortunately, justice exists to adjudicate between different faces. If ethics meets the other's face as incomparable and unique, justice makes it its business to "compare incomparables, uniquenesses" (*EN* 202). It represents a collective body—a Third that breaks the ethical dyad of self and other—that is capable of mediating between the potentially competing ethical demands of various faces. Furthermore, Levinas suggests that there are times when I must step into the role of the Third, when justice "takes precedence over the taking upon oneself of the fate of the other," with the result that "I must judge, where before I was to assume responsibilities" (*EN* 104). In other words, there are situations— for instance, when one face violates another—where I must allow justice to trump ethics. In this manner, Levinas grants me—the individual *I*—the capacity to judge but, again, it is unclear whether he would go as far as to condone my violence against the aggressor. Some fundamental questions thus persist: What if my decision to abstain from violence, to stay on the level of mere judgment, means that the violated other perishes in front of my eyes? And what if my judgment of who is being violated differs from that of someone else? What if the person I deem to be the persecutor is, in someone else's judgment, the persecuted?

If Levinas does not offer straightforward answers, it may be because no good ones exist: we have never been able to solve the problems that ensue from the fact that we cannot guarantee the neutrality of justice. But what is apparent is that justice, in Levinas's view, does what ethics cannot—should not even try to—do: it objectifies, thematizes, generalizes, and categorizes. In so doing, it reduces the uniqueness of the face "to the particularity of an individual of the human genus, to the condition of citizen" (*EN* 196). This is an important point that I will come back to below: particularity, for Levinas, is aligned with what is classifiable; somewhat counterintuitively, an individual is "particular" when he or she can be compared with other individuals. And the challenge of justice is precisely that

> behind the unique singularities, one must perceive the individuals of a *genus*, one must compare them, judge them, and condemn them. There is a subtle ambiguity of the individual and the unique, the personal and the absolute, the mask and the face. . . . To the Bible—the first to teach the inimitable singularity, the "semelfactive" uniqueness of each soul, there must be added the Greek writings, expert in species and genera. It is the hour of the Western World! (*EN* 229)

Levinas here combines the ethical legacies of the Judeo-Christian tradition with the juridical legacies of ancient Greece to define the "hour of the Western World": the glory of the West seems to be predicated on its ability to hold ethics and justice in tension without letting one eclipse the other. Ethics is what protects the singularity of each soul; justice, in turn, trades in species and genera. On the side of ethics we find the unique, the absolute, and the face; on the side of justice the individual, the personal, and the mask. This is why one of the difficult tasks of justice is to translate the uniqueness of the face into the mask of citizenship. This mask still showcases the idiosyncrasies of individuality, thereby preserving the impression of particularity even as it allows for comparisons to be drawn between it and other masks. But it hides the singularity of being that only ethics can honor. Justice, after all, is based on the idea of (formal) equality, the reciprocity of rights and duties, which, by definition, demands a degree of generalizability.

Although Levinas thus clearly acknowledges the necessity of justice, ethics for him remains primary in the sense that justice is ultimately derived from ethics: "It is always starting out from the Face, from the responsibility for the other that justice appears" (*EN* 104). Even though justice places the mask of citizenship over the face, it inevitably contains a residue of the face. In other words, behind justice reside the mercy and kindness of ethics: "It is in the name of that responsibility for the other, in the name of that mercy, that kindness to which the face of the other man appeals, that the entire discourse of justice is set in motion" (EN 229). Yet justice tends to lose track of its roots in mercy and kindness, which means that it needs to be continually perfected "against its own harshness" (EN 229); it needs to be reminded of its debt to ethics. Indeed, the virtue of democracy resides in the fact that it is ceaselessly remorseful about the failings of its justice and consequently capable of questioning itself. Because democracy knows that its justice is never just enough—that its justice cannot ever equal the mercy and kindness that inspire it—it is "always concerned about its delay in meeting the requirement of the face of the other" (EN 203). The justice of democracy—to the extent that it remains a genuine democracy—therefore suffers from bad conscience: it admits that it invariably falls short of its ideals, that the best it can do is to gradually, incrementally, close the gap between the principles of ethics and "the necessary calculations imposed by a multiple sociality, calculations constantly starting over again" (EN 230). In addition, when democracy suppresses its bad conscience—as present-day neoliberal capitalist democracy could be argued to do—it risks sliding into totalitarianism.

What Levinas means by democracy is thus closer to Derrida's "democracy to come"—an ideal of radical democracy that has not yet materialized in the real world—than it is to the current configuration of "democracy" under global capitalism. As a matter of fact, Levinas holds no illusions about the tendency of justice to go astray, to forget its ethical origins. As soon as a system, an institution, or an organization arises—as soon as there is a doctrine, a politics, a party, a state, or a church—there also arises the possibility of losing the face-to-face. The interhuman, which is based on a nonreciprocal logic, can, for instance, be lost in a political order founded on the expectation of reciprocity; the imposition of impersonal laws, edicts, and obligations between citizens can overshadow the pure altruism of ethical responsibility. As a result, not only is the "social contract" never a sufficient condition for ethics but its "neutrality" almost by definition extinguishes the other's singularity. Even more drastically, a totalitarian state can stifle the face-to-face by placing restrictions on relationality. This can be accomplished by laws that regulate who can interact with whom—as was the case in segregated America or apartheid South Africa—but it can also be accomplished by invisible forces of biopolitical control that place certain individuals beyond my relational reach, that, for example, render certain types of individuals invisible or untouchable. Such systems have lost their ethical legitimacy along with their capacity to question themselves, with the consequence that their justice is best characterized as a travesty of justice. Dictatorial states are obviously prone to such travesties, but nominal democracies are by no means immune to them in the sense that seemingly "just" systems frequently rest on institutionalized foundations of injustice, such as racism or economic inequality.

5

Levinas does not try to deny the religious, specifically Judaic, origins of his ethical stance, though he also seeks to universalize it beyond these origins:

> I am in reality responsible for the other even when he or she commits crimes, even when others commit crimes. This is for me the essence of the Jewish conscience. But I also think that it is the essence of the human conscience: All men are responsible for one another, and "I more than anyone else." One of the most important things for me is that asymmetry and that formula: All men are responsible for one another and I more than anyone else. (*EN* 107)

Along related lines, the ideal of chosenness—the ideal of being selected for suffering—contains unmistakable echoes of Judaism at the same time as the ideals of loving one's neighbor, of showing mercy and kindness to the other, and of dying for this other also gesture toward Christianity. More generally speaking, there is hardly any doubt that behind the Levinasian notion of the other as sacrosanct operates an image of divinity that demands unconditional humility from the faithful. Levinas is explicit about this: "The relation to God is presented there as a relation to another person. It is not a metaphor: in the other, there is a real presence of God. In my relation to the other, I hear the Word of God. It is not a metaphor; it is not only extremely important, it is literally true. I'm not saying that the other is God, but that in his or her Face I hear the Word of God"; the other as face, in sum, is "the way the word of God reverberates" (*EN* 110).

As an atheist with no religious background, I admit to a knee-jerk resistance to this aspect of Levinas. Yet I also find Levinas's explanation for the persistence of religion in his philosophy quite interesting. Levinas accounts for the traces of God in his ethical vision by claiming that ethics now carries the mantle of making sense of suffering that religion carried before Auschwitz. He observes that, in itself, suffering is senseless: it is "unassumable" to the regular flow of life because it is characterized by a quantitative "too-muchness" that feels unmanageable, by a sensorial "superfluity" that penetrates and disorients the dimensions of meaning that strive to make sense of it (*EN* 91). Suffering, as it were, explodes the ordinariness of meaning from within, making it impossible for meaning to mean properly; it represents a revulsion, a refusal, or a denial of meaning, "the *way* in which, within a consciousness, the unbearable is precisely not borne" (*EN* 91–2). Moreover, suffering connotes pure passivity, a submission of consciousness to woe. This passivity is not the opposite of activity—for instance, the active receptivity of the senses—but rather a primary vulnerability, helplessness, and solitude: "a pure undergoing" of evil that rends the humanity of those it cripples (*EN* 92). Most fundamentally, suffering "is the *impasse* of life and of being—their absurdity—in which pain does not just somehow innocently happen to 'color' consciousness with affectivity. The evil of pain, the deleterious per se, is the outburst and deepest expression, so to speak, of absurdity" (*EN* 92–3). That is, suffering is intrinsically useless, "for nothing" (*EN* 93).

The empirical experience of pain engrosses the subject's entire consciousness so that there are no resources left for the alleviation of pain; it confirms, precisely, the uselessness of suffering. To counter this, Western culture, like all other cultures, has devised various ways of making sense of suffering, of justifying and rationalizing it, of giving meaning to the meaningless. For instance, pain has been turned into a means to an end, so that by our suffering, we are expected to attain a goal of some kind: perhaps it will make us stronger, refine our character, make us more empathetic, or give us access to perspectives that would otherwise elude us. Pain, in short, is seen as a tool of personal growth. Moreover, it has often been deemed necessary for pedagogical, utilitarian, or other progress-oriented personal or social projects (as is evident in the everyday motto of "no pain, no gain"). But no social entity has been more powerful in conjuring away the meaninglessness of suffering than religion, for the believer is rewarded for his or her suffering by the kingdom of God (where all suffering finally ceases). "This is pain henceforth meaningful," Levinas remarks, "subordinated in one way or another to the metaphysical finality glimpsed by faith or belief in progress. Beliefs presupposed by theodicy! That is the grand idea necessary to the inner peace of souls in our distressed world" (*EN* 96). Religion explains worldly evil by a "grand design" that grants "a suffering that is essentially gratuitous and absurd, and apparently arbitrary, a meaning and an order" (*EN* 96). However, the problem faced by the European culture of Levinas's time was that God was so spectacularly absent from Auschwitz that it was hard to retain faith in the progress narrative of suffering: "The disproportion between suffering and every theodicy was shown at Auschwitz with a glaring, obvious clarity. Its possibility puts into question the multimillennial traditional faith. Did not Nietzsche's saying about the death of God take on, in the extermination camps, the meaning of a quasi-empirical fact?" (*EN* 97). As a result, religion was no longer able to justify or rationalize, let alone provide consolation for, suffering.

For the Western imagination, the twentieth-century totalitarian-isms of the right and left, Hitlerism and Stalinism, Auschwitz and the Gulag, put an end to the capacity of religion to render suffer-ing meaningful. These were instances of suffering inflicted deliber-ately, of the type of needless suffering that could not be redeemed by any recourse to theodicy. But, for Levinas, this end of theodicy only revealed all the more powerfully the unjustifiable character of the other's suffering, "the outrage it would be for me to justify my neighbor's suffering" (*EN* 98). As Levinas sums up the matter, even "if God was absent in the extermination camps, the devil was very obviously present" (*EN* 99). In other words, even though the atroci-ties of the camps revealed the impotence of religion to lend meaning to suffering, they highlighted our acute need for the kind of ethics that does not abandon the other in his or her suffering—that is, for exactly the kind of ethics of charity that the Judeo-Christian tradition had historically advocated. And although Levinas focuses on the destiny of the Jews specifically, he wishes to use the "ovens of the 'final solution' crematoria where theodicy abruptly appeared impossible" to ask a universally applicable question about ethics; he wishes to ask whether we are willing to "abandon the world to useless suffering, leaving it to the political fatality—or drifting—of blind forces that inflict misfortune on the weak and conquered, while sparing the conquerors, with whom the shrewd are not slow to align themselves" (*EN* 99–100).

At issue is nothing less than the fate of ethical accountability after the death of God. Levinas's somewhat paradoxical conclusion is that we must now, "in a faith more difficult than before, in a faith without theodicy, continue to live out Sacred History" (*EN* 100). Only Sacred History, according to Levinas, can guide us back to the kind of suffering that means something, that is "no longer suffering 'for nothing'" (*EN* 100). Predictably enough, Levinas believes that the only sort of suffering that means something is the suffering I suffer on behalf of the other: "a suffering for the suffering (inexorable though it may be) of someone else" (*EN* 94). Essentially, my ability to suffer for the suffering other translates the uselessness of my suffering into something potentially useful, bringing me into existence as a being of ethical capacity:

> It is this attention to the suffering of the other that, through the cruelties of our century . . . can be affirmed as the very nexus of human subjectivity, to the point of being raised to the level of supreme ethical principle—the only one it is impossible to question—shaping the hopes and commanding the practical discipline of vast human groups. (*EN* 94)

Though I have reservations about this celebration of suffering— reservations I will return to below—there is also something persuasive about the idea that suffering gives rise to an ethical principle that is, quite simply, "impossible to question." In other words, there is something poignant about Levinas's vision insofar as it offers a thoroughly universalist understanding of ethics while at the same time managing to sidestep at least some of the problems that have plagued earlier Western attempts to conceptualize a generalizable set of ethical norms. As posthumanist theory has so amply revealed, Western universalism in its metaphysical forms has often been nothing but an apology for the value systems of the powerful. Levinas attempts to neutralize this failing by resorting to the Judeo-Christian injunction to love one's neighbor irrespective of the identity of this neighbor. Žižek may be right that this injunction presupposes that we suppress the strangeness of the other—that the price we pay for it is our inability to meet the other's disconcerting jouissance. In addition, I am not convinced that monotheistic religions have ever been able to live up to their codes of compassion; it seems that the violence of monotheism has fairly consistently stifled its altruistic currents. But I admit that, as an ethical *ideal*, the injunction to love one's neighbor can be appealing precisely because it is supposed to apply to everyone without fail, making everyone (at least in principle) equally responsible for the well-being of everyone else. According to this vision, I cannot turn away from the suffering of the other just because I happen to have more power or money than this other, because I am of a different race, gender, or ethnicity than this other, or because I disagree with this other in some fundamental way. The basic Levinasian point is that I am obliged to help the other in need even when this other annoys, infuriates, disappoints, or threatens me.

There are of course other routes to this same conclusion, including the Kantian command that I exercise my reason to consider whether my actions can be raised to a universally applicable rule—a command that (again, at least in principle) should keep me from acting in ways that injure others. The Kantian categorical imperative, after all, tells me that my actions are ethically justifiable only if I can ask everyone to act in the same fashion. Those of us theorizing from a posthumanist perspective have had a hard time with this version of ethics in part because of our aversion to the rational subject of metaphysics—the kind of subject who is able to sit down and ask itself, "Can I rationally demand that every human being act in the way I act?" And we have also had a hard time with Kantian ethics because we are aware of the long-standing tendency to equate the categorical imperative with ethical principles derived from conventional morality. If Kant himself maintained that the categorical imperative should not be confused with preconceived notions of good and evil—that it should not be conflated with traditional edicts of right and wrong—this is exactly what frequently ends up happening in practice, so that the question of "What should I do?" gets recast as the question of "What do the mores of my society tell me I should do?" This is why Lacan, for example, accuses Kant of coercive moralism (a matter I will discuss in Chapter 4). But what remains somewhat uncertain is whether this means that the categorical imperative as such is corrupt or merely that it tends to be used in corrupt ways. Personally, I like to differentiate between the categorical imperative on the one hand and its misguided applications on the other, for it seems to me that, properly understood, it makes it refreshingly hard for me to define ethical conduct in self-serving ways; it alerts me to situations where my conduct might be driven by what Kant calls "pathological" determinants—such as the fact that I might wield authority in a given situation—by urging me to repeatedly return to the question of whether others could be expected to make the same choices as I do.

6

Levinasian ethics is hence not the only way to arrive at generalizable ethical principles. And, as will become clear in the course of my argument, I do not think that replacing rationalist ethical principles by religious (or quasi-religious) ones represents an improvement of either critical thought or political efficacy. At the same time, I recognize that Levinas succeeds where the Kantian approach—along with many other rationalist approaches—arguably fails, namely in his ability to address the key question of human suffering. As Julia Kristeva has recently proposed, one of the major flaws of secular societies wedded to the principles of Enlightenment rationalism is their inability to cope with this very question, with the consequence that religious extremism, including Christian and Islamic fundamentalism, is gaining ground. Essentially, Kristeva believes that as long as secularism is aligned with a heartless global capitalism that is more interested in making a profit than in alleviating suffering, as long as secularism only speaks the language of the dollar, there is no way to counter the tide of religious violence. To address this problem, Kristeva calls for "a more complex humanism"—a progressive secular humanism which would situate vulnerability at the center of the political project, which would, essentially, add "a fourth term (vulnerability) to the humanism inherited from the Enlightenment (liberty, equality, fraternity)."[6] Such revamped humanism would not be hostile to religions yet it would also not necessarily be "indulgent with them."[7]

In a striking moment of intellectual honesty, Kristeva revises her earlier poststructuralist stance against humanism as follows: "I belong to the generation that objected to soft humanism, this fuzzy 'idea of man,' devoid of substance, bonded to a utopian fraternity, which harked back to the Enlightenment and the postrevolutionary contract. Today it seems to me not just vital but possible to refashion these ideals" (NB 29). Kristeva in fact believes that this refashioning of the ideals of humanism is the only effective way to "inscribe in the concept of the human itself—and therefore in philosophy and political practice—the constitutive part of the destructivity, vulnerability, and imbalance that are integral parts of the identity of the human race and, singularly, of the speaking subject" (HF 42). Kristeva further insists that "political solidarity requires mental solidarity between those who suffer from various kinds of exclusion and those who have been relatively spared. This co-presence at the suffering of others, indispensable in order to 'change the gaze' and put such solidarity into effect, sends us back to the constitutive vulnerability of we human beings at the junction of biology and meaning" (NB 92). One might say that Kristeva's revamped humanism is her answer to the Levinasian question of how to salvage ethics from the wreckage of Auschwitz. Like Levinas, Kristeva acknowledges that an ethics that glosses over suffering is missing an essential ingredient. But she is less convinced than Levinas that the prolongation of Sacred History (beyond theocracy) represents a viable solution. Rather, given the choice between religious discourses of suffering and a more capacious secular humanism, Kristeva opts for the latter.

It is these days fashionable, among progressive intellectuals, to insist that secular humanism cannot escape its religious pedigree (and even that the absolutism of secularism is more oppressive than the absolutism of monotheistic religions). This "turn to religion" seems to have something to do with the mysterious spell that (the hugely conservative) Carl Schmitt managed to cast over key thinkers such as Derrida and Agamben. Schmitt proposed that all "significant concepts of the modern theory of the state are secularized theological concepts," which, through historical development, "were transferred from theology to the theory of the state, whereby, for example, the omnipotent God became the omnipotent lawgiver."[8] In this way, Schmitt suggested that Western Enlightenment secularism—with its ideals of justice, equality, reciprocity, and democratic process—represents a mere continuation of the Judeo-Christian tradition from which it arose. Convinced by Schmitt's reasoning, Derrida spent much of *The Politics of Friendship* outlining the progression of Western politics from the ancient Greek system premised on the equality of all free men (loosely conceived as brothers) to the universal "brotherhood" of Christianity to the secularized version of fraternity represented by the French revolution. Agamben pursued a similar line of inquiry in *The Kingdom and the Glory*, arguing that "glory" (of the divine, of the sovereign) represents the link between theology and politics, religion and government.[9] Butler has recently followed suit, proposing that we are mistaken if we believe that our efforts to privatize religion, to exclude it from public life, have been successful; we are mistaken if we think that Western secularism can be dissociated from its religious—specifically Protestant—origins. As Butler maintains, "If the public sphere is a Protestant accomplishment, as several scholars have argued, then public life presupposes and reaffirms one dominant religious tradition *as* the secular."[10] Butler therefore raises the possibility that one religion—Protestantism—has been able to dictate the contours of Western secularism. As she continues, "If we could not have the distinction between public and private were it not for the Protestant injunction to privatize religion, then religion—or one dominant religious tradition—underwrites the very framework within which we are operating" ("JZ" 71). In this sense, both the public and the private are "'in religion' from the start," with the result that "secularization may be a fugitive way for religion to survive" ("JZ" 71–2).

One might well ask how it can be true that the privatization of religion has failed if it is *also* true that Protestantism—which demands precisely this privatization—has triumphed as the form of secularism that underpins Western societies. Though I understand Butler's aggravation about the hegemony of Protestantism, I also find her argument—like the arguments of Derrida and Agamben— a little frustrating because it seems to me that it would be equally possible to posit, following Max Weber, that secularism represents a tremendous *break* from religious dogmas: the French revolution was not *just* a matter of bringing Christian tenets into a nominally secular space; in many ways it was a drastic deviation from these tenets. By this I do not wish to deny the continued power of religion in the public sphere. Leaving aside, for the moment, Christian and Islamic fundamentalism, it would, for instance, be possible to argue that many of the stumbling blocks of American politics—from its irrational fights over abortion and gay marriage to its expansionist foreign policy—stem from the fact that it remains a thoroughly Christian state. But this is different from saying that secularism is merely an adaptation of Christianity. Is not the problem, rather, that American secularism has not been able to purge itself of Christianity to the same extent as, say, Scandinavian secularism? As a matter of fact, the distinction between these versions of secularism reveals, precisely, the possibility of a secularism divorced from Christianity.

I am aware that in the current geopolitical environment, any argument for secularism risks coming across as an argument "for" the West and thus "against" the rest of the world (particularly Islam). But if the alternative is the idea that there is no way out of the heteropatriarchal, misogynistic, homophobic, and xenophobic legacies of monotheistic religions—legacies that have, precisely, made it impossible for these religions to live up to their principles of universal compassion—then this is a risk I must take. As someone who routinely teaches deeply religious undergraduates (Christians and Muslims alike), I am constantly reminded of these legacies. For instance, I learned a long time ago to suppress any mention of homosexuality in my undergraduate classrooms because it invariably led to the terrorization of the (closeted) gay, lesbian, and queer students in the room by religious students who deemed homosexuality to be a "sin" against God. Given that queer theory is one of my main theoretical resources—and that I teach it on the graduate level—I have found the necessity of this suppression suffocating and keep wondering if the progressive scholars criticizing secularism (and in some cases, advocating religion) are not experiencing the same reality or if they have merely found better ways to cope with it than I have. By this I do not mean to suggest that all of my religious students are close-minded, for many are emphatically not. But the problem is pronounced enough to make me receptive to Kristeva's argument regarding the need for a refurbished secular humanism, not necessarily as a *replacement* for religion but as a viable *alternative* to it. In other words, though I do not wish to categorically denounce religions (I trust that there are nonoppressive ways to live out one's religious beliefs), I also do not want to reject the ideal of humane secularism (secularism sufficiently attentive to human suffering) *a priori*, as if it were a conceptual and practical impossibility. There is no question that secular humanism has failed in a variety of ways—that it has, for example, frequently been usurped for the purposes of economic exploitation—but surely the antidote to these failures cannot be to throw it out of the window altogether in a fit of uncritical religious revivalism; surely the solution cannot be to argue that those who wish to strive for a progressive secularism are somehow intrinsically deluded in their conviction that there might be another way to live besides the God-centered one.

In this context, Kristeva is, once again, instructive, for she proposes that human beings have an unquenchable, prereligious "need to believe" in higher ideals of some sort, and that when a given society is incapable of producing such ideals, religious extremism steps in to fill the void.[11] This is not to downplay the sociopolitical and economic roots of religious fundamentalism—such as poverty, inequality, and Western imperialism—analyzed by critics such as Jasbir Puar.[12] If anything, Kristeva agrees with Puar on this, which is exactly why she believes that being able to address the depths of human suffering is the only way out of the current bind of violent religious clashes. With regard to the "need to believe," Kristeva, in turn, maintains that our yearning for ideals "is part and parcel of the speaking subject 'before' any strictly religious construction," so that it is only by taking this yearning seriously that we can "confront not only religions' past and present fundamentalist off-course drift but also the dead ends of secularized societies" (*NB* 12). As is the case with suffering, it is the lack of viable secular responses to our yearning for ideals that incites religious violence, which is why Kristeva believes that the best way of dealing with our collective malaise is to devise such responses.

Levinas, it seems to me, arrives at a similar—or at least compatible—solution: though Levinasian philosophy carries unmistakable religious undertones, including the appreciation for Sacred History I mentioned above, it does not aim to resurrect religion per se but rather to enable secular ethics to accomplish what religion used to be able to accomplish (or at least promised to accomplish). Because Levinas remains so explicitly tied to religious discourse, his approach may at first glance confirm the conviction of Schmitt, Derrida, Agamben, and Butler, among others, that secularism is merely a clandestine form of religiosity. But I would place the emphasis on his admission that religion failed at the extermination camps and that, therefore, the only way to proceed is to build an ethical model that moves beyond strictly religious edicts yet attains the same level of universality as these edicts have historically aspired to. If even the executioner, for Levinas, has a face, it is because Levinas needed a degree of universality that equaled the universality of the Judeo-Christian tradition that he both drew upon and sought to transcend.

7

I have already alluded to some of the ways in which Levinas gestures toward a universalist ethics even as he criticizes metaphysical notions of reason and subjectivity alike. His is obviously not a universalism based on the rational deliberations of a sovereign subject. Indeed, as I have illustrated, there is, in Levinas, no such thing as a sovereign subject because the subject's being (including its consciousness) is always "interrupted" by the other. To be sure, the figure of the rational subject does enter Levinas's theory on the level of justice in the sense that Levinas never loses track of the necessity of systematically arbitrating between the competing claims of different faces. As we have learned, to accomplish this goal, justice seeks to compare incomparables by grouping individuals within categories that facilitate normative assessments. This is why justice takes place in the register of particularity—a register that allows for classification even as it retains a degree of differentiation among those classified. Levinasian ethics, in contrast, takes place in the register of singularity: the face as self-identical, as what cannot be classified into (captured by) concepts. Most important, this singularity partakes in the universal—becomes the object of the kind of accountability that understands no exception—without any reference to the province of particularity. There is therefore something Hegelian about Levinasian ethics even though he does not acknowledge this influence, and even though quasi-Hegelian commentators such as Žižek criticize him for being stuck on the level of particularity (a point I will consider in Chapter 3). But what matters to us at this juncture is that, in Levinasian ethics, each face counts immediately and equally—without any detour through the normative considerations characteristic of justice—so that there is no such thing as favoring the singularity of one face over another.

This universalizing thrust of Levinasian ethics tends to be sidelined by commentators who fixate on the idea that Levinas advocates an ethics of alterity—of respecting the absolute otherness of the other. As a result, Levinas is often called upon to support a difference-based ethical orientation, as might be the case, for example, in poststructuralist or multiculturalist paradigms. Undoubtedly it is not incorrect to utilize Levinas in such a way. But what gets lost in this manner of summing things up is that Levinas's ethics is also one of leveling differences. If there is, in Levinas, an emphasis on singularity, there is also an emphasis on the parity of the various singularities. Beyond the Levinasian rhetoric of the irreducible alterity of the other—which has fed various discourses of difference—there is a deep preoccupation with universal accountability as well as with the fundamental sameness and equal worth of all human life. In a sense, what unites humans is that we are all, without fail, singular creatures. And it is the difficult task of ethics to cut through the cultural camouflage that covers over this singularity; it is the task of ethics to reach the other on a primordially "human" level, beyond the trappings of his or her social persona (particularity, individuality, personality). As Levinas specifies, ethics is a matter of "the human *qua* human" (*EN* 109).

Explaining the same idea in relation to his key concept of the face, Levinas posits that ethics asks me to revere "the presence of humanity in the eyes that look at me" (*TI* 208), to behold the face before the "plastic forms" (*EN* 145) of composure settle over its radical defenselessness. As he elaborates:

> Before all particular expression of the other, and beneath all expression that, being already a bearing given to oneself, protects, there is a bareness and stripping away of expression as such. Exposure, point blank, extradition of the beleaguered, the tracked down—tracked down before all tracking and all beating for game. Face as the very mortality of the other man. (*EN* 186)

This mortality is the basis of human kinship: "That all men are brothers is not explained by their resemblance, nor by a common cause of which they would be the effect, like medals which refer to the same die that struck them"; instead, it is "my responsibility before a face looking at me as absolutely foreign . . . that constitutes the original fact of fraternity" (*TI* 214). Or, as Levinas expresses the matter in a different context, "The sensible presence of this chaste bit of skin with brow, nose, eyes, and mouth, is neither a sign allowing us to approach a signified, nor a mask hiding it. The sensible presence, here, de-sensibilizes itself in order to let the one who refers only to himself, the identical, break through directly" (EN 33).

The face, in the ethical sense, is thus not a sign or a mask that connects its bearer to some human generality—to some familiar signified that we can hold onto in our attempts to relate to the other—but rather what allows the singular (the self-identical) to break through directly, without any mediation. This is one way to understand how Levinasian ethics manages to bypass the level of particularity, how it is able to reconcile the singular with the ideal of universal ethical accountability: by aiming at the "human" prior to its solidification into a socially intelligible entity, this ethics leaps directly from the singular to the universal. Along related lines, Levinas maintains that his ethics is intuitively accessible to everyone, that it is, for example, not specific to the West, is "not an invention of the white race, of a humanity which has read the Greek authors in school and gone through a specific evolution" (EN 109). That is, the ethical vision he endorses—one that grants primacy to the other even to the point of self-sacrifice—is one that transcends cultural difference: "The only absolute value is the human possibility of giving the other priority over oneself. I don't think that there is a human group that can take exception to that ideal" (EN 109). It is of course debatable whether this is actually true. For instance, many Westerners, trained in the individualistic doctrines of their culture, do not hold the other in such high regard. Yet there is a great deal to be said for the notion that there is something viscerally comprehensible about the universality of human vulnerability, that all of us, regardless of education, formation, socialization, or cultural background, can grasp what it means to be vulnerable.

There may be people in every society who seek to defend themselves against this vulnerability—perhaps by projecting it onto others, perhaps by pretending to be immune to it—but it is difficult to deny that we are all aware of it at least as a potentiality. We know that if a person is tortured, he will be in pain. And though we cannot grasp the acuteness of that pain, we can go some distance in imagining it, and thus in empathizing with those who have experienced it. Such base-level connectedness is arguably the strongest justification for universal human rights, as Levinas himself suggests when he aligns his ethical vision with a transpolitical, transnational defense of "the rights of man" (*EN* 203). Human rights discourses have recently come under attack from various quarters, including the most progressive, and this is for a good reason, for they have often been misused. I will return to this problem later in this book. But at this point in the argument, let me merely stress that human rights, for Levinas, gesture toward an ethical vision "beyond justice," functioning as "an imperious reminder" of the mercy and kindness that need to be added to the severity of justice, that cannot be reduced to the generalities of legislation (*EN* 203).

8

That Levinasian ethics tends toward universality while managing to sidestep some of the snares of more metaphysical ethical models does not mean that it is devoid of problems. Perhaps the most pronounced of these is its insistent masochism and its related inability to acknowledge that care for the other may be impossible without a degree of care for the self. Levinas talks as if the self's ethical resources were infinite, as if there were no limit to its ability to prioritize the other. To be sure, he does admit—as I discussed above—that justice alleviates the burden of ethics, yet the thrust of his philosophy is to foreground the responsibility that the self carries for the other (even to the point of self-sacrifice, even to the point of being willing to die for the other). Indeed, not only does Levinas relentlessly remind us of the asymmetry of our responsibility for the other, but he tends to debase the self in ways that border on self-hatred. The Levinasian subject does not merely surrender its sovereignty but enters into an economy of self-chastisement in "its modality of detestable self" (*EN* 147). As I have already noted, the Levinasian self is always already guilty, which, ironically, may make it harder to determine whether it might actually be guilty of a concrete misdeed. After all, if guilt is predetermined and omnipresent, how do we judge a situation where the self is guilty of something specific? How do we add new guilt into a base-level layer of guilt that cannot be expiated by any means?

I have emphasized that Levinas insists that even the executioner has a face, and that this face, like all other faces, is inviolable. Along related lines, he claims that "I am responsible for the other even when he bothers me, even when he persecutes me" (*EN* 106). And though he adds that he hopes that this will not become "a rule of daily usage" (*EN* 106), he also remarks that to be persecuted is "the obverse of a universal responsibility—a responsibility for the Other [*l'Autre*]—that is more ancient that any sin" (*DF* 225). Levinas is here speaking of the Jewish history of persecution specifically, yet to the extent that Judaism functions as a constant backdrop for his ethics, the idea that responsibility arises from the experience of persecution gets elevated to a general principle. In the final analysis, when stripped of its specifically Jewish connotations, the term *persecuted*, for Levinas, seems to function as a synonym for the realization that we are intrinsically "interrupted" by the other in the manner I have outlined; that is, there seems to be a link between the crisis of sovereignty brought on by the inherently relational nature of subjectivity and the notion that we are "persecuted" by the other. As we will see in the next chapter, this is how Butler chooses to interpret the matter. But the danger of using the term *persecuted* in such a loose sense is that it makes it difficult to differentiate the relational ontology of human beings from more specific forms of persecution, including the Jewish history of persecution. If being touched by otherness is automatically a matter of being "persecuted" by the other, what happens to acute forms of persecution? If the idea that I am always already guilty makes it harder to isolate the moments when I am concretely guilty of something, the idea that I am always already persecuted makes it harder to isolate the moments when I am concretely, violently persecuted. Levinas's point, of course, is that my responsibility for the other does not emerge from my "agency" as a self-sufficient subject but from my devastating dependence on the other. Yet there is still something rather chilling about statements such as, "In suffering, in the *original traumatism* and return to self, where I am responsible for what I did not will, absolutely responsible for the persecution I undergo, outrage is done to me."[13]

Butler notes that "it is possible, even easy, to read Levinas as an elevated masochist."[14] The implication is that because reading Levinas as a masochist is easy, we should not do so. But I would say that there may be no way around this reading, and that if Butler accepts Levinas's masochism (rather than criticizing its excessiveness), it may be because she herself gets a great deal of theoretical mileage out of it—a matter I will comment on at various points in this book. But let me identify my main quarrel with this masochism immediately: even if we concede that in saying that I am responsible for my persecutor, Levinas does not mean that I have somehow caused my persecution—that I have prompted my persecutor to persecute me—but merely that my responsibility for the other extends to my persecutor, his formulation arguably places too big a burden on those who have been victimized. He keeps quoting Dostoyevsky: "We are all guilty for everything and everyone, and I more than all the others" (*EN* 105). Yet this is simply not always the case. There are circumstances where some people are much more guilty than others. As a consequence, if the Ku Klux Klan burns a cross on my yard, a multinational corporation poisons my water supply, or a gay-hating gang assaults me in a dark alley, my stance of unconditional generosity toward my persecutor would only feed power structures that have historically made some lives unbearable while simultaneously justifying various social atrocities. Žižek in fact goes as far as to postulate that Levinas displaces his personal guilt about having survived the Holocaust onto the persecuted:

> Although Levinas is often perceived as the thinker who endeavored to articulate the experience of the *Shoah*, one thing is self-evident apropos his questioning of one's own right to be and his emphasis on one's unconditional asymmetrical responsibility: this is not how a survivor of the *Shoah*, one who effectively experienced the ethical abyss of *Shoah*, thinks and writes. This is how those think who feel guilty for observing the catastrophe from a minimal safe distance.[15]

I would not go quite this far. But I admit to being suspicious of the fact that Levinasian ethics privileges my responsibility for the other over the other's responsibility for his or her actions, for this emphasis makes it difficult to counter the abuses of power. Levinasian ethics might work perfectly in an ideal world devoid of power differentials—in a world where everyone in fact did respect everyone else equally—but in the real world, in the world that we inhabit, it all too easily rewards the victimizer by demanding that those who have been victimized by him humanize his face regardless of how vehemently he has dehumanized theirs. In an extreme formulation, the idea that the persecuted are responsible for their persecutors implies that the targets of racism, sexism, homophobia, and other forms of violence remain responsible for their tormentors, or that, say, Muslim immigrants singled out by Islamophobic citizens remain responsible for these citizens. This is a bizarre kind of ethics—one that absolves the persecutor of all accountability by shifting the ethical onus entirely onto the persecuted. On the one hand, Levinasian ethics relies on the meta-norm that the other's face is inviolable. But, on the other, it offers no normative resources for dealing with situations where people do not abide by this rule; it is, in short, an ethics wholly devoid of normative content in the sense that the other—even the persecutor—can never be condemned in ways that would reduce my responsibility for him or her. As I have attempted to show, Levinas makes a valiant effort to get around this problem by carving out a separate sphere of justice where condemnation becomes possible. But this does not change the fact that his ethics asks the victimized to display a staggering degree of compassion for their victimizer.

In addition, might there not be a certain hubris to the idea that I have been "chosen" for a wholly asymmetrical responsibility for the other? Is there not something rather arrogant about the idea that no matter how abusively the other behaves, I am able (even if I struggle with the matter) to meet his abuse with empathy? Levinas states, "I have always thought that election is definitely not a privilege" (*EN* 108). This is obviously true in the sense that it is difficult to read being elected for suffering as an existential bonus. Yet there is also a degree of roundabout egotism to the idea that I am capable of the kind of superhuman suffering that those who have not been elected cannot bear. Levinas might counter this by insisting that all of us have been similarly elected. But this does not solve the core issue at hand, namely that suffering, in Levinasian ethics, carries the insignia of nobility, which is precisely why I retain reservations about this ethics even as I understand the need for an ethical paradigm that is able to address suffering in a world that is full of it. My reservations persist primarily because it seems to me that there is a very short step from the valorization of suffering to the utterly apolitical notion that we do not need to remedy the world's suffering—say, poverty—because it coats the anguished masses with a patina of special grace. Monotheistic religions have always respected this relationship between suffering and grace, which is precisely why Marx characterized them as the opiate of the masses. I suppose I worry that Levinasian ethics could become another such opiate: a tool of appeasement rather than of political consciousness.

9

A less drastic political problem arises from Levinas's valorization of the other's opaque unintelligibility and unknowability. Those of us—myself included—who have wanted to counter the humanistic idealization of inner transparency have found this valorization of opacity constructive.[16] But recently I have had to revise my position on the matter because I have come to see how common it is to fetishize intersubjective opacity and even to turn it into a weapon by which power is amassed in relationships, particularly in intimate relationships. For example, in surveying the contemporary North American romantic culture, what strikes me most forcibly is the degree to which people routinely resort to the trope of opacity (ambivalence, ambiguity, vagueness, uncertainty, and so on) in order to gain control of their partners or prospective partners. Simply put, the one who stays unreadable remains powerful, whereas the one who becomes transparent loses in the game of romance. Among other things, the idea that ethical relationality entails my ability to tolerate the opacity of the other leads to the expectation that I remain infinitely patient with his or her indecision or emotional elusiveness. Any request for clarity, for a resolution of any kind, that I might make is immediately coded as unethical, even violent. In the context of a gendered biopolitical and heteropatriarchal environment where women are habitually asked to put up with men's murkiness, and even to actively care for this murkiness by hefty doses of "understanding," this is a questionable dynamic; in a society that deems women to have more emotional intelligence than men, and that therefore holds women responsible for the success of relationships, the call for forbearance in the face of ambivalence feeds the hegemonic system instead of offering an ethical counterpoint to it. Granted, a degree of opacity is a psychological given; obviously none of us can know ourselves completely, let alone always act reliably. But there are those who consciously manipulate—and are even socially encouraged to manipulate—the patience of others. And to the extent that the Levinasian ethical paradigm focuses on my responsibility for the other rather than on the ethical valences of the other's actions, it cannot even begin to address such manipulations.

This digression into the realm of intimate relationships may seem trivial, yet it is precisely in this realm that thinkers such as Irigaray have made Levinasian inroads, raising our reverence for the indecipherable other to the pinnacle of ethical virtue. What I am saying is that a greater degree of attention to the systematic power differentials that permeate the field of intimacy reveals the (unintended) cruelty intrinsic to this model. Likewise, a greater degree of attention to the inequalities of power in both national and international contexts might disclose the (again, unintended) brutality that adheres to an ethics premised on a masochistic subject who, as Levinas states, "has promised itself that it will carry the whole responsibility of the world" (DF 89). Indeed, the hyperbolic pitch of Levinasian ethics could be argued to hide its political impotence (a point that is not unrelated to the point about suffering and pacification I made above). This ethics—which Levinas, let us recall, describes as our "chance for holiness" (EN 202)—appears to operate in such a saintly or divine register, appears so far removed from lived experience, that it risks losing its ability to speak to the material concerns of the world. If anything, because our failure to approximate the ideals of this ethics seems inevitable, we might be tempted to discard these ideals as inherently unachievable (and thus not worth the effort).

Against the backdrop of Western metaphysics, the Levinasian approach is deeply political in its rejection of the autonomous, self-sufficient subject. Yet it is also potentially paralyzing. By this I do not wish to suggest that I see no value in utopian thinking. I agree with critics from Kristeva to Alenka Zupančič and José Esteban Muñoz, who have pointed out that our world is impoverished by its lack of higher ideals, and that what we, consequently, need is not a more realistic attitude but rather a more idealistic one.[17] But when it comes to ethics specifically, there may be something about impossible-to-attain ideals that creates a loophole that conveniently allows us to flee from them; paradoxically, when our ethical ideals become so lofty that we cannot reach them, they may become more or less meaningless. Or, to state the issue differently, if Levinasian ethics lets the callous perpetrator off the hook—if it refuses to condemn those who choose to abuse the weakness or generosity of others—it at the same time places such an insufferable burden on those who aspire to ethical conduct that they might abandon their cause out of sheer hopelessness.

10

One could say that Kant secretly hovers in the background of Levinasian ethics in the sense that this ethics is driven by a regulative ideal that is supposed to lead the ethical subject to ever more purified forms of conduct; in Levinasian ethics, as in Kantian, we are forever caught up in the bind between an ideal we aspire toward and an imperfect reality that keeps falling short of this ideal. This furtive Kantianism in fact becomes obvious in Derrida's appropriation of Levinasian ethics, particularly in his provocative claim that genuine forgiveness forgives the unforgivable. In Derrida's view, forgiveness that only forgives the forgivable is not pure, nor is forgiveness that seeks an end of some kind (salvation, redemption, reconciliation, and so on). And Derrida is particularly scornful of forgiveness that "aims to re-establish normalcy (social, national, political, psychological) by a work of mourning."[18] Forgiveness, he specifies, "is not, it *should not be*, normal, normative, normalising. It *should* remain exceptional and extraordinary, in the face of the impossible: as if it interrupted the ordinary course of historical temporality" (CF 32).[19] In making this argument, Derrida attempts, among other things, to subvert the notion that forgiveness should be predicated on the punishment (and the consequent repentance) of the perpetrator, for such a notion, for Derrida, relies on a problematic economy of exchange that creates a false symmetry between punishing and forgiving (as in, "I will be able to forgive you if you are first punished and learn to repent").

Like Levinasian ethical accountability, pure forgiveness here remains the kind of ideal that we can rarely, if ever, attain. Moreover, in the same way that Levinas distinguishes between justice and ethics, Derrida distinguishes between the domain of judgment, punishment, and reparation (justice) on the one hand and the domain of forgiveness (ethics) on the other. As Derrida explicitly states, forgiveness exceeds "the measure of any human justice" (CF 33). As a result, when a collective body charged with dispensing justice—for example, the post-apartheid South African state—grants forgiveness, it intrudes into the domain of ethics where only the victim can forgive the perpetrator in a (literal or virtual) face-to-face encounter. For Derrida, the state can judge but not forgive. Indeed, the quasi-automatic conferral of forgiveness by the state can be used to elude the demands of justice (so that, for example, if I feel that I have been forgiven, I might no longer worry about offering reparation to those I have harmed). The flipside of this is that justice can obscure the fact that forgiveness has not been granted, that the perpetrator having been punished does not necessarily mean that he or she has been forgiven. After all, it is possible to bring the perpetrator to justice—and even to punish her—without having any intention of ever forgiving her. Yet the ideal of forgiving the unforgivable remains, for Derrida, a necessary ideal because only forgiving the forgivable would be too easy, would in fact render the very notion of forgiveness meaningless.

The danger here is the same as in Levinas, namely that a notion of forgiveness that no one can even begin to live up to may disintegrate into mere empty rhetoric without any real-life political bearing. Derrida's solution to the problem is the same as that of Levinas: he strives to keep ethics (the domain of forgiving the unforgivable) separate from the collective domain of justice even as he recognizes that the two domains bleed into each other. As Derrida explains:

> These two poles, *the unconditional and the conditional*, are absolutely heterogeneous, and must remain irreducible to one another. They are nonetheless indissociable: if one wants, and it is necessary, forgiveness to become effective, concrete, historic; if one wants it to *arrive*, to happen by changing things, it is necessary that this purity engages itself in a series of conditions of all kinds (psychosociological, political, etc.). It is between these two poles, *irreconcilable but indissociable*, that decisions and responsibilities are to be taken. (*CF* 44–5)

That is, Derridean ethics, like Levinasian ethics, is unconditional, whereas justice is conditional, and though the two are indissociable, they are also irreconcilable.

It seems to me that the only way to alleviate the political shortcomings of Levinasian ethics, such as its tendency to shift the burden of ethical responsibility to the victimized, is to insist on this point, is to insist on the fact that ethics and justice are irreconcilable—"irreducible to one another"—even as they are indissociable from each other. In more concrete terms, the only way to rescue Levinasian ethics from political disasters brought on by its inability (or unwillingness) to account for the functioning of social power is to enforce justice as a realm where normative judgments remain possible. Levinas recognizes this, as does Derrida. However, in Butler's model of precarious life, which I discuss in the next chapter, the matter becomes more ambiguous. On the one hand, Butler's impressive history of theorizing social power makes her more acutely attentive to systematic inequalities than either Levinas or Derrida. On the other, her resistance to anything that even vaguely hints at Enlightenment rationalism, and particularly her aversion to the kinds of *a priori* norms of right or wrong that accompany this rationalism, causes her to shun the definition of justice that Levinas still takes for granted. More specifically, Butler seeks to build a paradigm of social justice, including global justice, on the basis of Levinasian *ethics*, with the result that the distinction between ethics and justice gets lost. By this I do not mean that Butler does not condemn injustice, for her critique of the hegemonic geopolitical attitudes of both the US government and the Israeli state is notorious. My point, rather, is that such moments of condemnation cannot be sustained by her overall political model, for this model is based on Levinasian ethics, which—as I have shown—functions on a level of immediacy prior to normative content (and thus to any possibility of condemnation). As a consequence, whenever Butler resorts to normative judgments, she tends to slide into a discourse of liberal humanism that seems completely incongruous with her otherwise posthumanist political vision. To be sure, Levinas also speaks the language of liberal humanism whenever he speaks about justice. But he never sought to discredit this language in the context of justice in the first place. Butler, in contrast, discredits it fairly categorically, which means that when she needs to make a normative judgment of any kind, she has no place to go, except a backhanded deployment of the very language she ridicules.

Levinas did not seem to have a problem with the idea that justice relies on *a priori* normative judgments. But Butler resists this idea, which is precisely why she clings to Levinasian ethics—the part of Levinasian theory where *a priori* norms have no role to play—as the blueprint for her politics. But in so doing, Butler risks falling into the very trap that Derrida cautions us against, namely the tendency to think that ethics automatically addresses the concerns of politics (or justice), so that, for instance—to return to the example I gave above—if I feel that I have been forgiven, I might conclude that I no longer need to offer reparation to those I have injured. Butler in fact takes this line of logic a step further by arguing that, due to the inner opacity that renders me partially unintelligible to myself, I am not fully accountable for my actions, and can therefore expect the forbearance of those I have wounded; I am, as it were, to be forgiven (according to the edicts of ethics) rather than judged for the rightness or wrongness of my actions (according to the edicts of justice). This implies, among other things, that justice is entirely secondary to ethics—in this case, to forgiveness. I do not think that this is what Butler intends to assert, yet I would like to raise the possibility that the turn to Levinasian ethics in contemporary theory—including in Butlerian theory—represents a privatization of politics, so that what matters now are not the kinds of structural changes that could be achieved by collective action (inspired by normative judgments of right and wrong) but rather the intricate details of how we ethically relate to others in face-to-face (that is, fairly private) scenarios. Is this not precisely the kind of shift of emphasis that our neoliberal capitalist system thrives on? Is it not the case that as long as we remain mired in the specifics of relationality, including the complexities of forgiveness, we do not have much energy for worrying about global social change? Again, I am not saying that Butler does not worry about global social change, for she clearly does so intensely. My point is merely that there may be an irresolvable tension between this worry and the Levinasian ethical arsenal with which she seeks to tackle it.

2

The ethics of precarity:
Judith Butler's reluctant
universalism

*I want to argue that if we are to make broader social
and political claims about rights of protection and
entitlements to persistence and flourishing, we will
first have to be supported by a new bodily ontology,
one that implies the rethinking of precariousness, vulnerability, injurability, interdependency, exposure,
bodily persistence, desire, work and the claims
of language and social belonging.*

JUDITH BUTLER[1]

1

In her theorizing from the last decade, Judith Butler combines
Levinasian insights about the primacy of the other with psychoanalytic
insights about the intersubjective formation of human beings to
devise a post-Enlightenment, postmetaphysical ethics that—as she
explains in the above quotation—is supported by "a new bodily
ontology" based on a rethinking of precariousness, vulnerability,

injurability, interdependency, and exposure, among other basic components of life. If Levinas sought to break "the obstinacy of being" by showing that we owe our very existence to the other, and that we are therefore irrevocably responsible for the other as face, psychoanalysis reveals the ways in which our primary infantile relationships linger into adulthood, repeatedly derailing any sense of coherence we might attain. In other words, psychoanalysis reminds us that the other dwells within the self—through the unconscious, through the repetition compulsion, and even through our bodily drives—in ways that render us constitutionally incomplete, disoriented, out-of-joint, and riven by alterity. Most importantly for Butler's purposes, our formative exposure to the other—what she, following Jean Laplanche, describes as our primordial impingement by the other—is involuntary and always potentially traumatizing. Even when we are not treated badly, we are treated unilaterally, which means that we are completely at the mercy of others. And when we *are* treated badly—when we are handled brutally, abandoned, neglected, or tormented—our masochism is inevitable in the sense that we are forced to cathect to those who harm us; because our very survival depends on such wounded attachments, being injured—and injurable—becomes the status quo of our lives. As Butler states, it seems better "to be enthralled with what is impoverished or abusive than not to be enthralled at all and so to lose the condition of one's being and becoming."[2]

Butler thus replaces the metaphysical model of self-contained subjectivity by a Levinasian-psychoanalytic model of relational ontology. To "be" a subject, for Butler, as for Levinas, is to be "interrupted" by otherness, by relationality. This is why Butler's model asks (autonomous) "being" to yield to (intrinsically nonautonomous) relationality. As she explains, "The kind of relationality at stake is one that 'interrupts' or challenges the unitary character of the subject, its self-sameness and its univocity. In other words, something happens to the 'subject' that dislocates it from the center of the world."[3] Or, as she puts the matter in *Precarious Life*:

> If I am confounded by you, then you are already of me, and I am nowhere without you. I cannot muster the 'we' except by finding the way in which I am tied to 'you,' by trying to translate but

finding that my own language must break up and yield if I am to know you. You are what I gain through this disorientation and loss. This is how the human comes into being, again and again, as that which we have yet to know. (*PL* 49)

The "human" here is the name for the disorientation and loss that results from being "broken" by the other; I am, from the start, seized by, or mired in, otherness for the simple reason that my relation with the other is what "I" am. And because my capture by the other—which precedes the formation of my self—includes an unconscious element, I remain partially opaque to myself: I cannot fully access the history of my own formation, nor can I entirely grasp how the enigmatic messages of the outside world have shaped, and continue to shape, the contours of my inner world. In addition, I am interpellated into collective systems of normative meaning that inform the outlines of my existence, even my bodily experience, in impossible-to-reverse ways. I am, in short, not the author of the norms that determine the contours of my destiny. Nor am I the author of the language I speak. And because I can only persist, let alone flourish, in such contexts of social crafting, my attempts to claim sovereignty are always fantasmatic, unable to conjure away my constitutive passivity in relation to the surrounding world.

Butler's conceptualization of our relational ontology is somewhat extreme in implying that there is nothing about our being that can be separated from the other, so that our experience of ourselves as quasi-bounded entities is purely fictitious, or worse, arrogant and violent. It is also somewhat one-sided in assuming that we are invariably overwhelmed rather than, say, enabled, by others. As she writes, "That we are impinged upon primarily and against our will is the sign of a vulnerability and a beholdenness that we cannot will away. We can defend against it only by prizing the asociality of the subject over and against a difficult and intractable, even sometimes unbearable relationality."[4] Below I will return to the problematic nature of the idea that our relationship to others is first and foremost one of being impinged upon and that our efforts to fight off this impingement invariably result in the asociality (arrogance and violence) of the self-sufficient subject. But what is important to recognize at this point is that our unwilled relationality becomes the underpinning of Butler's ethics of precarity, an ethics that takes "the very unbearability of exposure as the sign, the reminder, of a common vulnerability, a common physicality and risk" (*GA* 100). Butler is here quite close to the Kristevian revamped humanism I discussed in the previous chapter in the sense that, like Kristeva, she wishes to place vulnerability at the center of her ethics; though she might not share Kristeva's humanistic aspirations, she wishes to remind us of our ethical responsibility to attend to the suffering of others, who, like us, are exposed to the always potentially violent touch of the surrounding world. In other words, Butler accepts Levinas's conclusion that our ontological condition of being bound to the other, and particularly our condition of being "interrupted" by someone else's longing and suffering, gives rise to the kind of accountability that cannot, under any circumstances, be conjured away. Butler's ethics of precarity is, in short, premised on a shared bodily condition of helplessness, on a return "to the human where we do not expect to find it, in its frailty" (*PL* 151).

2

One of the strengths of Butler's ethical vision is its capacity to negotiate the relationship between the universal and the singular in ways that do justice to both. Simply put, precariousness is a universal condition of human life, yet we experience it in highly singular ways. Regarding the universal reach of her ethics, Butler states, "Precariousness has to be grasped not simply as a feature of *this* or *that* life, but as a generalized condition whose very generality can be denied only by denying precariousness itself." "The injunction to think precariousness in terms of equality," she continues, "emerges precisely from the irrefutable generalizability of this condition" (*FW* 22). It is thus the generalizability of precariousness that makes it a suitable foundation for a universal ethics of equality. At the same time, Butler takes pains to stress that she does not wish to "deny that vulnerability is differentiated, that it is allocated differentially across the globe" (*PL* 31), which suggests that it may be difficult to draw an analogy between one experience of vulnerability and another; it may be hard to find a vocabulary that would allow us to compare different experiences of suffering. This is due not only to the difficulty of translating from one context to another but also— and centrally—to the ways in which biopolitical and necropolitical forces distribute precariousness unevenly so that some individuals and populations are much more precarious than others. Such differentiation can take place within one society, so that, it would, for instance, be difficult—even dangerous—to try to compare the precariousness of a white Wall Street trader and that of the Puerto Rican woman who cleans his house. Butler's focus, however, has been primarily on global inequalities—some racist, some capitalist, some nationalist—that have historically maximized the precariousness of some populations and minimized that of others. It is this unequal allocation of precarity that, for Butler, forms the point of departure "for progressive or left politics in ways that continue to exceed and traverse the categories of identity" (FW 3).

Because Butler's social ontology asks us to take stock of our dependence on others, as well as of the interdependence of human beings on a global level, it urges us to object to violence aimed at others even when these others are far away from us or do not seem to share any of our values. Precariousness, as it were, offers a basis for identification, and identification, in turn, offers a basis for ethical indignation: I oppose injustice done to the other because, on a very basic level, I can place myself in the other's position— because I see that, under different conditions, the injustice aimed at the other, or at least something akin to this injustice, could be aimed at me. As Butler asks, "From where might a principle emerge by which we vow to protect others from the kinds of violence we have suffered, if not from an apprehension of a common human vulnerability?" (PL 30). This is why she insists that speculations on the vulnerability-inducing formation of the subject "are crucial to understanding the basis of non-violent responses to injury and, perhaps most important, to a theory of collective responsibility" (PL 44). Speaking of the Vietnam War specifically, Butler notes that it was the apprehension of the precariousness of the lives that the United States Army was destroying—particularly graphic pictures of children "burning and dying from napalm"—"that brought the US public to a sense of shock, outrage, remorse, and grief," and that led to the widespread protests against the war (PL 150). There is a great deal one could say here about the special status that the image of the innocent but suffering child holds in the American psyche,[5] but Butler's point is that the pictures—which the American public was not supposed to see—reminded Americans of what geopolitical structures of power try to make them forget, namely that the other is just as woundable as they are; it reminded this public of the core of sameness that unites human beings despite their vast cultural, ethnic, and religious differences.

One of the obvious dangers in raising precariousness to a universal human condition—a danger Butler is clearly aware of—is that it could function as a way for relatively privileged Western intellectuals to imply that we are all equally vulnerable, oppressed, deprived, and harassed. Butler counters this danger with a sustained attention not only to the unequal distribution of precariousness but also to the global structures of power that make it difficult for us to acknowledge, let alone empathize with, the precariousness of those who do not inhabit our immediate, intimate lifeworld. The American public may have been outraged at the images from Vietnam in the same way that many were outraged at the images from Abu Ghraib, but this ethical response depended on a momentary failure of power: people saw pictures they were not meant to see. As Butler deftly demonstrates, one of the ruses of power is to delimit the domain of grievability so that—under normal circumstances—we are prevented from mourning the suffering (or death) of those deemed different from, or inferior to, ourselves. According to Butler, it would be easy to enumerate "a hierarchy of grief" (*PL* 32) that determines which lives count as mournable and which do not, and even—and perhaps most fundamentally—which lives are recognizable as human and which are not:

> We seldom, if ever, hear the names of the thousands of Palestinians who have died by the Israeli military with United States support, or any number of Afghan people, children and adults. Do they have names and faces, personal histories, family, favorite hobbies, slogans by which they live? What defense against the apprehension of loss is at work in the blithe way in which we accept deaths caused by military means with a shrug or with self-righteousness or with clear vindictiveness? To what extent have Arab peoples, predominantly practitioners of Islam, fallen outside the "human" as it has been naturalized in its "Western" mold by the contemporary workings of humanism? What are the cultural contours of the human at work here? How do our cultural frames for thinking the human set limits on the kinds of losses we can avow as loss? After all, if someone is lost, and that person is not someone, then what and where is the loss, and how does mourning take place? (*PL* 32)

As we all know, one of the violences of traditional Western humanism is that it has historically barred the majority of the world's population (women, nonwhite men, poor white men) from its definition of the human. This is one reason that this kind of humanism cannot provide a foundation for an ethics of precarity, for recognizing the precariousness of others depends on our ability to first recognize them as human; it is why an ethics of precarity is, as Butler explains, "not a matter of a simple entry of the excluded into an established ontology, but an insurrection at the level of ontology, a critical opening up of the questions, What is real? Whose lives are real?" (PL 33).

The derealization (through dehumanization) of the enemy is one of the basic strategies of warfare. It is easier to kill those we do not consider fully human, or human in the same way as we are, and it is also easier to deny that the loss of such people is a real loss and therefore something that should be mourned. Violence against such people, Butler explains, "leaves a mark that is no mark" (PL 36). In the place of public acts of grieving, there will be silence (of the newspapers, of television, of the government), for grieving presupposes "a life worth noting, a life worth valuing and preserving, a life that qualifies for recognition" (PL 34). Butler is talking about a systematic erasure of those who do not qualify as fully human, an erasure that makes violence invisible to us, which convinces us that "there never was a human, there never was a life, and no murder has, therefore, ever taken place" (PL 147). In this sense, the prohibition on grieving prolongs the violence of killing, adding a new layer of brutality to the original brutality, so that we are caught up in a vicious cycle where some lives are deemed ungrievable because they are considered less than human and where, conversely, some people are considered less than human because they are deemed ungrievable. On the one hand, the discourse of mourning "our" losses can be exploited for nationalist purposes; on the other, the denial of "their" losses aids in the dehumanization of the other. The antidote to this is not just to shift our frames of perception so that we come to see those we do not usually see— and, then, perhaps, to mourn those we do not usually mourn—but also to alter the modalities of representation that portray some types of individuals (or groups) as inherently good and others as inherently evil. After all, when an individual is presented to us as a personification of evil, we find it difficult to identify with him or her, let alone recognize any trace of precariousness in him or her, which is why Butler argues that no understanding of humanization can take place "without a consideration of the conditions and meanings of identification and disidentification" (*PL* 145).

3

Basing an ethics on our capacity to identify with the suffering of others rather than, say, on *a priori* principles of human rights, carries some risks, the first of which is that the failings of identification are so endemic that such an ethics might end up being unacceptably erratic. Though I wholeheartedly agree with Butler's contention that global power imbalances make it difficult for Westerners to acknowledge the equal humanity of non-Westerners, I do not think that the matter is quite this simple, for if Americans have a hard time mourning the Iraqis and Afghans killed by the US military, Iraqis and Afghans might also have a hard time mourning those who are far away from them, including each other. Or, to approach the matter from a slightly different perspective, the fact that Americans, generally speaking, do not grieve those killed by the US military does not mean that such casualties are not grieved at all; presumably they are grieved deeply by people close to them. As a result, one could argue that in painting a portrait of the non-Western "other" as intrinsically ungrievable, Butler is inadvertently participating in the very dynamic of othering the other that she is trying to escape; on a certain level, her discourse implies that the non-Western subject is always an other—is never a subject—when in fact this other, within his or her own society, *is* a subject (someone with a name and face, personal history, family, hobbies, and perhaps even slogans by which he or she lives).

Moreover, though Butler is undoubtedly right in suggesting that we identify with the suffering of some people more than that of others because their names and faces are familiar to us in the sense of being culturally and ethnically similar to us, there are alternative ways that alliances based on familiarity are forged, ways that cut across cultural and ethnic differences. For instance, that my friend is black, my colleague is Chinese, and my downstairs neighbor is Muslim does not change the fact that if this friend, colleague, or neighbor is harmed or killed, I—a white atheist woman—will mourn more intensely than I would mourn another white atheist woman harmed or killed somewhere in Sweden. In other words, there seems to be an important link between familiarity (and thus our ability to mourn) on the one hand and intimacy, proximity, and shared history on the other that is not necessarily in any way based on similarity of culture or ethnicity. From this perspective, the ability to mourn the other may be too haphazard, too random, a basis for ethics.

The second risk that accompanies an ethics based on our ability to identify with the suffering of others is that it can replace political action by a paralyzing grief. Grief can be privatizing, and thus potentially depoliticizing, because it tends to result in a retreat from the social world. This retreat may, in part at least, be a defense against our own vulnerability, for grief reminds us of the immensity of our dependence on others: the fact that we can be undone by the loss of others highlights the flimsiness of our fantasies of sovereignty. Indeed, besides acute bodily suffering, there are few things in life that "interrupt" the coherence of our being more than the anguish we feel when we have lost someone who feels irreplaceable to us. If desire, intimacy, and sexuality already challenge our aspirations of autonomy, grief often results—at least momentarily—in the utter dissolution of the self. In Butler's words, "Perhaps . . . one mourns when one accepts that by the loss one undergoes one will be changed, possibly for ever. Perhaps mourning has to do with agreeing to undergo a transformation (perhaps one should say *submitting* to a transformation) the full result of which one cannot know in advance" (*PL* 21). Through this process we are deconstituted in ways that are beyond our control. As Butler correctly remarks, we cannot "invoke the Protestant ethic when it comes to loss"; we cannot decide how the task of grieving is to be performed or when it is going to come to an end (*PL* 21). Rather, we are forced to ride waves of sadness that mock our attempts at self-mastery, that call us back to prior experiences of dispossession. Some of these experiences relate to losses we can name but, ultimately, what grief touches is the unnameable kernel of melancholia that connects us to our constitutive inability to attain closure (to disavow our dependence on others). Butler describes such melancholia as a kind of timeless enigma that "hides" in each loss we mourn (*PL* 21–2), as an indelible trace of a primary vulnerability that we can no longer access directly but that our losses approach indirectly. In a more Lacanian vein, one could say that every loss reanimates the primary loss—the loss of *das Ding* (the primordial nonobject of desire)—that constitutes the melancholy foundation of our being. That is, when we lose another person, we not only mourn that loss but we also mourn, with renewed energy, our own incompleteness, our own helplessness, even if we are not aware that this is what we are doing.

Butler asserts: "On one level, I think I have lost 'you' only to discover that 'I' have gone missing as well" (*PL* 22). This can be understood to mean that when I lose you, I no longer know who I am because who I am is so intimately tied to you that the loss of you makes me unintelligible to myself. But it can also be understood to mean that in losing you I have come against melancholy reaches of my being that I usually keep at bay through my efforts to lead a self-governing and reasonably organized existence. Butler implies that there are ethical lessons to be learned from such an encounter with melancholia in the sense that my heightened sensitivity to my own precariousness leads (or should lead) to my heightened sensitivity to the precariousness of others. As she posits, "Despite our differences in location and history, my guess is that it is possible to appeal to a 'we,' for all of us have some notion of what it is to have lost somebody. Loss has made a tenuous 'we' of us all" (*PL* 20).

Unquestionably, this is a poignant way to characterize the solidarity of suffering. But would it not be equally possible to argue that melancholia might lead to the kind of preoccupation with the self, the kind of solipsistic turning-inward that excludes all others from the self's sacred crypt of sadness, that represents the very antithesis of ethical accountability? Melancholia, even more than mourning, fends off others; it sacrifices present and future objects for the sake of the one that has been lost. As Freud already noted, the melancholic copes with his or her loss by incorporating the lost object into his or her psyche, thereby translating a loss in the external world into an internal possession, with the result that the psyche, for the time being, becomes closed to other objects. The memory of the lost object, as it were, crowds out the possibility of new affective ties, which is why, for instance, we find it hard to cathect to a new love object when we are still mourning a lost one. In this sense, while grief may well function as an ethical resource in the way that Butler suggests, the melancholia that grief awakens may pull us in the opposite direction, away from others, from alterity, from the stimulation of new bonds. In addition, melancholia is difficult to translate into the vocabulary of ethical intervention because it arrests action; it is hard to get a depressed person out of bed, let alone into a political rally.

4

Though grief may be a potent source of indignation, as an ethical resource, it may be somewhat unreliable precisely insofar as it conjures up the melancholy ghosts of our constitutive despair. Moreover, it would be relatively easy to stage a critique of Butler's ethics of mourning akin to the one that Wendy Brown stages in relation to Western liberal notions of tolerance, namely that mourning—like tolerance—can function as a distraction from political and economic solutions to global problems.[6] In the same way that discourses of tolerance make us feel that we are accomplishing something when in fact nothing has changed in concrete terms, the ethics of mourning can obscure the fact that mourning by itself does not transform things. If anything, as long as we get to focus on our grief, we do not actually need to *do* anything; we can feel good about ourselves because we experience ourselves as benevolent Western subjects who feel the appropriate remorse about the suffering and death of those far away from us. One could even propose that Brown's contention that tolerance is what the powerful extend to the less powerful—that tolerance merely debases the tolerated even further—applies to grief as well in the sense that the objects of our grief may become all the more disempowered (pitiable, pathetic) by that grief.

Along related lines, there might be an argument to be made about the potentially patronizing tenor of Butler's suggestion that Western subjects are somehow uniquely responsible for grieving those who are less fortunate. Though she does not state the matter in these terms exactly, the implication of much of her discussion of shared precarity is that it is the Western subject in particular who must develop its capacity to mourn the violated other. The non-Western subject is, in this model, invariably the one who is the more violated, the more victimized, and therefore in need of "our" grief, while we, the Westerners, do not deserve the grief of non-Westerners, but should, first and foremost, feel our guilt. There are of course excellent historical reasons for this line of reasoning. Obviously the West should feel guilty about its colonial past and about the ways in which its ongoing imperialistic aspirations of empire-building directly and indirectly contribute to the suffering of non-Westerners. Yet there is also something questionable about the branding of the Western subject as one who is supposed to be racked by grief while it is the lot of the non-Westerner to be the suffering object of this grief. One could even say that, within this model, grief becomes the way in which Western subjects suffer. Does this mean that other forms of suffering have, once again, been relegated to the rest of the world (so that, say, "they" have their poverty while "we" have our grief)?

At the end of the last chapter, I raised the possibility that the turn to Levinas in contemporary ethics might represent a flight from politics. The same could be said about the fetishization of grief as the ethical sentiment *par excellence*. Yet Butler is also right in insisting that, under certain circumstances, grief can furnish a sense of political community, and that it can furthermore do so on a basis that is both more fundamental and more complex than mere identitarian identifications. If our goal is to transcend identity politics without thereby discarding our understanding of the reasons for which various individuals and populations have sought shelter under identitarian labels (black, Muslim, queer, and so on), then shared grief is a potentially powerful place to start. If I can get to the point where the other's grief becomes my grief, then the other's outrage about her oppression also becomes my outrage, with the consequence that I may be willing to overlook the differences between self and other to act on behalf of this other. There are alternative ways to arrive at the same place, and these include my rational assessment that the other has been unjustly treated, but Butler is correct in suggesting that there is something viscerally powerful about the grief we feel when the other's vulnerability, particularly the other's bodily vulnerability, has been exploited. Accounts of genocide, torture, and rape, for instance, tend to move us even when we have no personal connection to the victims, which is precisely why Butler is right in criticizing the ways in which the media keep us from having to face the graphic violence not only of war but also of the unbearable destitution of marginalized populations. If violence is, in Butler's words, "a touch of the worst order" (*PL* 28), an insidious infringement by which human vulnerability is abused, sometimes from hatred, often from creed, then the first step to being able to intervene in such a touch is to be able to witness the havoc it causes. When this havoc is concealed, so is the touch, which means that there is no foundation for grief, let alone outrage and action. This is why Butler's call for a rethinking of grievability as a foundation for alleviating the power imbalances of the global order strikes a chord, why her ethics of precarity makes such intuitive sense, why it is hard to deny her basic insight that "there can be no equal treatment without a prior understanding that all lives have an equal right to be protected from violence and destruction" (*PW* 21).

This is precisely why public acts of grieving are so important, why it is vital to see the pictures, to apprehend the names and faces of those who have been wounded even when these names and faces are not immediately familiar to us. As Butler explains, "I am as much constituted by those I do grieve for as by those whose deaths I disavow, whose nameless and faceless deaths form the melancholic background for my social world, if not my First Worldism" (*PL* 46). "If those lives remain unnameable and ungrievable," Butler concludes, "if they do not appear in their precariousness and their destruction, we will not be moved. We will not return to a sense of ethical outrage that is, distinctively, for an Other, in the name of an Other" (*PL* 150). The prohibition against mourning is, in this sense, one aspect of the derealization of loss, of the indifference we are asked to display with respect to the other's suffering or even death. At the same time, we are encouraged to mourn the losses that are avowed, that "count," as expediently as we can, so as to leave no debilitating residue of sadness that might impede the nation's general robustness, let alone interfere with capitalism's demand for efficiency; we are urged to grieve quickly, to get back on our feet, to brush ourselves off, to get back on track, to get "back to business." After a catastrophe, such as 9/11, there is a haste to return the world to its previous order, whether by sending people back to work, by resorting to nationalist slogans of renewed prowess, or by staging flamboyant architectural competitions to prove technological (and, by implication, military) invincibility. In the Western world, money, the Protestant work ethic, and extravagant displays of power are used to bandage the wounds of violence, to reestablish the fantasy of being inviolable, beyond the reach of dangerous, "irrational" others. This is one reason Butler claims that there might be "something to be gained from grieving, from tarrying with grief, from remaining exposed to its unbearability and not endeavoring to seek a resolution for grief through violence" (*PL* 30).

5

I appreciate Butler's claim that overcoming grief too quickly might eradicate one of our most important ethical resources. But I also want to note the masochistic tendencies of her ethical model because these tendencies, in my view, complicate the task of theorizing (let alone attaining) social justice. On the one hand, I understand the reasons for Butler's Levinasian conviction that ethics is (or should be) a matter of contesting "sovereign notions of the subject" (*PW* 9)—notions that, as Adriana Cavarero argues, are based on "individualistic doctrines, which are too preoccupied with praising the rights of the *I*" (quoted in *GA* 32). After all, the critique of "the ontology of individualism" (*FW* 33) characteristic of the humanist subject, particularly of the Enlightenment subject, has always been central to posthumanist theory. And in recent years, this critique has found a new target: the narcissistic neoliberal subject for whom the fantasy of impermeability and self-sufficiency is foundational. On the other hand, I think that the question of sovereignty is more complicated than Butler allows for, and that this complexity is revealed by accounts of extreme oppression, such as Frantz Fanon's *The Wretched of the Earth*,[7] which voice the need of a traumatized collectivity to reestablish its autonomy and self-determination in the face of subordination. Likewise, individual trauma narratives— Holocaust memoirs, chronicles of rape, and so on—often emphasize that being able to recover a sense of agency over one's life is an essential part of surviving trauma. In other words, they reveal that the quest for sovereignty is not invariably a synonym for arrogant individualism. And they also reveal the problematic nature of the Levinasian ethical injunction to revere the other regardless of how brutally this other has behaved—that is, regardless of any normative considerations.

We have learned that Levinas maintains that our responsibility for the other is unconditional and inescapable, that the other as face is inviolable and that, unfortunately for us, even the executioner, even the Nazi guard, has a face. We may feel tempted to attack such a face, but ethics demands that we resist this temptation. This seems reasonable: I do not take issue with the idea that I should not counter murder with murder, particularly as Levinas emphasizes that it is the task of justice—as opposed to ethics—to arbitrate between different faces. However, as I have argued, the fact that Levinasian ethics places no normative limits on the behavior of the victimizer makes an unreasonable demand on the victimized; it shifts the ethical burden entirely from the victimizer to the victim, so that ethics no longer assesses the actions of the victimizer but rather the responses of the victim. A similar charge could be leveled against Butler, whose fairly uncritical adoption of Levinasian ethics—coupled with her relative neglect of Levinasian justice—causes her to claim that "our responsibility is heightened once we have been subjected to the violence of others" (*PL* 16). In this vision, assigning responsibility—in the sense that normative justice strives to do—becomes impossible.

Consider also the following assertion from *Parting Ways*: "The responsibility that I must take for the Other proceeds directly from being persecuted and outraged by that Other. Thus there is violence in the relation from the start: I am claimed by the other *against my will*, and my responsibility for the Other emerges from this subjection" (*PW* 59; emphasis added). This assertion is not as crazy as it may seem when taken out of context, for what Butler is getting at is the Levinasian connection between my relational ontology and my ethical responsibility. The basic idea is that because the other "interrupts" the coherence of my being, impeding my self-closure, I am, in a sense, always "persecuted" and "outraged" by the other; yet because the other is always already an ingredient of my self, I cannot denounce my responsibility for this other. In this model, responsibility is the reverse of being impinged upon by the other in ways that sometimes feel persecuting and outrageous. As Butler reminds us, according to Levinas, "precisely the Other who persecutes me has a face" (*GA* 90). Consequently, "I cannot disavow my relation to the Other, regardless of what the Other does, regardless of what I might will" (*GA* 91). Responsibility, in this sense, is "not a matter of cultivating a will, but of making use of an unwilled susceptibility as a resource for becoming responsive to the Other": "Whatever the Other has done, the Other still makes an ethical demand upon me, has a 'face' to which I am obligated to respond" (*GA* 91). Simply put, if the individualistic ethical theories that Butler resists praise the "rights of the *I*," Butler's relational ethics, like its Levinasian counterpart, values the other's well-being over the subject's self-preservation. In Butler's words, "One of the problems with insisting on self-preservation as the basis of ethics is that it becomes a pure ethics of the self, if not a form of moral narcissism" (*GA* 103).

I understand why Butler's Levinasian ethics represents an effective decentering of the sovereign Enlightenment subject. But does it not swing too far to the other extreme, making a virtue out of masochism? Is there not, say, from a feminist perspective, something quite uncomfortable about the idea that I am responsible for others who violate me "against my will." Butler writes:

> Given over from the start to the world of others, [the body] bears their imprint, is formed within the crucible of social life; only later, and with some uncertainty, do I lay claim to my body as my own, if, in fact, I ever do. Indeed, if I deny that prior to the formation of my "will," my body related me to others whom I did not choose to have in proximity to myself, if I build a notion of "autonomy" on the basis of the denial of this sphere of a primary and unwilled physical proximity with others, then am I denying the social conditions of my embodiment in the name of autonomy? (*PL* 26)

Physical vulnerability is here what "saves" me from the demon of autonomy. Does this mean that my attempts to protect myself physically render me unethical? If Butler raises the self's reverence for the other to an ethical virtue, there might also be some virtue in being able to recognize one's own self as worth fighting for, particularly if that self is one that has been socially denigrated. From a Levinasian perspective, the quest for self-preservation is the antithesis of ethics; but from an alternative ethical perspective—a more straightforwardly feminist, antiracist, or anticolonial one—it might be one of the pillars of an ethical world.

More generally speaking, one of the problems with Butlerian ethics is that it consistently sets up a rigid dichotomy between bad autonomy and good relationality. Indeed, one could say that this is an instance where a vehemently antiessentialist thinker falls into the kind of poststructuralist essentialism where some possibilities—such as the idea that autonomy might sometimes be an important component of human life—become unthinkable. Butler often talks as if the fact that we are not fully autonomous creatures meant that we have no capacity for autonomy whatsoever. Yet in the same way that having an unconscious does not erase the conscious mind but merely complicates its functioning, our lack of seamless autonomy does not render us completely devoid of it. Moreover, as Jessica Benjamin, among others, has illustrated, autonomy is not always the repugnant antithesis of relationality.[8] Quite the contrary, a degree of autonomy might actually be necessary for respectful relationships with others at the same time as relationality might sometimes be a means of building autonomy. Autonomy and relationality, in this sense, are not mutually exclusive but rather mutually constitutive of each other, so that Butler's portraiture of autonomy—of any attempt at recentering the self—as intrinsically evil seems too one-dimensional. Butler asserts that there is "no recentering of the subject without unleashing unacceptable sadism and cruelty": "To remain decentered, interestingly, means to remain implicated in the death of the other and so at a distance from the unbridled cruelty . . . in which the self seeks to separate from its constitutive sociality and annihilate the other" (GA 77). I agree that self-assertion can take place at the expense of others. And I agree that the fantasy of sovereignty can promote contempt not only for others but also for alternative, more relational modalities of being. But I am not convinced that the subject who seeks to recenter itself is automatically sadistic and cruel, driven to annihilate the other.

Butler's enthusiasm for relationality as a *substitute* for autonomy, rather than as its counterpart, causes her to cut off a considerable part of human experience, including the fact that we *do* usually have a sense of ourselves as semiautonomous individuals who possess a degree of agency, and who are consequently not indiscriminately subjected to the will and actions of others. That we are not fully agentic does not mean that we have no agency at all; that the other dwells within our constitution does not mean that our relationship to the other is all we are; that our personal history cannot be divorced from the social and intersubjective currents around us does not mean that we can be reduced to these currents—that we have no conception of ourselves as discrete individuals with discrete personal histories.

In *Frames of War*, Butler criticizes Melanie Klein for privileging the ego:

> Why the ego? After all, if my survivability depends on a relation to others, to a "you" or a set of "yous" without whom I cannot exist, then my existence is not mine alone, but is to be found outside myself, in this set of relations that precede and exceed the boundaries of who I am . . . who "I" am is nothing without your life. (*FW* 44)

This characterization of the self-other relationship certainly fits Butler's larger theory. But does the fact that my existence is not "mine alone" really mean that *nothing* of it is "mine"—that it takes place *wholly* "outside myself"? Is it really the case that I am *nothing* without the other? In addition, even if the ego is not the most important (or admirable) part of me, surely I have one, and surely it serves a purpose. For one thing, it allows me to talk to you on these pages as if I had something meaningful to say.

Moreover, it is not merely the self that is the casualty of Butler's approach, but ultimately—and paradoxically—the other as well, for the more the other is elevated above the self, the more menacing, the more ominous, he or she becomes. The other may, in Butler's model, be as vulnerable as I am, but because of the other's capacity to persecute me, she is always also potentially someone who can hurt me; if my subjectivity is a matter of the other impinging upon me against my will, then the other is an automatic agent of aggression. Let me requote the passage from *Parting Ways* I already quoted above, this time allowing Butler to complete her thought:

> The responsibility that I must take for the Other proceeds directly from being persecuted and outraged by that Other. Thus there is violence in the relation from the start: I am claimed by the other against my will, and my responsibility for the Other emerges from this subjection. If we think about the face as that which commands me not to be indifferent to the death of the other, and that command as what lays hold of me prior to any choice I might make, then this command can be said to persecute me, to hold me hostage—*the face of the Other is persecutory from the start*. And if the substance of that persecution is the interdiction against killing, then *I am persecuted by the injunction to keep the peace*. (*PL* 59; emphasis added)

There is arguably a kind of paranoid fantasy at play here where the other, the entire world of others, persecutes me against my will; there is no such thing as a nonpersecutory face. But what is perhaps even more disturbing is that Butler—who has always had the tendency to see the external world as inherently predatory[9]—manages to turn even the other's vulnerability into a weapon of persecution aimed at me: the other's vulnerability prohibits killing, and I am persecuted by this "injunction to keep the peace," which, ultimately, implies that I am persecuted by the other's vulnerability. As Butler adds:

> Of course, the commandment not to kill is, paradoxically, imposed upon me violently: it is imposed against my will and so is violent in this precise sense. . . . If the face is "accusatory," it is so in a grammatical sense: it takes me as its object, regardless of my will. It is this foreclosure of freedom and will through the command that is its "violent" operation, understood variously as persecutory and accusatory. (*PL* 59)

The commandment not to kill carries a violence that is persecutory and accusatory, and because it is the fragility of the other as face that imposes this commandment on me, I am, as it were, violated by the other's very helplessness.

I am, then, impinged upon not just by the aggression of others but by their dependency as well. Or, more properly, their dependency is what makes them aggressive. Furthermore, Butler's model overlooks the fact that the individuals who facilitated my formative coming-into-being are not necessarily the same as those I interact with as an adult. I may have started my life in a state of interpersonal vulnerability that made it impossible for me to dissociate myself from those who chose to wound me, but what keeps me from doing so now? I may owe an existential debt to those who have over the years made my life viable, but does this condemn me to an indiscriminate patience with everyone I meet irrespective of any normative considerations? Surely there is a distinction between the idea that I am inhabited by an ontological otherness that I cannot denounce—that I only have a self to the extent that I partake in structures of intersubjectivity—and the idea that I cannot (or should not) sever my connection to *specific* others who injure me. Although it is true that my infantile experiences will always exert an influence over my life, it is inaccurate to assert that, as an adult subject, my relationship to the world of others is always (or primarily) one of being persecuted and outraged. More abstractly speaking, if we are to look for a universal constituent of subjectivity, primordial impingement, dispossession, and precariousness are a good place to start. But I do not think that it makes sense to restrict the human condition to these traits. Undoubtedly there are other characteristics, such as the capacity for rational thought, the potential for creativity, or the aptitude for pleasure—and not *just* the susceptibility to pain—that *also* unite us. Butler consistently downplays the difference between the constitutive vulnerability of the child and the psychic realities of adult subjectivity, failing to consider the possibility that our infantile defenselessness does not necessarily translate into lifelong helplessness. We undoubtedly carry the imprint of our formative vulnerability to our graves. But surely this is not the whole story, or even the main story; surely we are also deeply enabled by others.

6

My larger point is that Butler's adoption of Levinasian masochism leads her down some murky conceptual alleys. Consider, for instance, what happens when Butler combines the nonnormative thrust of Levinasian ethics with psychoanalytic insights about the intrinsically opaque nature of subjectivity to exhort me to forgive those who have wounded me. According to Butler, I am ethically obliged "to offer forgiveness to others, who are . . . constituted in partial opacity to themselves" (*GA* 42). More specifically, I need to recognize that others are driven by unconscious motivations that remain beyond their reach, which means that they do not always know what they are doing. Nor are they capable of giving a full account of their actions, with the result that my request for such an account constitutes a form of ethical violence. As Butler proposes:

> The recognition that one is, at every turn, not quite the same as how one presents oneself in the available discourse might imply, in turn, a certain patience with others that would suspend the demand that they be self-same at every moment. Suspending the demand for self-identity or, more particularly, for complete coherence seems to me to counter a certain ethical violence,

which demands that we manifest and maintain self-identity at all times and require that others do the same. (*GA* 41–2)

My opacity to myself should therefore make me patient with the other's opacity; my disorientation should make me patient with the other's disorientation; and my noncoincidence with myself should make me patient with the other's noncoincidence with herself. Butler suggests that "a new sense of ethics" emerges from such a recognition of the inevitability of mutual ethical failure:

> As we ask to know the other, or ask that the other say, finally or definitively, who he or she is, it will be important not to expect an answer that will ever satisfy. By not pursuing satisfaction and by letting the question remain open, even enduring, we let the other live, since life might be understood as precisely that which exceeds any account we may try to give of it. (*GA* 42–3)

Butlerian ethics thus implies that I only "let the other live" when I remain lenient with her inability to give an accurate account of herself. On the flip side, I can expect similar leniency from others. As Butler proposes, "I will need to be forgiven for what I cannot have fully known" (*GA* 42). In this way, Butler turns my inner opacity into a semiautomatic grounds for forgiveness. To be sure, she admits that this opacity should not be taken as license to do whatever I want to. But in principle it deserves the patience, forbearance, and forgiveness of others. Even more pointedly, Butler maintains that because my prehistory—the part of my infantile formation that I cannot, as an adult, reconstruct—keeps interrupting any story I tell of myself, it constitutes "my failure to be fully accountable for my actions, my final 'irresponsibility,' one for which I may be forgiven only because I could not do otherwise" (*GA* 78–9). As a consequence, she concludes, "If we speak and try to give an account from this place [of opacity], we will not be irresponsible, or, if we are, we will surely be forgiven" (*GA* 136).

Is this not a little too convenient for us? Butler reads the psychoanalytic insight about our inner opacity to mean that we cannot be held fully responsible for our actions but will, instead, "surely" be forgiven. I would say that this is a fairly self-serving way to interpret the fact that we are often motivated by unconscious currents that we do not entirely understand. I would indeed be tempted to reverse Butler's formulation to argue that I am fully responsible for my actions even when I cannot comprehend how the ghosts of my formative experiences goad me to these actions. Freud's point about making the unconscious conscious, after all, was not that I should resign myself to riding the pulse of the repetition compulsion for the rest of my life; rather, his point was that by developing an active relationship to my unconscious, I might be able to foster the capacity to intervene in this compulsion whenever it threatens to hurt either me or others. By this I obviously do not mean that I expect to master my unconscious. If nothing else, I remain a good Lacanian. But I believe that psychoanalysis teaches me, has taught me, that I am responsible for my actions even—and perhaps *particularly*—when they are unconsciously motivated. In this sense, my opacity does not absolve me of responsibility but rather asks me to become more vigilant in relation to my unconscious patterns. That I have a prehistory that I cannot control does not mean that I have no say over my actions in the present. Nor does my lack of self-transparency mean that I cannot attain a degree of self-understanding. This is why I cannot see my opacity as a get-out-of-jail-free card; rather, I see it as an invitation to a radical form of self-responsibility.[10]

"My unconscious made me do it" may be a tempting excuse, but it places too heavy a burden on those who have been harmed by my actions. Likewise, though I appreciate Butler's impulse to remain generous with the inner opacities of others, I am not as quick to absolve them of their wrongdoings as Butler. If anything—and here I return to a concern I already raised in relation to Levinas— I think that there is something questionable about Butler's call for patience, forbearance, and forgiveness in a biopolitical context where some people—say, women—are already expected to offer such patience, forbearance, and forgiveness more than others. I am not at all certain that uncritical charity with respect to others is either ethically prudent or psychoanalytically sound. Indeed, nothing is easier than abusing this charity. From the neoliberal subject who cannot commit to anything, and who therefore expects others to tolerate her ambivalences indefinitely, to the rapist who claims that his victim "provoked" him, the world is full of people who are used to getting away with more than they should. The refusal to condemn them in the name of a more capacious ethics merely gives them permission to continue their hurtful behavior;

indeed, this refusal directly contradicts Butler's own view that we should oppose any and all attempts to exploit human vulnerability. Moreover, looking back, one might ask whether feminism, the Civil Rights movement, anticolonial struggles, resistance to apartheid, and so on, would have been possible if those involved had decided to be forgiving rather than furious. Butler argues that "it may be that only through an experience of the other under conditions of suspended judgment do we finally become capable of an ethical reflection on the humanity of the other, even when that other has sought to annihilate humanity" (*GA* 45). Does this mean that if I condemn a person who has "sought to annihilate humanity," I fail at the task of being ethical?

Butler flees from ethical condemnation—a k a normative judgment—because it supposedly props up the condemning subject's righteousness by disavowing commonality with the one who is being condemned. As she argues, "Condemnation is very often an act that not only 'gives up on' the one condemned but seeks to inflict a violence upon the condemned in the name of 'ethics'" (*GA* 46). Butler here—awkwardly enough—judges the violence of judgment to be more violent than the violence of the act that is being judged. I concede that there are situations where the normative moral order inflicts violence by its judgments—and even misjudges—but it seems like an overstatement to suggest that, in condemning those who commit acts of violence, I "lose the chance to be ethically educated or 'addressed' by a consideration of who they are and what their personhood says about the range of human possibility" (*GA* 45). Butler maintains that condemnation "takes aim at the life of the condemned," among other things because "punishment works to further destroy the conditions for autonomy, eroding if not eviscerating the capacity of the subject addressed for both self-reflection and social recognition, two practices that are, I would argue, essential to any substantive account of ethical life. It also, of course, turns the moralist into a murderer" (*GA* 49). It is difficult to escape the irony of the fact that this is one of the few places in her entire body of work where Butler openly appreciates autonomy and the capacity for self-reflection. The one who condemns becomes a murderer because she destroys the autonomy of the perpetrator of violence, whereas the perpetrator—even the murderer—becomes a victim by virtue of being condemned. Pushed to an extreme, Butler's vision could be argued to imply that those who murder cannot quite help themselves but those who condemn them are culpable of (soul)-murder.

Undoubtedly, Butler's reading of our relational ontology as a foundation of ethical generosity represents an important attempt to rethink ethics in a postmetaphysical world. In a way, Butler asks: how can we understand ethical accountability in the context of partially opaque inner lives and even more opaque interpersonal relationships; how can we conceive of ethics when the very status of the human being is uncertain? Yet her resistance to the notion of agency makes it difficult to conceptualize responsibility beyond a kind of kinship of vulnerability. At a key point in *Giving an Account of Oneself*, Butler asks:

> According to the kind of theory I have been pursuing here, what will responsibility look like? Haven't we, by insisting on something nonnarrativizable, limited the degree to which we might hold ourselves or others accountable for their actions? . . . Have we perhaps unwittingly destroyed the possibility of agency with all this talk about being given over, being structured, being addressed? (*GA* 83; 99)

My response to this is, "Yes, we have." Or, more precisely, *you*—Judith Butler—have. I am still doing my best to hold onto some agency. This does not mean that I am about to dust off the skeleton of the Enlightenment subject. I understand the problems—the ethical violence—that this subject represents. But I also think that, for many of us, the lived realities of subjectivity tend to be quite far from the hubris of this subject. Butler sometimes sounds as if she were conducting a witch hunt against enormous egos. But where exactly are these king-sized egos? My sense is that many of us are trying quite hard to scrape together a modicum of ego strength, a modicum of autonomy, a modicum of self-determination. And those who have been acutely traumatized are working overtime at this for the simple reason that their egos, autonomy, and self-determination have been violently stomped on. I do not think that an ethics of masochism would help them—would help any of us—lead more manageable lives. And it certainly does not do anything for our capacity to take responsibility for the pain that we may, often inadvertently, inflict on others.

7

Butler's resistance to the idea that agency, including autonomy and the capacity for self-reflection, may be a valuable feature of human life explains, in part at least, her hostility to *a priori* principles of right and wrong. This hostility is of course endemic in posthumanist theory because this theory views ethics primarily as a matter of questioning hegemonic normative paradigms. From the Frankfurt School to Lacan, Foucault, Barthes, Derrida, and Butler, among others, there has been an attempt to unearth the violence intrinsic to our dominant ethical models: the fact that their claim to objectivity rests on a number of constitutive exclusions (say, the exclusion of women, or the exclusion of racialized others). One could indeed say that this is what critical theory—my own field—consists of: it reveals the oppressive underbelly of the norms that we have been taught to take for granted. I have always been—and continue to be—a huge supporter of this type of theorizing. But I have also come to see that sometimes the vehement critique of norms obscures the fact that we still need them. And it also obscures the fact that there is no reason to assume that our *a priori* norms must be metaphysically founded. As feminist philosopher Amy Allen has argued persuasively, *a priori* norms are always historically specific in the sense that they arise in particular social contexts. This, however, does not mean that they are invariably worthless; that is, the loss of metaphysical foundations for our normative systems does not automatically invalidate them but merely reveals their historicity. Any *a priori* set of principles, Allen explains, is by definition "our historical a priori," yet rejecting such principles wholesale "would mean surrendering intelligibility. We have no choice, after all, but to start from where we are."[11]

I will return to Allen's argument in Chapter 5. At this point, let me merely emphasize that the lack of normative limits—of *a priori* ethical principles—in Butlerian theory, as in Levinasian ethics, makes it hard to avoid the conclusion that I am supposed to actively sustain those who hurt me, and that this is the case regardless of whether they are sexists, racists, neo-Nazis, or homophobic religious fundamentalists. Indeed, the extreme lengths to which Butler is willing to go to defend the Levinasian notion that even the executioner has a face are revealed in *Parting Ways*, where she discusses the condemnation of Eichmann that Hannah Arendt stages at the end of *Eichmann in Jerusalem*.[12] In this text, Arendt is critical of the ways in which Israel uses the Eichmann trial for its political ends, yet she also holds Eichmann responsible for his crimes, stating in closing that he deserves to be hanged for these crimes. Butler proposes that at the moment that Arendt judges Eichmann, "some disposition of language binds them both together; she is part of a human plurality with him—indeed, with the likes of him. And yet the effect of her address to him is to exclude him from that very domain of plurality" (*PW* 171). The implication is that Arendt, in judging Eichmann, fails to live up to her own ideal of plurality. In a strictly abstract sense this may be true. But the charge also illustrates the problematic nature of an ethics that operates wholly without norms, where literally nothing a person does renders him or her worthy of ethical censure. Yes, we need to revere plurality. But we also need some way to decide which types of actions are acceptable. Eichmann emphatically did not respect plurality. I am consequently not sure if it was Arendt's responsibility to extend to him the courtesy of respecting his (though I do not support the death sentence, I think Arendt had the right to condemn Eichmann). Butler has so much trouble with the idea of normative judgments that she comes close to defending Eichmann against Arendt's insensitivity; though she is not saying that Eichmann is not guilty, she implies that Arendt is *also* guilty for not including him in the plurality of humanity.

Interestingly, Butler's resistance to *a priori* values, even ones derived from the Enlightenment, dissipates in the context of her critique of Israeli state violence against Palestinians, for she argues that Palestinians have the right to have basic rights, such as the right not to be dispossessed of land, due to their membership in a global human community. More specifically, and following Edward Said, Butler calls for a binational, pluralistic solution to the Israel-Palestine conflict that would be based on democratic principles of equality and inclusion rather than on the nationalist policies of Israel. Regarding Palestine's claim "to the lands that rightfully are its own," she writes: "One could formulate the right in light of international law or on the basis of moral and political arguments that may or may not be framed within a specific version of the nation-state" (*PW* 205). I happen to agree with this stance: I also think that Palestinians should have basic human rights regardless of whether or not they belong to a nation-state. But Butler's argument also reveals the limits of her capacity to utilize Levinasian ethics as a blueprint for social justice, for there is nothing about this ethics—an ethics that explicitly shuns rights-based approaches—that supports her sudden turn to the kind of liberal cosmopolitanism that can be traced, through Arendt, all the way back to Kant.

I have explained that Levinas himself solves this dilemma by keeping ethics and justice separate—that Levinasian justice allows for the kinds of *a priori* normative principles that his ethics eschews. In other words, Levinas's critique of metaphysics does not extend to Enlightenment-based legal edicts that seek to adjudicate between different faces and that can consequently be used as a foundation of rights-based discourses. Butler, in contrast, has spent much of her career recoiling from any affiliation with the Enlightenment, including its principles of justice, so that her sudden reliance on such principles seems to come out of nowhere. I do not take issue with the idea that *a priori* principles of equality, freedom, reciprocity, and democratic process should apply to the Israel-Palestine conflict. But let us not pretend that these principles arise directly from a Levinasian ethics of precarity rather than from the Enlightenment; let us recognize that if Butler stayed faithful to Levinasian ethics, she would not be calling for equal rights for Palestinians but rather saying that self-preservation should not be a priority for them, that, indeed, there might be something profoundly unethical about their quest for sovereignty and self-determination. One could of course argue that the Enlightenment does not own the notion of equal rights, that it is possible to think about equal rights beyond their humanistic context, as Derrida does when he claims that "what remains irreducible to any deconstruction" is "an idea of justice— which we distinguish from law or right and even from human rights—and an idea of democracy—which we distinguish from its current concept and from its determined predicates today."[13] But Derrida's elusive definition of justice and democracy is not what Butler is working with when she, in a Kantian vein, calls for international law that recognizes the rights of individuals not on the basis of their attachment to nation-states but rather on the basis of their humanity.

8

It seems to me that Butler cannot have it both ways, that if she is going to remain resistant to the rights-based values of the Enlightenment, including its values of autonomy and rational self-reflexivity, then she cannot resort to its cosmopolitan norms of justice whenever these happen to suit her political purposes. A similar sliding—a similar confusion between seemingly incompatible theoretical positions—takes place with regard to Butler's attitude toward the universalist implications of her ethics of precarity. As I have emphasized, Butler explicitly acknowledges the universal reach of her paradigm: the fact that precariousness is a generalizable condition of human life. Yet her relationship to this universality is ambivalent, even reluctant, no doubt because it is difficult to talk about universality in the context of ethics without raising the very specters of the Enlightenment—including its reliance on *a priori* norms—that Butler is trying to outwit. This ambivalence is, once again, most pronounced in *Parting Ways*, where Butler performs an awkward retraction of her earlier rhetoric of generalizability by claiming that her analysis of shared human precariousness aims at pluralization rather than universalization. Under pluralization, she writes, "Equal protection or, indeed, equality is not a principle that homogenizes those to whom it applies; rather, the commitment to equality is a commitment to the process of differentiation itself" (*PW* 126). Speaking of suffering specifically, Butler adds that, unlike universalization, pluralization recognizes that even though all of us are defenseless against suffering, any given experience of suffering is so unique that the attempt to compare various forms of suffering is bound to founder. If, as I stressed at the beginning of this chapter, Butler's earlier work included a sustained effort to navigate the (admittedly challenging) tension between universality and singularity, she now presents this tension as more or less insurmountable: "If we start with the presumption that one group's suffering is *like* another group's, we have not only assembled the groups into provisional monoliths—and so falsified them—but we have launched into a form of analogy building that *invariably fails*" (*PW* 128; second emphasis added).

Butler's ambivalence about using the trope of universalism in *Parting Ways* is understandable, for in this text she is walking a tightrope between arguing, on the one hand, that the Jewish history of exile, violation, and dispossession should yield insight into the experiences of exile, violation, and dispossession of others, including the Palestinians, and insisting, on the other, that we should not conflate these two experiences. In other words, however critical Butler is of Israel's policies toward Palestinians (and she is very critical), she wants to make absolutely sure that she cannot be accused of claiming that these policies are akin to Hitler's National Socialism; she does not want to imply that "Zionism is like Nazism or is its unconscious repetition with Palestinians standing in for Jews" (PW 29). Such an analogy, she notes, would "fail to consider the very different modes of subjugation, dispossession, and death-dealing that characterize National Socialism and political Zionism" (PW 29). Her goal, instead, is

> to ask how certain kinds of principles might be extrapolated from one set of historical conditions to grasp another, a move that requires an act of political translation that refuses to assimilate the one experience to the other, and refuses as well the kind of particularism that would deny any possible way to articulate principles regarding, say, the rights of refugees on the basis of a comparative consideration of these and other instances of historical dispossession. (PW 29–30)

Butler thus wants to avoid both the kind of universalism that levels distinctions and the kind of particularism that makes it impossible to compare experiences of violation. On the one hand, she—again, following Said—urges Jews to draw upon their history of persecution and diaspora to build a sense of kinship with other persecuted and diasporic peoples, including the Palestinians; because the Jews have suffered so much hardship, she argues, they may be capable of "ethical solidarity" (PW 49) toward others who have had comparable experiences. On the other hand, she specifies that it is important not to understand this convergence of experiences "as a form of strict analogy" (PW 121). Again, one can see why the context of Butler's discussion calls for repeated disclaimers about strict analogies, and why it therefore complicates the discourse of generalizability that she uses more freely in her earlier books. The rhetorical challenges of Butler's analysis in this text are formidable because she does not want to downplay the specificity of the Nazi genocide, yet she seeks to build a model of political responsibility that would recognize convergent modes of dispossession; she wishes to acknowledge that "there are historically specific modalities of catastrophe that cannot be measured or compared by any common or neutral standard" (*PW* 29), yet she also strives to leap from one history of oppression to another. As she maintains, "In thinking about the history of the oppressed, it seems imperative to recognize that such a history can and does apply to any number of people in ways that are never strictly parallel and tend to disrupt easy analogies" (*PW* 100).

I can certainly understand why Butler insists that histories of oppression can be convergent without being equivalent. I agree with her resistance to the kind of universalization that would erase important distinctions. And I would never endorse an ethical model where one history of suffering would negate another, where the specificity of suffering would be lost. Yet there is also something unconvincing about Butler's sudden attempt to replace universalization by pluralization, and particularly about her claim that, when it comes to experiences of suffering, analogies "invariably fail." Given that the ability to draw analogies between different forms of suffering constitutes the very crux of her ethics of precarity, it is difficult to see how this ethics can survive the collapse of this ability. If anything, it seems that this collapse would instantly undermine the most radical potential of Butler's ethics, namely its ability to compete with other universalizing paradigms, such as transcendental Enlightenment paradigms. Nor does Butler's hesitation about universalism seem theoretically necessary, for drawing an analogy does not cancel out the distinctiveness of the entities being compared. As she herself postulates in *Precarious Life*, "When analogies are offered, they presuppose the separability of the terms that are compared. But any analogy also assumes a common ground for comparability, and in this case the analogy functions to a certain degree by functioning metonymically" (*PL* 72). Exactly. If I draw an analogy by saying that you and I both have two eyes, this does not mean that our eyes are therefore identical: my eyes will still be blue while yours will still be brown. But what is important is the understanding that if someone throws acid in our eyes, we will both scream. Likewise, if I say that bodily vulnerability is something that you and I share, I do not mean to suggest that we experience this vulnerability in the same way.

A universalist ethics of precarity based on analogies does not demand a similarity of experiences but merely that we are able to recognize points of contact between different experiences. Let us recall that even the most banal forms of universalism, such as the neoliberal rhetoric of "different but equal," do not ask that we all have the *same* experiences but merely that—as human beings—we possess the capacity to recognize the correspondences, the often quite abstract resemblances, between different experiences. When it comes to suffering, for instance, universalism does not presume that my suffering is *like* yours but merely that I am able to draw a parallel between your suffering and mine. In this sense, Butler's fear that universalization is *intrinsically* homogenizing seems somewhat misplaced, and in fact directly contradicts her own statements elsewhere in *Parting Ways*, such as the following: "It is only possible to struggle to alleviate the suffering of others if I am both motivated and dispossessed by my own suffering" (*PW* 127). Likewise, Butler explicitly posits that one history of suffering provides "the conditions of attunement to another such history," so that "one finds the condition of one's own life in the life of another where there is dependency and differentiation, proximity and violence" (*PW* 130). I have already expressed my reservations about the idea that ethics should be based on something as unreliable as my capacity to be moved by the suffering of others. But if such an ethics is going to work at all, we must presuppose that the common experience of precariousness provides a ground for translating from one experience to another in ways that enable a degree of universalization—that even though each human life is unique, there is a kernel of sameness that makes identification (and therefore ethical indignation, outrage, and action) possible.

I am not saying that Butler does not recognize this. As I have tried to show, she admits that one experience of suffering might reverberate with another experience of suffering without it being the case that the two experiences are the same. My point, rather, is that there is something perplexing about her rhetorical vacillation between universalism and antiuniversalism, and that I suspect that this vacillation is motivated more by what I earlier characterized as her desire to remain "a good poststructuralist" than by any genuine philosophical exigency. More specifically, it is due to an unacknowledged conflict between her ideological commitments—which tell her to steer clear of universalization at all costs—and the fact that her entire ethical paradigm is predicated on her capacity to move between different experiences of oppression in ways that are inherently universalizing. Furthermore, if it is *Parting Ways* that most clearly showcases this conflict, it is because this text quite simply cannot attain its stated aims without a process of rigorous universalization. After all, the book's (tenaciously reiterated) goal is to derive a generalizable set of ethical principles from the Jewish heritage. As Butler writes, "It may seem to be a paradox to say that there is a Jewish route to the insight that equality must be secured for a population regardless of religious affiliation, but this is the consequence of a universalization that mobilizes an active trace of that formation with another, as well as a break with its original form" (*PW* 18).

That universal ethical principles are extracted from a specific cultural resource—in this case, the Jewish tradition—does not, Butler explains, "mean that they belong exclusively to [the] tradition from which they are derived" (*PW* 3). She in fact suggests that only principles that demonstrate applicability outside their tradition of origin are able to yield strong enough ethical and political edicts to begin with, so that being able to depart from a given tradition is a precondition of ethical and political effectiveness. As she asserts, "It would seem that other sorts of values and political aspirations did and do emerge in the light of the Nazi genocide, ones that seek to understand and forestall *all* forms of fascism and *all* efforts at coercive dispossession" (*PW* 26; emphasis added).[14] Universalization, in other words, is built into the very methodology of Butler's text in ways that render the moments when she resorts to the rhetoric of antiuniversalization quite bewildering. I appreciate her persistent attention to singularity—her vigilant efforts to safeguard plurality, diversity, and difference against the homogenizing impulses of universalization—because this reminds us that even though precariousness is a universal condition of human life, it is always experienced in singular ways, and that there are consequently times when the temptation to compare two singularities might augment rather than alleviate violence. Yet Butler's overemphasis on the incommensurability of oppressions at times threatens to undercut what is most inspired about her ethics of precarity, namely its capacity to combine a posthumanist understanding of subjectivity with a universalist model of ethical accountability.

9

One reason for the theoretical inconsistencies of Butler's analysis is that even though her ethics of precarity implies that the individual is the proper unit of ethical and political deliberation, her discussion of the virtues of pluralization (as opposed to universalization) tends to privilege groups, particularly "the Jews" and "the Palestinians," as the appropriate unit. As a consequence, it becomes harder for her to keep her eye on the kernel of similarity that unites the units in question. She comes close to admitting this when she writes, "Through elaborating a series of such broken or exhausted analogies, the communitarian presumption that we might start with 'groups' as our point of departure meets its limit, and then the internally and externally differentiating action of pluralization emerges as a clear alternative" (PW 128).

Butler is right that analogies between groups will always be broken or exhausted, for groups will always be defined in part by their differences. And within each group, there is going to exist so much differentiation that no degree of universalization can reveal the ontological principle that causes the group to cohere as a group. As a matter of fact, it is precisely the quest for such an ontological principle that leads to violent ethnonationalisms and religious fundamentalisms; there is always something totalitarian about the search for an ontological foundation for group solidarity. Such a solidarity can be politically constructed in useful ways, but trying to ground it in some kind of an ethos of blood and soil is a recipe for disaster. This is one reason that cosmopolitan theory has long advocated the individual—rather than, say, the nation-state or religious community—as the relevant unit of ethical and political consideration. As Seyla Benhabib expresses the matter, "Why should members of the same ethnic group share a comprehensive worldview? Cannot one be Russian as well as an anarchist, a communist, or a slavophile? Can one not be black as well as a separatist, an integrationist, or an assimilationist?"[15] In principle, Butler agrees. As we saw above, she proposes—in a moment of cosmopolitanism that Benhabib might appreciate—that Palestinians have the right to have basic rights by virtue of their humanity rather than by virtue of their group identity.[16] Yet when it comes to the conflict between pluralization and universalization, Butler tends to revert to group-based thinking, which is one reason she ends up rejecting universalization in favor of pluralization.

Butler's tormented relationship to universalism becomes particularly evident when she attempts to deny the universalizing force of the Levinasian concern for the other as face. More specifically, Butler maintains that because every face makes a singular claim upon me, the face inevitably subverts universalism; it disrupts the kind of universalizing "formalism" that "would have me treat each and every other of *equal* concern" (*PW* 57). But I am not sure how one can, in the Levinasian context, get from the idea that every face makes a singular claim upon me to the idea that I am not expected to treat each and every face with equal concern. Isn't the implication the exact opposite, namely that even if the claim of each face comes to me in a singular fashion, I am equally responsible for all faces? That is, each face has an *equal* singular claim upon me. When Butler asks, "Can the face serve as an injunction against violence toward each and every individual?" (*PW* 57), the answer seems entirely obvious: yes, that is exactly what the face does, which is why it is, for Levinas, a site of nonnegotiable accountability. Yet Butler proposes—and it is at moments such as this that I get bothered by her excessive allegiance to poststructuralist dogmas—that on the basis of my responsibility toward the other, "a demand is delivered to me that is precisely not universalizable," that the singular form of the other's address automatically "undoes the universality of the claim" (*PW* 66). Butler seems here to be stuck in the same conceptual tangle as when she suggests (against her own statements to the contrary) that analogy implies the equivalence of experience. In contrast, I would posit that in the same way that analogy does not require that the units of comparison are equivalent, the universal weight of the Levinasian injunction to heed the call of the face does not in any way erase the singularity of the faces that might, at any given moment, be making a claim on me. Or, to put the matter more abstractly, it is completely possible for a singularity to partake in a universality without thereby losing its singular character.

Speaking of the commandment not to kill, Butler writes, "For Levinas, we are the ones who are singularly interpellated by the commandment and thus differentiated from one another in such a way that universality is made impossible" (*PW* 66). The obvious question, once again, is why Butler thinks that the singularity of the interpellation cancels out the universality of the commandment not to kill. If Levinas goes as far as to assert that even the SS man has a face, then obviously he is not saying that sometimes it is acceptable to kill. Yet Butler maintains that any "codification" of the Levinasian obligation to the other would immediately betray the "anarchism" of this obligation (*PW* 67). This anarchism, she explains, has to do with that fact that human relationality is not rational but links "human destitution to a certain responsibility to shelter the life of others. It is as if, or precisely because, we are transient, dust and ashes, that we must shelter life" (*PW* 67). But how is this responsibility to shelter life—in its Levinasian valence— not a universal injunction? That it is based on precarity rather than reason does not make it any less universal. If anything, the fact that it refers to a prerational realm of human existence seems to make it *more* universal.

In rational ethical approaches, there may be some question about the accuracy and consistency of reason, and therefore about ethical injunctions based on reason, whereas in Levinasian ethics, there is no ambiguity about our ethical accountability. If, say, in Kant, there is a great deal of analysis of how ethical conduct—or practical reason—can be corrupted by various "pathologies" such as personal interests, in Levinas there is no space for falling short of the ethical obligation to place the other's well-being before our self-preservation, though, of course, in practice we do constantly fail at this. Yet Butler inexplicably asserts that the obligation that emerges from the perishable character of life is "emphatically nonuniversalizable":

> The "one" who is asked to follow the commandment is also vanquished ontologically by this address . . . it becomes nothing other than this obligation and is held in life by the commandment itself, and so sustained and vanquished by this address. This means that the self is no substance and that the commandment is no codifiable law, each exists only in the manner of an address that singles out, vanquishes, and compels. (*PW* 67)

Besides the quasi-religious mystification that happens here with the self that has no substance and the commandment that is no law, what is so bizarre about all of this is the idea that the so-called "vanquishing" of the subject somehow makes its obligation to the other less universal. Isn't the point rather that everyone is "vanquished," everyone is decentered, everyone is interrupted, and that it is precisely because of this shared predicament that we are all equally, universally, responsible for everyone else? Indeed, Butler's position here seems to directly contradict her entire ethics of precarity, for it seems paradoxical, to say the least, to maintain that vulnerability is a generalizable condition of human life but that the ethics based on this vulnerability is "emphatically nonuniversalizable."

10

The kinds of paradoxes I have outlined are not mere momentary lapses of logic in Butlerian theory: as I have sought to show, they arise, in part at least, from a violent clash between Butler's poststructuralist sensibilities—sensibilities that cause her to automatically reject certain conceptual possibilities, such as universalism, as ideologically untenable—on the one hand and the deeply universalizing (even humanist) ethos of her ethical vision on the other. The ambivalence generated by this clash reaches to the very core of her ethics of precarity. As a final example, let us recall that—as I explained at the beginning of this chapter—Butler strives to base her ethics on "a new bodily ontology, one that implies the rethinking of precariousness, vulnerability, injurability, interdependency, exposure." As a critical response to Enlightenment rationalism, this makes a great deal of sense. But what follows does not, for Butler goes on to qualify her statement as follows: "To refer to 'ontology' in this regard is not to lay claim to a description of fundamental structures of being that are distinct from any and all social and political organization" (FW 2). That is, Butler wishes to convince us that she can offer us a "bodily ontology" that tells us nothing about the "fundamental structures" of human being. Yet this stance is nonsensical—an instance of mere rhetorical tap-dancing—for obviously her "bodily ontology" *does* tell us something "fundamental" about human life, particularly about human woundability. If it did not, there would be no basis for her ethics of precarity.

In preparation for the next chapter, I want to note that Butler's disclaimer regarding bodily ontology—which mirrors the disclaimers about the universalizing "formalism" that I analyzed above— hearkens back to a long-standing quarrel between Butler and Žižek regarding whether or not it is legitimate to talk about "formal" structures of being, such as the Lacanian symbolic, imaginary, and real. Where Žižek defends Lacanian formalism, Butler insists that any attempt to describe the universal building blocks of human life takes place at the expense of sociopolitical specificity, including the various axes of inequality that shape our existence. That is, Butler wants to dissociate herself from the kinds of formalistic theories of subjectivity—such as Lacan's—that (in her view) presuppose a general structure that is then filled with particular content, that is, theories that (in her view) do not pay sufficient attention to the ways in which variable social and political forces infiltrate subjectivity from the get-go.

But such a reading of Lacan is utterly misleading. Take Butler's contention that the Lacanian symbolic is a static, ahistorical edifice which precludes our capacity to understand sociopolitical specificity. Here I must side with Žižek, who writes in response to Butler:

> This notion of the Real . . . enables me to answer Butler's criticism that Lacan hypostasizes the 'big Other' into a kind of pre-historical transcendental a priori: when Lacan emphatically asserts that 'there is no big Other [*il n'y a pas de grand Autre*]', his point is precisely that there is no a priori formal structural scheme exempt from historical contingencies—there are only contingent, fragile, inconsistent configurations.[17]

In other words, the Lacanian subject, like any subject, is constituted in relation to context-specific collective forces, including sociopolitical inequalities; its "fundamental structures of being" are, as it were, always molded by the external stimuli it (variably) encounters in the world. This is why there is no Other of the Other, no ultimate guarantee of the symbolic's hegemony—why the symbolic remains a battleground for ever-shifting sociopolitical antagonisms.

Consider also the Lacanian idea that we are all wounded by language, that our interpellation into the symbolic order generates a constitutive lack. Butler appears to presume that this means that Lacan believes that we are all wounded in the same manner. Yet there is room, in Lacanian theory, for the recognition that the signifier wounds us in various ways based on our social placement in the network of signification, so that, for example, a sexist or racist comment will impact us differently depending on our subject position. As a consequence, even though we all feel lacking, we do not experience this lack in the same way (or to the same degree). There is, for instance, nothing incompatible about the Lacanian notion of lack and Butler's own reading of melancholia, for the latter—as I illustrated above—can be traced all the way back to the loss of *das Ding*, that is, to our foundational dispossession by the signifier (even if it cannot be reduced to this dispossession). Moreover, given that desire, in Lacanian theory, arises from our lack, it is the singularity of our experience of lack that explains the singularity of our experience of desire. Yet the fact that we all experience desire in singular ways does not cancel out our ability to refer to "desire" as a theoretical concept—one that allows us to understand something "fundamental" about human life.

It seems to me that in the same way that the universal, when it is a genuine universal, can accommodate a host of singularities that are all granted equal status (so that the universal does not automatically violate singularity), the notion of "fundamental" (or "formal") structures of being can accommodate an endless number of permutations. And, as we will discover in the chapters that follow, Lacan's "formalist" theory of subjectivity opens to realms of postmetaphysical autonomy that make agency much more thinkable than Butler's Levinasian ethics—an ethics that, while being a gripping account of our devastating vulnerability, does not grant a whole lot of space for self-assertion. I will in fact try to demonstrate that Lacan, ironically enough, offers better resources for feminist, queer, and other progressive political struggles than (the more overtly political) Butlerian discourse, for he gives us a subject who is capable of defiance rather than just mourning.

3

The Lacanian rebuttal: Žižek, Badiou, and revolutionary politics

[Butler's] last book, although it does not mention Badiou, is de facto a kind of anti-Badiou manifesto: hers is an ethics of finitude, of making a virtue out of our very weakness, in other words, of elevating into the highest ethical value the respect for our very inability to act with full responsibility.

SLAVOJ ŽIŽEK[1]

1

In my discussion this far, I have focused on the universalizing underpinnings of Levinasian and Butlerian ethics because I want to question the idea that a postmetaphysical ethics must be intrinsically relativistic. This manner of reading Levinas and Butler required me to reach beneath the valorization of otherness that represents one of the cornerstones of their philosophies. In so doing, I did not mean to discredit their undeniable respect for alterity, difference, and singularity, nor did I mean to downplay the importance that they—Butler perhaps more than Levinas—place on particularity. Moreover, I am aware that much of the most fertile theorizing about ethics in poststructuralist, postcolonial, feminist, and queer theory has galvanized around the burdens of particularity in ways that I would never wish to obliterate. As I hope to illustrate in this chapter, I continue to be theoretically and politically aligned with those who believe that the specificity of subject position matters, that social power creates the kinds of systematic inequalities that make it impossible to ignore the ways in which race, gender, sexuality, class, ethnicity, and religion, among other identity markers, impact not only our variable self-perceptions but also the concrete life choices that are available to us. Such power takes visible form in institutionalized practices of racism, patriarchy, homophobia, and economic disparities, including the brutal practices of global capitalism. But it also infiltrates our lives in hidden currents of biopower that dictate our understanding of "common sense," that naturalize certain ways of being in the world while rendering others seemingly impossible. In this manner, we are guided to specific existential choices, specific destinies even, without being aware of the extent to which our so-called "choices" originate from outside of ourselves, guided by the invisible hand of biopolitical control. I agree with those who recognize that the ways in which this hand touches us—whether it slaps us in the face or caresses us into complacency—is related to where we are situated in the social hierarchy. The particularity of subject position, in short, signifies the kind of difference that makes an enormous difference.

I do not, then, see my attempt to locate the kernel of universality in the work of Levinas and Butler as a refutation of the trope of otherness that has been so crucial to their thinking as well as to the thinking of related critics such as Derrida and Irigaray. At the same time, I have expressed my reservations about the masochistic, disempowering tendencies of both Levinasian and Butlerian ethics, and these reservations are what steer me to the more rebellious Marxist-Lacanian ethical paradigms of Žižek and Badiou. The central paradox of this chapter is that even though Žižek and Badiou are vehemently critical of progressive political movements such as feminism, antiracism, and queer solidarity—a matter I will return to below—I believe that their Lacanian approach nevertheless offers such movements a more robust model of agency than either

Levinas or Butler. Lacan was as staunch a critic of the sovereign subject of Enlightenment rationalism as Levinas and Butler but, unlike them, he did not conflate the downfall of this subject with the loss of agency; he did not engage in the kind of vilification of autonomy that we have witnessed in Levinas and Butler. Admittedly, he theorized this autonomy in ways that may at first glance make it difficult to recognize it as such, but there is no doubt that his version of psychoanalysis was designed to facilitate the emergence of defiant subjects—the kinds of subjects who are able to take a degree of critical distance from their social surroundings and, when necessary, even to sever their ties to the hegemonic dictates of these surroundings.

What I mean by this will become clear as my discussion progresses, but let me say right away that this basic Lacanian stance manifests itself in the theories of Žižek and Badiou as the conviction that the point of ethics is not to fixate on our entrapment in hegemonic power but, rather, to make the impossible possible. In other words, if Butler tends to underscore the impossibility of breaking our psychic attachment to wounding forms of social power, Žižek and Badiou insist on our ability to do precisely this. They have no patience with the idea that the human being is a default victim, which is why Žižek often accuses Butler—as he does in the statement I placed at the beginning of this chapter—of making a virtue out of weakness, "of elevating into the highest ethical value the respect for our very inability to act with full responsibility." Badiou, in turn, has launched comparable accusations against Levinas, mocking Levinasian ethics for being a matter of a "prophetic submission to the Law of founding alterity."[2] According to Badiou, Levinas "has no philosophy—not even philosophy as the 'servant' of theology"; rather, his philosophy is "*annulled* by theology" (*E* 22–3).

2

Perhaps the best way to spell out the disagreements between Levinas and Butler on the one hand and Žižek and Badiou on the other is to start with the Levinasian face. Both Žižek and Badiou have put a great deal of pressure on the idea that the precarity of the face could serve as a basis for ethics. Furthermore, both have ridiculed ethical paradigms based on "respect" for the diversity of the faces found in the world—paradigms, that, explicitly or implicitly, draw on Levinas, and that have, among other things, fueled the celebration of multiculturalism. Both Žižek and Badiou, somewhat vexingly, see multiculturalism as an enemy of class-based (Marxist) politics, claiming that its difference-based approach and local squabbles about "equal rights" distract us from what really matters, namely the relentless march of global capitalism. In addition, Žižek and Badiou maintain that the Western multiculturalist rhetoric of respecting differences is deeply hypocritical, falling apart the moment the other is *too* different, the moment the other is no longer the "good" other—the other with whom we can empathize because, on some fundamental level, he or she is just "like" us. Within the multiculturalist model, Badiou writes, "I respect differences, but only, of course, in so far as that which differs also respects, just as I do, the said differences. Just as there can be no 'freedom for the enemies of freedom', so there can be no respect for those whose difference consists precisely in not respecting differences" (*E* 24). That is, the multiculturalist respect for differences applies only to those differences that are more or less compatible with the West's conception of liberal democracy and human rights. Any vigorously defended difference—any difference that deviates too drastically from the West's "humanistic" vision—is automatically deemed "barbaric," "totalitarian," or "terroristic." As Žižek sums up the matter, multiculturalism collapses the minute the other reveals itself as a "*faceless monster*" (*N* 185).

Badiou and Žižek do not seem to be aware that similar critiques can be found within difference-based theories, that the problems of multiculturalism—and of identitarian political movements, more generally speaking—have already been theorized by the very critics Badiou and Žižek brand as their adversaries, and that these adversaries have arguably done so with a greater degree of sophistication than Badiou and Žižek have managed.[3] Indeed, as we have seen, even Butler's ethics of precarity contains an intricate critique of the ways in which some faces are recognized as human while others are not; her ethics is, precisely, aimed at correcting the fact that our frames of perception cast some people as faceless monsters. Interestingly, Butler arrives at this insight at least in part through Levinas, whereas Badiou and Žižek *reprimand* Levinas for the failings of multiculturalism, implying that Levinas is not fully able to theorize the more menacing aspects of the other. Žižek, for example, maintains that Levinas cannot account for the fact that the other, in a Lacanian vein, is never just a symbolic or imaginary entity—someone we can safely relate to through processes of signification and narcissistic identification—but always also the terrifying, uncontrollable locus of jouissance.[4] That is, Žižek believes that the Levinasian face is too placid, too reassuring, functioning as an ethical lure that gentrifies the threat posed by the other by distracting us from the realization that, underneath the face, the other is radically unknowable (even to himself). As Žižek asserts, "Levinas fails to include into the scope of 'human' . . . the *inhuman* itself, a dimension which eludes the face-to-face relationship" (N 158).

While there may be some truth to this claim, it also overstates the issue because, as I explained in Chapter 1, Levinas does not actually depict the face as a locus of straightforward identification. Rather, he describes it as "a being beyond all attributes" (EN 33), as what escapes the kinds of conceptual and perceptual categories that would allow us to reduce it to what is familiar to us. The face is a site of utter singularity, of utter self-sameness, which means that it by definition defeats our attempts to classify it.[5] Consequently, far from facilitating immediate empathy, the face alerts us to the limits of empathetic affinity, which is exactly why it elicits unqualified responsibility—why, in Levinasian terms, we are supposed to protect the other regardless of how this other appears to us, regardless of whether or not we experience the other's face as benevolent.

This combination of the singularity of the face and the universality of its sanctity—the idea that every face, regardless of how threatening it may seem, demands our unconditional responsibility—is a matter that Žižek conveniently sidesteps. In other words, even if Žižek's critique of the shortcomings of multiculturalism is correct (and below I will return to why it might not be), he is mistaken in thinking that Levinas is to blame for these shortcomings. At the same time, Žižek's larger point is worth considering: like Badiou, he wishes to demonstrate that multiculturalism works only as long as the other is someone with whom we can identify (and let us not forget that Butler's ethics of precarity calls for exactly this type of identificatory capacity); Žižek reminds us that multiculturalism makes sense as long as the other possesses qualities, ideals, or values we can relate to but that matters become complicated when the other no longer makes any sense to us, when the other is, say, a suicide bomber who does not hesitate to kill random civilians for the sake of his or her cause. In this manner, Žižek raises an important question, namely how we should ethically relate to a face that seems to be out to injure, or even murder, us.

This question has arguably, in the aftermath of 9/11, the US-led war on terror, Guantánamo Bay, the conflicts of Iraq and Afghanistan, and so on, emerged as one of the biggest dilemmas of contemporary ethics, destabilizing the tenets of liberal tolerance that many of us had learned to take for granted. We have in fact had to confront the problematic Badiou highlights, namely that despite our rhetoric of respecting differences, it is difficult for us to respect those who refuse to respect differences. To state the problem succinctly: if we resolve to do what Butler suggests and widen our horizon of who counts as a legitimate face, what do we do with the face of someone who, in turn, chooses to denigrate the faces of others (Eichmann being a good example)? How do we respond to the face of the Christian or Islamic fundamentalist who shows contempt for the faces of women or gays? How do we meet the face of the racist who thinks that black faces are the devil? Are there not situations where the Levinasian respect for the face is overrated and it would be better to heed Žižek's call to smash the other's face (N 142)?

3

As we have learned, Butler's answer is: absolutely not. Her Levinasian response is that each and every face is our ethical responsibility and that we must avoid responding to aggression with aggression. Instead, we need to recognize the generalized precarity of human life: the fact that we are all radically injurable, defenseless, and prone to suffering. This is why the Butlerian solution is to humanize those faces that have been deprived of their human resonance by both global and more local structures of power. Žižek's strategy is the exact opposite in the sense that justice, in his opinion, calls for a radical *de*humanization of the subject—a move away from the face. According to Žižek, the problem with our ethical paradigms is that we are unable to abstract from the face in favor of impersonal justice; we keep focusing on the specifics of the face instead of applying the same neutral principles to everyone without exception. Because it is, practically speaking, impossible for us to consider all faces equally, justice cannot be a function of agitating for this or that face but rather of remembering "the faceless many left in shadow" (N 182). In other words, justice begins when I recall the distant multitude that eludes my relational grasp. When justice prevails, everyone is equally my neighbor so that my "actual" neighbor is no more important to me than my "virtual" neighbor. While interpersonal empathy implies that I elevate the object of my concern over all others, justice demands the reverse: it asks that I set aside my inclination to grant a special status to those I know, identify with, feel compassion for, or even love. This insight, Žižek claims, brings us to a radically "anti-Levinasian conclusion": "The true ethical step is the one *beyond* the face of the other, the one of *suspending* the hold of the face, the one of choosing *against* the face, for the *third*" (N 183). "This coldness *is* justice at its most elementary" (N 183), Žižek continues, for justice is a matter of transcending the fetish of the face so as to uphold the impartial letter of the law. Along related lines, Badiou asserts that it is not respect for differences but rather a kind of studied *in*difference to them that founds ethics. As he boldly proposes, "The whole ethical predication based upon recognition of the other should be purely and simply abandoned. For the real question—and it is an extraordinarily difficult one—is much more that of *recognizing the Same*" (E 25). Since difference, infinite alterity, "is quite simply *what there is*" (E 25), politics and ethics alike need to be centered around what is valid for all of us. As Badiou sums up the matter, "Philosophically, if the other doesn't matter it is indeed because the difficulty lies on the side of the Same" (E 27).

What we have here is a clash between the Levinasians and the Lacanians, the defenders of the face and those who see the aesthetics of the face as a decoy that distracts us from impartial justice. While Butler wants us to stretch our frames of perception so that we are able to see everyone as a face, Žižek and Badiou want us to look past the face for the sake of justice. To some extent, this clash is artificially orchestrated by Žižek, who overlooks the fact that Levinas himself distinguishes between ethics and justice—the self-other dyad and the "third"—and specifies that while ethics relates to the face, justice must dissociate itself from the idiosyncrasies of the face in order to arbitrate between the claims of different faces. But what most interests me is that, despite their obvious disagreements, both sides of the clash, in this particular instance at least, seem to be on a quest for a universal foundation for ethics. After all, whether we are looking to make every face count equally, or to studiously ignore every face, we are striving for a general principle that levels distinctions between individuals; we are trying, in our divergent ways, to say that either everyone matters or no one does.

I have illustrated that Butler's relationship to the question of universalism is, generally speaking, quite conflicted. And I ended the previous chapter by discussing the ways in which she seeks to deny the universalizability of the ethical demand that arises from the Levinasian face. Yet I have also stressed—against Butler's own protestations, as it were— that her ethics of precarity cannot work without a degree of universalization. Žižek and Badiou, in turn, do not make any attempt to hide their allegiance to universalism, even if they approach it from a very different perspective. I call attention to this convergence of theoretical preoccupations in order to mark a shift that may currently be taking place in posthumanist theory: after decades of intense theorizing about differences, we are witnessing a resuscitation of the category of the Same—an attempt to figure out what unites human beings so as to determine a genuinely egalitarian starting point for ethics.

From a cynical perspective, one might suspect that this trend signals the triumph of universalist neo-Marxist theories, such as those of Žižek and Badiou, over more multiculturalist, antiracist, feminist, or queer ones, for Marxism has, in the post-'68 context, remained one of the strongholds of universalism. For instance, Ernesto Laclau has long been interested in the processes of "hegemonization" through which the political claims of a particular social group—such as the workers—attain universal status so that everyone, and not merely members of this group, comes to recognize the validity of these claims.[6] Likewise, Michael Hardt and Antonio Negri argue in *Commonwealth* that what they call "the experience of the common" is the only effective foundation of sociopolitical and economic transformation. This experience of the common unifies people around a shared political goal in ways that allow them to transcend the particularities of their identity positions; it is a matter of a multitude of singularities coming together to form a new kind of universal—not the transcendent universal of Western humanism but a universal that is built from the bottom up, that is brought into existence by the collective action of individuals who are willing to push aside what divides them in order to access the power of what they have in common.[7] Add to this the ongoing efforts of Žižek and Badiou to disparage difference-based critical approaches from poststructuralism to multiculturalism, feminism, antiracism, and queer theory, and it might be tempting to see a Marxist (white straight male) conspiracy against the "rest" of us.

In a moment, I will return to some aspects of Žižek and Badiou's theories that point to this possibility. But as an overall assessment of the situation, suspecting a Marxist conspiracy would be overly simplistic, given that Laclau, Hardt, and Negri have all made admirable attempts to reconcile their Marxism with the aforementioned difference-based approaches. Hardt and Negri, for example, spend considerable energy lamenting the ways in which classical Marxist analyses have been antithetical to feminist and antiracist struggles. Equally important, critics for whom Marxism is not a significant resource seem to be finding their way to universalism as well. For instance, Leo Bersani proposes in *Intimacies* that if we refused to approach others through the lens of their psychological particularity, or through categories such as race, ethnicity, gender, or nationality, we would discover that what is different about them is "merely the envelope of the more profound . . . part of themselves which is our sameness."[8] Likewise, Butler's reluctant universalism is an indication that a degree of disillusionment regarding relativistic discourses may have crept into progressive criticism. Liberal critics—from Rawlsians to Habermasians to neo-Kantian cosmopolitans—have, of course, long been invested in universalist ethical paradigms, but what interests me in this book is the revival of the rhetoric of universalism among left-leaning critics specifically. As should be clear by now, this universalism is emphatically not a return to traditional humanistic notions of subjectivity; we are not talking about an attempt to revive the Enlightenment subject of rational deliberation. Quite the contrary, if there is something that even Butler, Žižek, and Badiou all seem to agree on, it is that human beings are *not* fully rational creatures. Žižek's quasi-Kantian call for disinterested principles of justice perhaps comes the closest to liberal humanism (at the same time as his Marxism takes him in a very different direction). Yet his strongly Lacanian conception of the subject as an entity that is inhabited by the unruly drive energies of the bodily real—by energies that effectively undermine the subject's efforts to lead a "reasonable" life—simultaneously discredits the unitary, sovereign subject of humanism.

My main point is that the postmetaphysical critics I have chosen to analyze in detail are all, in one way or another, willingly or not, attracted to the idea that there might be a way to theorize a universalist ethics even in the absence of the sovereign humanist subject. However, where they diverge is in how they conceptualize the relationship between the singular and the universal. As we have learned, Butler struggles with the tension between the singularity of experience and the universality of ethical principles, sometimes to the degree of theoretical paralysis; because Butler both desires and resists the universal, she arrives at conceptual contradictions that at times appear insurmountable. Žižek and Badiou, in contrast, see no contradiction between singularity and universality; as their statements about the "coldness" of justice (Žižek) and the "indifference" of ethics (Badiou) indicate, they believe that the universal can, potentially at least, accommodate a multitude of singularities. However, I want to be careful here to specify that I do not think that Žižek and Badiou have adequately thought through this relationship between the singular and the universal. The flip side of their cavalier rejection of "identitarian" political movements is that they falsely assume that every singularity automatically has equal access to the universal. Žižek explains this perspective as follows: the singular "immediately participates in universality, since it breaks through the idea of a particular order. You can be a human immediately, without first being German, French, English, etc."[9] This is why "in every great philosopher there is the theme of the direct participation of singularity in universality, without the detour via particularities, cultures, nationalities, gender differences and so forth" (PP 75). In a different context, Žižek further specifies that the Hegelian dialectical procedure which he favors "can be best described as a direct jump from the singular to the universal, bypassing the mid-level of particularity."[10]

The problem with this formulation should be obvious, namely that the majority of the world's people—women, nonwhite men, queer subjects, and so on—have historically had to fight quite hard to be considered fully human (let alone "German, French, English"). Žižek and Badiou take it for granted that every singularity can claim an immediate membership in the universal. Yet nothing could be less true. Singularity, for most of the world's population, has not gained them admission to the universal but has rather marked them as inherently inadmissible. This is because their singularity has been eclipsed by the "particularity" of their subject position, by the fact that they have always been read through this subject position rather than through the coordinates of their singularity. In practice, this means that women have always had trouble transcending their coding as female first, human second; blacks have always had trouble transcending their coding as "colored" first, human second; gays have always had trouble transcending their coding as "deviants" first, human second; non-Westerners have always had trouble transcending their coding as "other" first, human second, and so on. This is the dynamic that Žižek and Badiou ignore in their wholesale rejection of all "identitarian," group-based political movements, such as feminism, antiracism, queer solidarity, and anticolonial struggles.

Let me state the matter slightly differently. I think that Žižek and Badiou are on the right track in trying to revive a universalist ethics. They are also on the right track in recognizing that the human is always derailed by a kernel of what Žižek calls the "inhuman" so that what unites us—what makes us "same"—is not something comfortably human but rather what "exceeds humanity," what causes us to be fundamentally out of joint with our so-called humanity (PP 76). And I even have a degree of sympathy for their efforts to erect the singular as an antidote to the particularity of identity politics. The reason they want to go *directly* from the singular to the universal is that they see the identitarian focus on particular identity categories such as race, gender, sexuality, religion, and nationality as a "reactionary" political stance (PP 75)—one that at best traps individuals in narrow and self-serving preoccupations, and at worst leads to the extreme violence of nationalist uprisings, ethnic cleansings, and religious fundamentalisms. However, Žižek and Badiou do not adequately distinguish between different identitarian movements, so it becomes difficult to see the difference between the Civil Rights movement and National Socialism. Obviously, if one is to use National Socialism as an example of a particularistic "identity politics," as Žižek and Badiou often do, it makes sense to argue that it would be preferable to circumvent particularity by moving directly from the singular to the universal. But the problem is that Žižek and Badiou do not acknowledge that there are significant differences between different identitarian movements, that there are circumstances in which such movements can serve progressive rather than ethnonationalist (or fascist) aspirations. Their approach, in short, leaves no space for historical specificity, nor does it show any awareness of the fact that if many people have historically taken cover under various identity categories, it is precisely because they have been *unable* to translate their version of singularity into the universal.

4

The anti-identitarian attitude of Žižek and Badiou also does not admit what is obvious to those of us who have been politically aligned with some of the movements they malign, which is that many of them are actually not identitarian at all but often work quite diligently to forge cross-identitarian or postidentitarian alliances. For instance, contemporary feminism, at least in its more theoretical valences, is rarely a movement for the liberation of "women," understood in some essentialist sense, but one that questions the very meaning and construction of gender and sexuality. Moreover, such feminism usually strives to combine an analysis of heteropatriarchy with an analysis of other related forms of social inequality, such as racism and class disparities. Žižek and Badiou tend to talk as if feminism were exclusively a movement that sought to ensure that women have equal access to the dominant neoliberal capitalist system. Yet this is hardly how many feminist activists, let alone most academic feminists, would define their struggle.

It is of course true that there have been moments in the history of feminism when it has broken from the class struggle in order to insist on the importance of heteropatriarchal oppression. Some second-wave feminists, for example, got fed up with the ways in which the political imagination of the male-dominated left was focused so narrowly on economic exploitation that other genres of oppression—such as gender oppression—became invisible. As a result—and I would say, understandably—they chose to focus on patriarchy instead. But many contemporary feminists aim at a radical liberation from the various hegemonic forces that subjugate us, including neoliberal biopolitics and global capitalism. In this sense, there is something thoroughly uninformed about Žižek and

Badiou's insistence that, in contrast to the universal reach of class politics, feminism (along with related "identitarian" movements) remains stuck on the level of the particular.[11] Moreover, it is not even clear to me how the effects of demolishing patriarchy (or, say, racism) would be any less universal than the effects of demolishing capitalism. Given that patriarchy governs gender relations in virtually every society, dissolving it would surely have fundamental repercussions for many aspects of our lives, including their economic organization; it might even be that redistributive justice presupposes gender justice. By this I do not mean to suggest that feminism is more important than class politics—not at all—for what most bothers me about the approach of Žižek and Badiou is precisely that they engage in such a counterproductive ranking of political causes. And, unfortunately, their efforts to elevate the class struggle over all other political struggles give the impression that what is, in the final analysis, at stake for them is an old-fashioned Marxism that seeks "universal" emancipation for white men while being entirely willing to leave everyone else behind.

Interestingly, this is exactly the complaint leveled against Žižek by Laclau, who notes the same problem I have just outlined, namely that the idea that the class struggle is somehow more intrinsically universal than other political struggles, such as multiculturalism, is based on a spurious ranking of political causes. In Laclau's opinion, not only is it possible to demonstrate the potentially universalist appeal of the causes that Žižek labels "identitarian," or "particularist," but it is also possible to show that the class struggle is no less identitarian than any other struggle, centered as it is on the worker's self-understanding of himself as having a particular identity—an identity that can be undermined in various ways. The class struggle, on this view, arises when the worker feels that his identity is somehow threatened, for instance, when he fears that below a certain level of wages, he cannot live a decent life. As a result, Laclau declares that his "answer to Žižek's dichotomy between class struggle and identity politics is that class struggle is just one species of identity politics, and one which is becoming less and less important in the world in which we live."[12] Indeed, given the stark realities of global capitalism, one could argue that anticolonial and anti-imperialist struggles are just as much struggles against capitalism as the traditional class struggle. Conversely, one could easily propose that the traditional class struggle is *more* identitarian than some of the struggles that Žižek groups under "postmodern identity politics" ("CS" 97), for the latter have consistently sought to transcend the particularity of identity categories by seeking partnerships with other progressive movements, whereas the white men involved in the traditional class struggle have had notorious—even infamous—trouble with this. From this perspective, that the traditional class struggle has a privileged universal standing over more "particular" movements is an illusion based on it being a white male movement (not a particularly original problem).

This is not to say that Žižek's fears regarding "today's postmodern politics of multiple subjectivities" ("CS" 108) are not to some extent founded. In positing that the postmodern celebration of diversity reflects "the specific ideologico-political constellation of Western late capitalism" ("CS" 107), Žižek calls attention to the ways in which the postmodern valorization of diversity, and its attendant glorification of contingency, hybridity, flexibility, and flux, mirrors the logic of capitalism, which thrives on the proliferation and dispersion of identities; simply put, postmodern politics replicates capitalism's dislike of boundaries. Žižek may therefore be right in claiming that postmodernism is not "political enough, in so far as it silently presupposes a non-thematized, 'naturalized' framework of economic relations" ("CS" 108). As he continues, "I think one should at least *take note* of the fact that the much-praised postmodern 'proliferation of new political subjectivities', the demise of every 'essentialist' fixation, the assertion of full contingency, occur against the background of a certain silent *renunciation* and *acceptance*: the renunciation of the idea of a global change in the fundamental relations in our society" ("DC" 321).

I am certainly sympathetic to Žižek's point that there may well be something about postmodernism that causes us to lose track of the background of capitalism that sustains its endless array of choices, with the consequence that class inequalities become undetectable and unaddressed. Yet I would also like to ask him why he thinks that a politics that shuns boundaries and worships fluidity—that, as he himself admits, calls for "the demise of every essentialist fixation"— ends up being a "postmodern identity politics." I have never quite understood how Žižek leaps from postmodernism to the fixity of identitarian politics, given that at the core of postmodernism resides the wish to deconstruct rigid identity categories of all kinds.

That said, I agree with him that when capitalism functions as an unquestioned framework for political struggles, these struggles either become mere palliative measures, or worse, become complicit with the hegemonic system. In this sense, Žižek is correct in positing that the left needs a new political imaginary which is able to transcend incremental approaches that merely agitate for equal rights within the existing system; he is correct in asking for more comprehensive social transformation. However, Žižek is misguided in assuming that only the Marxist tradition is able to envision such a transformation. Indeed, it would be possible to show that many of the very "postmodern" approaches that he attacks have arrived at exactly the same conclusion.

Consider, for example, queer theory's recent critiques of "homonormativity." These critiques are leveled against the attempts of relatively affluent white gays and lesbians to use rights-based political issues—such as gay marriage—as a means of purchasing their way into "normalcy" at the expense of those who cannot be so easily assimilated: poor queers, racialized queers, gender-variant queers, immigrant queers, and so on. In other words, critics of homonormativity maintain that the mainstreaming of gays and lesbians not merely shifts, but also intensifies, lines of social marginalization, so that while some gays and lesbians now "make it" to dominant culture, others are all the more irrevocably excluded (and exploited).[13] Even more fundamentally, queer critics of homonormativity question the mainstream LGBTQ movement's desire to "make it" in dominant culture in the first place. They problematize the narratives of success promoted by neoliberal capitalism, pointing out that such narratives blind us to structural inequalities such as poverty, racism, sexism, and homophobia which make it impossible for some people to succeed no matter how hard they try. Essentially, if the neoliberal creed tells people that their individual efforts can surmount any and all obstacles, queer critics of neoliberalism emphasize that this creed is just a convenient way to gloss over the fact that some people will never attain the American dream.

In many ways we are dealing with a rift that has always complicated progressive politics, namely the battle between those who want to improve the existing system by making it more inclusive and those who want to blow this system into smithereens and replace it with something completely different. That is, we are dealing with a division between rights-based political approaches on the one hand and more revolutionary approaches on the other: the supporters of gay marriage want equal rights within the system, whereas queer critics of gay marriage see marriage as the corrupt foundation of a thoroughly corrupt system. Indeed, queer critics recognize that the LGBTQ movement's attempts to gain entry to a marriage-based system—a system that automatically vilifies those who reject monogamy—threaten to wipe out queer subcultures that have historically been organized around promiscuous, anonymous, and fleeting sexual encounters. For many queer critics, the disappearance of such subcultures equals the death of queer culture as such. Ironically, it is because the LGBTQ movement has managed to make gays and lesbians seem "just like" straight people, eager to endorse the family values of married monogamy, that it has made such tremendous political strides. Essentially, the gay and lesbian subject has been stripped of his or her disturbing "otherness" in order to make him or her more palatable to straight society. For many queer critics, this is a short-sighted victory that drastically undermines more radical efforts to gain social justice.

If Žižek bothered to read queer theory, he would know that its attacks on heteropatriarchal capitalism—as well as on the tendency of incremental political movements to ensure that their supporters become obedient members of society just like everyone else—rival his own (a topic I will return to in the next chapter). Nor is it true, as Žižek seems to believe, that gays, lesbians, queers, feminists, antiracists, multiculturalists, and other "identitarians" are any more easily co-opted by the capitalist system than the worker. As Laclau points out, the worker is no exception to being susceptible to bribery by the system, which can appease him, for instance, by raising his wages, cutting his working hours, improving his working conditions, offering various consumer compensations, or by being willing to tolerate a flourishing trade union network. In this manner, the worker's demands can be integrated into the system just as seamlessly as the demands of other political actors. This is why Laclau concludes that "one cannot avoid the feeling that the notion of class is brought into Žižek's analysis as a sort of *deus ex machina* to play the role of the good guy against the multicultural devils" ("SHP" 205).

5

It seems largely futile to pit class politics against other political movements. As Nancy Fraser has observed, if a theory of justice

> is to avoid foreclosing demands in advance, the theory must be able to entertain claims that presuppose non-standard views of the "what" of justice. Erring on the side of inclusiveness, then, it should begin by assuming that injustice comes in more than one form and that no single view of the "what" can capture them all. Rejecting social-ontological monism, it should conceive justice as encompassing multiple dimensions, each of which is associated with an analytically distinct genre of injustice and revealed through a conceptually distinct type of social struggle.[14]

Arguing that such a multidimensional view of justice would recognize the equal importance of the axes of economic redistribution, social recognition, and political representation, Fraser concludes that whoever dogmatically forecloses the domain of justice by excluding any one of these axes "declares his or her thinking inadequate to the times" (*SJ* 59). Somewhat amusingly, this is exactly Laclau's charge against Žižek, for he remarks that Žižek's theory is "schizophrenically split between a highly sophisticated Lacanian analysis and an insufficiently deconstructed traditional Marxism" ("SHP" 205); according to Laclau, Žižek's "way of dealing with Marxist categories consists in inscribing them in a semi-metaphysical horizon which, if it were accepted—a rather unlikely event—would put the agenda of the Left back fifty years."[15]

Perhaps even more damning is Laclau's contention that Žižek's revolutionary rhetoric is mere empty talk, that there is no actual content to Žižek's anticapitalism. In response to Žižek's accusation that he (along with Butler) silently accepts the premises of the capitalist market economy and the liberal democratic regime—that he and Butler fail to envision the possibility of a radically *different* system—Laclau writes:

> The reader must excuse me for smiling at the naïve self-complacency this r-r-revolutionary passage reflects. For if Butler and I are not envisioning "the possibility of a thoroughly *different*

economico-political regime," Žižek is not doing so either. In his previous essay Žižek had told us that he wanted to overthrow capitalism; now we are served notice that he also wants to do away with liberal democratic regimes—to be replaced, it is true, by a thoroughly different regime which he does not have the courtesy of letting us know anything about. One can only guess. Now, apart from capitalist society and the parallelograms of Mr Owen, Žižek *does* actually know a third type of sociopolitical arrangement: the Communist bureaucratic regimes of Eastern Europe under which he lived. Is that what he has in mind? Does he want to replace liberal democracy by a one-party political system, to undermine the division of powers, to impose the censorship of the press? . . . And if what he has in mind is something entirely different, he has an elementary intellectual and political duty to let us know what it is. Hitler and Mussolini also abolished liberal democratic political regimes and replaced them by "thoroughly different" ones. Only if that explanation is made available will we be able to start talking politics, and abandon the theological terrain. Before that, I cannot even know what Žižek is talking about—and the more this exchange progresses, the more suspicious I become that Žižek himself does not know either. ("CU" 289)

Similar passages pepper Laclau's responses to Žižek, but suffice it to sum up the matter as follows: in Laclau's view, Žižek's so-called "class analysis" consists of a succession of dogmatic assertions that do not amount to any kind of a coherent political program; Žižek's complaint that other progressive critics accept capitalism as "the only game in town" ("SHP" 205) means nothing because it is not accompanied by an alternative vision of any kind.

  Žižek responds by insisting that in today's pragmatic neoliberal world, it is doubly important to hold alive the utopian dream of radical social transformation, even if this dream remains empty of content; our motto, he asserts, should be "*Soyons réalistes, demandons l'impossible!*"[16] This is a rousing rallying cry—one that I in principle appreciate—but what makes me suspicious of it is that my many years of teaching graduate seminars on contemporary theory have taught me that it tends to speak almost exclusively to white male students prone to Hegelian chest-thrusting, Lacanian muscle-flexing, and other stock tactics of classroom terrorization.

These are students who usually have not read much Hegel or Lacan, whose eyes glaze over at the mention of Hannah Arendt, Luce Irigaray, or Julia Kristeva, who believe that their online porn addiction is an important anticapitalist posture, and who spend their afternoons talking revolutionary strategy over their Starbucks lattés (one of my friends, Chris Gilmore, dubbed them "Starbucks revolutionaries").

Predictably, they are fascinated by Žižek's contention that one of the problems with neoliberalism is that it resorts to a maturation story according to which "just as a young man has to learn to accept the loss of grand enthusiastic adolescent plans and enter the everyday adult life of realistic compromises, the collective subject has to learn to accept the withering-away of global utopian ideological projects and the entry into the post-utopian realist era" ("HP" 324). I can see why this critique of neoliberalism might be appealing to young men who are in no hurry to grow up, but it does not do much for those of us who are asked to play the all-forgiving mother to their adolescent arrogance. In addition, that their revolutionary attitude tends to be accompanied by an explicit disdain for political struggles that do not reach a similarly radical pitch makes it all the more disturbing: in waiting for the revolution—which, conveniently for these privileged young men still eating out of their parents' fridges, never comes—one is absolved of any responsibility for participating in more "particular," actually existing, struggles, such as feminism or antiracism. Indeed, one is at liberty to follow Žižek's practice of standing in the sidelines and actively *ridiculing* the short-sightedness of such "identitarian" movements. In my opinion, there is nothing, absolutely nothing, innocent about this.

6

Žižek's dismissal of the ways in which the particularity of subject positions continues to matter cannot be divorced from his resistance to defining the human being as a victim—a resistance that he shares with Badiou. In other words, what creates a chasm between Butler in the Levinasian camp on the one hand and Žižek and Badiou in the Lacanian camp on the other is the latter's rejection of the premise of constitutive precariousness, the very premise that is central to Butlerian ethics. Žižek has attacked Butler explicitly on this issue on several occasions,[17] but let me approach the matter more obliquely, through Badiou's argument that to equate the human with the victim—to reduce the human being to the fragility of his constitution—is to deny the rights of the "immortal."

The "immortal," for Badiou, is not a theological concept, though it certainly carries some theological undertones. On the most basic level, Badiou is talking about the idea that human beings are more capable of courageous, spirited actions than we might be accustomed to believe. Badiou essentially distinguishes between two levels of human existence. The first is the ordinary, everyday domain organized by the pursuit of personal interests such as wealth, success, acclaim, happiness, or rewarding relationships. The second is the exceptional domain of truth-events—of moments when the subject is seized by an epiphanic vision so powerful that it is momentarily dislodged from its ordinary life (or "situation"). During such sudden surges of insight, the subject—who in fact only becomes a subject through the truth-event—is able to perceive the world from an angle that is foreclosed by its customary mode of being. And it is able, momentarily at least, to rise above its own interests in order to reach for something higher. In this sense, the realm of the truth-event is by definition one of innovation: an unexpected occasion for something previously unimaginable to shatter the status quo. As Badiou asserts—echoing Žižek's *Soyons réalistes, demandons l'impossible!*—the event opens up the "possibility of the impossible" (*E* 39).

Perhaps most important, the truth-event represents an ethical opportunity that allows the subject to pierce the canvas of the established order of things so as to identify what Badiou calls "the void" of the situation. Badiou derives his notion of the void from the Lacanian real, which explains why he sees it as a locus of antihegemonic insight: in the same way that the real represents the stumbling block to the symbolic order's fantasy of consistency and legitimacy, the void reveals the repressed irritant that makes the system (or "situation") struggle, malfunction, and sometimes fail. At the same time, the void is necessary for the system's "proper" functioning. As Žižek has pointed out, social animosities often secretly structure the very reality that they appear to fissure. In this sense, the void which seems to impede the comfortable closure of a given social hegemony is in fact what ensures its perpetuation. What is so revolutionary about the event, then, is that it reveals that what might seem like a (mere) contingent obstacle to the system's smooth operation is in fact what, ultimately, guarantees its viability; it shows that the obstacle in question is in reality a systemic necessity without which the situation's "logic" would disintegrate. In this manner, it might, for instance, suddenly become clear that the poor, the homeless, the "illegal" immigrants, the drug addicts, the inner city youth, the prostitutes, the gang members, and so on, who constitute the "void" (the invisible underside) of American society in fact facilitate the confident running of this society (its "business as usual"); it might become obvious that these individuals represent the underprivileged "stain" that perpetuates privilege as one of the defining characteristics of the dominant ideology of what it means to be American.

In unveiling the void of a given situation, the truth-event creates an ethical opening, an opportunity to see and do things differently. At the same time, Badiou admits the possibility of false events—or simulacra—that carry the same revolutionary fervor as the authentic event, and that are consequently capable of galvanizing people around a cause of some kind, but that do not in fact possess any genuinely liberatory content. National Socialism is one example of such a false event: Hitler seemed to realize the goal of translating the impossible into the possible by violating the basic norms of the established social order. As Žižek asks, "Did not a respectable middle-class *petit bourgeois* who, as a guard in a concentration camp, tortured Jews, also accomplish what was considered impossible in his previous 'decent' existence and acknowledge his 'passionate attachment' to sadistic torture?" ("CS" 124). The answer is *yes* but, as Žižek explains, this rupturing of the social edifice did not represent an authentic event because it did not arise from the void of the situation but rather served to reinforce the hegemonic system's fantasy of unity and self-mastery: the extermination of the Jews was supposed to lead to a stronger national character purified of all "external" irritants. In Lacanian terms, Nazism did not disturb "the fundamental fantasy" of a world without social antagonisms but merely avoided confrontation with such antagonisms by displacing them onto the figure of the Jew, which it, then, sought to destroy in order to eradicate the specter of collective rifts as such. As Žižek specifies, the inauthentic event "legitimizes itself through reference to the point of substantial fullness of a given constellation (on the political terrain: Race, True Religion, Nation . . .): it aims precisely at obliterating the last traces of the 'symptomal torsion' which disturbs the balance of that constellation" ("CS" 125). According to this logic, political uprisings that seek to create a new Whole by obliterating social antagonisms are intrinsically false, and Badiou admits that the threat of such false events (ethnonationalist uprisings, religious fundamentalisms, and so on) is ever-present. Yet he also believes that if we let our fear of false events overpower us to the extent that we are incapable of authentic ones, we shut down the possibility of truly transformative political interventions, reconciling ourselves to the kinds of purely incremental agendas that both he and Žižek eschew.

Badiou believes that when we categorize the human as a victim, we effectively shut down the possibility of authentic events: we make it impossible for new ways of interpreting things to enter the world. We, as it were, sacrifice the rights of the immortal for those of the mortal, denying that it is only as something "other than a victim," something "other" than a mortal being, that man accedes to the status of ethical subjectivity. This is why Badiou concludes that defining man as a victim only ensures that he will *"be held in contempt"* (E 12). Badiou further asserts that the victim, in the Western imagination, tends to be associated with the disempowered postcolonial subject, so that behind the Levinasian outlook that underscores our responsibility for the (suffering) other hides "the good-Man, the white-Man" (E 13). This is a powerful critique, yet it also raises the question of whether the "contempt" Badiou assumes will fall on the victim is an inevitable result of victimization or merely the outcome of a colonial logic that blames—and disparages— its victims for their lot. From the perspective of whom are the victimized automatically "held in contempt"? What is awkward about Badiou's formulation is its implication that victimization is something that can be avoided or rejected at will. It may be that Badiou does not mean to vilify the victimized themselves but merely ethical models—such as that of Levinas—centered around the notion of victimization. But this distinction is not always easy to uphold, with the result that Badiou at times sounds as if he thought that some people "allow" themselves to be victimized, whereas others (those capable of truth-events, those we admire rather than hold in contempt) are heroic enough to resist it. The problem is akin to the one I noted above with regard to Badiou and Žižek's assumption that every singularity has equal access to the universal. Though I am just as keen to escape the shortcomings of identity

politics as Badiou and Žižek are, I am not willing to ignore the
historical legacies of oppression—legacies that have *forced* various
people to assume undesirable subject positions, including those of
the victimized—to accomplish this escape.

7

Badiou's rhetoric of immortality oversimplifies not only the realities
of power but also the radical permeability of our bodies and psyches
alike—the very permeability that Butler foregrounds. At the same
time, his theory of the event counters Butler's trademark tendency
to read subjectivity as a site of disempowerment. This is exactly
why Žižek juxtaposes Badiou and Butler, arguing that Butler's
ethics of precarity represents a sort of "anti-Badiou manifesto."
Badiou himself has not responded to Butler, but Žižek is able to see
the contrast between these two thinkers so clearly in part because
there are obvious parallels between Badiou's event and the so-called
Lacanian ethical "act"—which Žižek has long criticized Butler for
misunderstanding. These parallels arise from the fact that Badiou,
as I indicated above, derives his notion of the void (which gives rise
to the event) from the Lacanian real, for the real, in turn, is what the
subject, in Lacanian theory, comes up against in the ethical "act." In
this sense, both the event and the act relate to the real as a kernel
of rebellious energy that reveals the inconsistencies of the dominant
system (the big Other). It is the possibility of such a kernel of
rebellious energy that Butler keeps rejecting, with the consequence
that she is not able to theorize the prospect of the kinds of radical
acts in which subjects—sometimes heroically, sometimes suicidally,
sometimes in both ways—reject the normative dictates of the big
Other by plunging into the jouissance of the real.

For Lacan, Antigone is the quintessential example of a subject
who commits such an act: because Antigone would rather die
than obey Creon's ban on burying her brother Polyneces, because
she stubbornly insists on her desire in the face of Creon's efforts
to intimidate her, she—in Lacan's eyes—becomes an ethical
heroine of a quasi-sublime status. More specifically, by defying
Creon, Antigone manages to assert her absolute autonomy vis-
à-vis Creon's symbolic law. As Lacan puts the matter, "When she
explains to Creon what she has done, Antigone affirms the advent

of the absolute individual with the phrase 'That's how it is because that's how it is.'"[18] Generally speaking, anyone who refuses to abide by the rules of the hegemonic symbolic, anyone who is willing to sacrifice his or her social viability—and sometimes literally his or her life—for the sake of a cause, could be said to commit an ethical act of this kind. In this sense, the act is the negative, self-destructive counterpart to Badiou's truth-event: if the event aims to bring a new—and presumably more just—social order into being, the act could just as well end in tragedy. This is why Žižek often accuses Badiou of downplaying the suicidal, death-driven aspects of the act. At the same time, even Žižek admits that the act, like the event, *sometimes* introduces the possibility of radical sociopolitical transformation; under certain circumstances—circumstances that cannot be predicted ahead of time—the act annihilates the old order so as to create space for a completely different one. Alternatively, the act may puncture the subject's coordinates of being in ways that allow for their fundamental reconfiguration; it may bring about an entirely new attitude toward the process of living.

Žižek's main criticism of Butler—one that I too share—is that she does not leave any space for such daring acts of sociopolitical or private rebelliousness. My annoyance at the hollow rhetoric of many young Žižekians notwithstanding, I appreciate the ideal of the kind of defiance that breaks, rather than merely reproduces, our psychic attachment to oppression, and this type of defiance is what Butler has found it difficult to conceptualize. Indeed, whether we are talking about Butler's early theories of social subjection and subversive reiteration, or about her later theories of precariousness and woundability, there is arguably a certain conservatism (or at least cautiousness) to her outlook precisely in the sense that it does not allow for the possibility of an uncompromising revolt on either the collective or personal level. Consider, for instance, this characteristic statement:

> In a Foucauldian perspective, one question is whether the very regime of power that seeks to regulate the subject does so by providing a principle of self-definition for the subject. If it does, and subjectivation is bound up with subjection in this way, then it will not do to invoke a notion of the subject as the ground of agency, since the subject is itself produced through operations of power that delimit in advance what the aims and expanse

of agency will be. It does not follow from this insight, however, that we are all always-already trapped, and that there is no point of resistance to regulation or to the form of subjection that regulation takes. What it does mean, however, is that we ought not to think that by embracing the subject as a ground of agency, we will have countered the effects of regulatory power.[19]

Butler essentially reads subjectivity as a function of subjection, suggesting that even our sense of agency is an effect of regulatory power. Though this does not mean that we are "always-already trapped," it does imply that the parameters of our resistance have been shaped by the very power we seek to oppose. Our only respite is that power sometimes has unintended effects, effects that we might—through reperformance, resignification, and reiteration— be able to exploit to our advantage; because we cannot overthrow the system, our only choice is to subvert it from within.

In progressive North American criticism at least, Butler's Foucault-inspired approach has been so influential that it is difficult to envision alternatives. As Wendy Brown remarks in relation to gender performativity:

> Gender is regarded (and lived) by contemporary young scholars and activists raised on postmodernism as something that can be bent, proliferated, troubled, resignified, morphed, theatricalized, parodied, deployed, resisted, imitated, regulated . . . but not emancipated. Gender is very nearly infinitely plastic and divisible, but as a domain of subjection with no outside, it cannot be liberated in the classical sense, and the powers constituting and regulating it cannot be seized and inverted or abolished. In one crucial respect, then, gendered regimes can be seen to share a predicament with global capitalism: each is available to almost any innovation and possibility except freedom, equality, and collective human control.[20]

Brown here comes close to Žižek's point about "postmodern" politics being the kind of politics that valorizes fluidity for its own sake without any regard for whether or not this fluidity in the final analysis holds any actual liberatory promise. Writing in a different context, and from a different theoretical orientation, Fraser expresses something similar when she argues that though Butler's approach "reveals the contingent, performatively constructed character of what passes for necessary and unalterable," "its internal normative resources—reification of performativity is bad, dereification is good—are far too meager for feminist purposes."[21] Neither Brown nor Fraser would be likely to deny the insightfulness of Butler's understanding of social subordination, wounded psychic attachments, and the constitution of gendered (and sexed) subjectivity, for both are supportive of Butler's overall vision—as I also tend to be. But their statements gesture toward a problematic that Butler has struggled in vain to resolve, namely that, in her theory, everything, including resistance, must be done *in relation to* power rather than in direct opposition to it: resistance, rather than being a matter of insubordination, is a matter of *negotiating* with power.

In some ways, we may merely be dealing with divergent definitions of insubordination, for obviously reperformance, resignification, and reiteration can also operate as forms of defiance. For many, the fluidity of gender and sexuality, for example, feels like a radically liberatory reality. A generous reading of Butler would therefore assert that her approach is no less emancipatory than the Marxist-Lacanian one of Žižek and Badiou—that she merely understands resistance differently. But a more critical reading would say that Butler's relationship to hegemonic power is far too respectful. Consider her claim that her theory of performativity emphasizes "the way in which the social world is made—and new social possibilities emerge—at various levels of social action through a *collaborative relation with power*."[22] Butler's wording here is telling: we are asked to collaborate with power rather than to topple it. Butler in fact readily acknowledges her complicity with power when she asserts that "such complicity is, for me, the condition of agency rather than its destruction."[23] No wonder, then, that Butler believes that the price we pay for our subjectivity is our passionate attachment to our own subjection. While Foucault was still a theorist of agency, and even of freedom, Butler is on some level a theorist of resignation in the sense that she views our defeat in relation to power as a foregone conclusion. This resignation can be detected in statements such as the following: "The salience of psychoanalysis comes into view when we consider how it is that those who are oppressed by certain operations of power also come to be invested in that oppression, and how, in fact, their very self-definition becomes bound up with the terms by which they are regulated, marginalized, or erased from the sphere of cultural life" ("CU" 149). As much as I appreciate the notion that biopower and other invisible modalities of power infiltrate our psychic lives in ways that we cannot control, I have never been convinced that those who are oppressed are invariably "invested in" their oppression. Some may be, but others surely are not. Many are able to take a degree of critical distance from their oppression—a distance that often leads them (deeply and quite consciously) to resent their oppressors even when they, out of self-preservation, "go along" with their oppression. And sometimes this critical distance even leads to overt acts of defiance.

I understand how Butler's Foucaultian understanding of resistance can lead to the conclusion that complicity with power is the prerequisite of agency, but there is arguably something quite conformist about the idea that in order to resist power, we need to work with it. This is why Žižek and Badiou, despite their troubled relationship to progressive political movements other than the class struggle, offer a thought-provoking counterpoint to Butlerian resignation. If Butler views subjectivity as more or less equivalent to being interpellated by hegemonic power, Žižek and Badiou see it as the *antithesis* of interpellation: the subject comes into being when interpellation *fails*, when the individual manages to take distance from social power or directly challenges this power. As Žižek explains, "Not only does the subject never fully recognize itself in the interpellative call: its resistance to interpellation (to the symbolic identity provided by interpellation) *is* the subject" ("CS" 115). In other words, if for Butler, the subject consists of a nexus of ideological forces, for Žižek and Badiou, the subject emerges when ideology falters; the subject represents a gap in the structure of ideology.

In the same way that the Lacanian real ruptures the complacency of the symbolic, rendering it less securely authoritative than it pretends to be, the subject—through the act, through the event—ruptures the complacency of ideology, revealing its fault lines and internal contradictions. This is why there is no Other of the Other: the ideological edifice of the big Other may work overtime to conceal its fissures, to posit a compelling origin for its fantasies of coherence, but this is a losing battle, for the real will always interrupt the functioning of power; it is why the moment when the subject hits the real through the act or event represents a counterintuitive moment of freedom. As Žižek observes, "The bar of the Real is Lacan's way of asserting the terrifying abyss of the subject's ultimate and radical *freedom*, the freedom whose space is sustained by the Other's inconsistency and lack" ("DC" 258). This is to say that the subject's constitutive incompleteness—the fact that its symbolic façade is always fractured by the energies of the real—ensures that there always remains a part of its being that has not been completely taken over by the dominant order; the bar of the real designates the subject's freedom because it gives rise to the subject's capacity to stage acts of defiance—or, in Badiou's terms, to participate in truth-events—which reveal the contingent and ultimately fraudulent status of the symbolic order.

8

Because Butler does not acknowledge the possibility of anything that might elude the grasp of power, she insists that even the real is a symbolic construct; for Butler, the very notion that there could be something that resists symbolization is itself symbolically produced—one ideological fantasy among others. Žižek, in contrast, insists that the real is the internal limit to the symbolic, the "bone in the throat" that makes the symbolic cough. This does not mean that the real has not been shaped by the symbolic but merely that this shaping is never entirely successful. Think, for example, of instances when the body "malfunctions," when its jouissance betrays the subject's symbolic projects, impeding its "proper" functioning. Something similar takes place in the act, except that the impact is more drastic in the sense that the act produces a subject who, however momentarily, opts out of the symbolic altogether, who is no longer embarrassed by its inability to adhere to the rules of social behavior but instead embraces—or feels compelled to embrace—the destructive energies of the real.[24] Such a subject is not interested in trying to solve its problems within the parameters of the system but rather insists on changing the game entirely, on defying the very structuring principles of the system. This is one way to understand what it means to make the impossible possible, what it means to open a gateway to what might, from the perspective of the established order, seem completely inconceivable (or even a little crazy). This is why the act does not "express" the subject's "inner nature" but rather radically reconfigures the coordinates of its identity; at its most authentic, the act reaches the core of the fundamental fantasies that, on the most basic level, determine the subject's being. As Žižek states, "An act does not merely redraw the contours of our public symbolic identity, it also transforms the spectral dimension that sustains this identity, the undead ghosts that haunt the living subject, the secret history of traumatic fantasies transmitted 'between the lines', through the lacks and distortions of the explicit symbolic texture of his or her identity" ("CS" 124). The act, in short, breaks the passionate attachment to subjection that Butler sees as intractable, thereby releasing the subject from its faithfulness to its repetitive efforts to negotiate with power.

This is what Žižek is getting at when he asserts that even though Butler frequently accuses Lacan of being a spokesman for heteronormative phallocentrism, Lacan actually offers a much more radical theory of agency than Butler herself does, thereby making it possible to imagine alternatives, among other things, to heteronormative phallocentrism. As Žižek explains, if the Butlerian subject's resistance is limited to the subversion of hegemonic norms—a subversion that, by definition, is "doomed to perpetual defeat" ("DC" 220)—Lacan "allows for a much stronger subjective autonomy: insofar as the subject occupies the place of the lack in the Other (symbolic order), it can perform separation (the operation which is the opposite of alienation), and suspend the reign of the big Other, in other words, separate itself from it" (N 137). The main idea here is that the subject who steps into the real—the place of the lack in the Other—severs its ties with the symbolic order. But what is perhaps most interesting about Žižek's statement is the claim that the separation that the act accomplishes is "the opposite of alienation." This means that the subject who commits the act follows the pulse of its own desire rather than acquiescing to the normative expectations of the big Other; if the subject is usually alienated from its desire by the desire of the Other, in the act, its abrupt separation from the Other breaks this alienation: suddenly, if only fleetingly, the subject is united with its desire rather than alienated from it. As Žižek observes, "Alienation *in* the big Other is followed by the separation *from* the big Other" ("DC" 253). In this sense, "the big Other is unassailable only in so far as the subject entertains towards it a relationship of alienation, while separation precisely opens up the way for . . . an intervention" ("DC" 255).

Separation—an adamant *No!*, *Enough!*, or *Fuck You!* aimed at the big Other—is the Lacanian antidote to alienation and thus an opening to intervention; like Antigone's defiant *No!* to Creon, it signifies the subject's radical autonomy. A contrast between Butler and Žižek will once again clarify that matter. As we have discovered, Butler believes that our inability to control the collective symbolic field into which we are inserted—along with our inability to access the opaque history of our own formation—renders us partially incomprehensible to ourselves and therefore inherently incapable of giving a full account of ourselves. In response, Žižek writes:

> The limit of such a reference to the impenetrable background into which we are thrown and on account of which we cannot be taken as fully accountable and responsible for our acts is the negativity of freedom: even when the entire positive content of my psyche is ultimately impenetrable, the margin of my freedom is that I can say No! to any positive element that I encounter. This negativity of freedom provides the zero-level from which every positive content can be questioned. Lacan's position is thus that being exposed/overwhelmed, caught in a cobweb of preexisting conditions, is *not* incompatible with radical autonomy. Of course, I cannot undo the substantial weight of the context into which I am thrown; of course, I cannot penetrate the opaque background of my being; but what I can do is, in an act of negativity, "cleanse the plate," draw a line, exempt myself, step outside of the symbolic in a "suicidal" gesture of a radical act—what Freud called "death drive" and what German Idealism called "radical negativity." (*N* 140)

That I cannot control the social context into which I am thrown is a given, as is my inability to recreate the opaque history of my own formation. But this does not consign me to an endless process of bargaining with power. I always retain the freedom to say *No!* to my predicament. This is the "negativity of freedom" I possess, which is why I have a degree of autonomy even when I feel overwhelmed by the webs of power that surround me. However, I can only activate this autonomy if I am willing to surrender my symbolic supports, if I am willing—even temporarily—to genuinely not give a damn about what is expected of me.

That I, in this instance, find Žižek's reading of Lacan persuasive reveals the crux of my overall disagreement with Butler: if Butler believes that I would rather form wounded attachments than no attachments at all—that the recognition granted by the Other (or an array of others) is so important to me that I am willing to harm myself to attain it—I believe that there are situations where I might be capable of cutting my connection to what wounds me even if this means risking my status as a socially (or interrelationally) intelligible being. Butler might argue that the price of my Lacanian attitude is too high, that the annihilation of social ties does not offer a viable alternative to the kind of more incremental change that Butler herself tends to advocate. Yet, as those who have conjured up the courage to walk away from an oppressive collective arrangement or from an enthralling but painful intimate relationship know, it can be tremendously liberating to leave behind what has been traumatizing. The trauma will linger, of course, but its impact will be different from what it would be if we tried to negotiate with its source. In part Butler asks us to negotiate because she does not believe that we can ever truly extricate ourselves from power. But in part she asks us to negotiate because her Levinasian approach implies that sociality is intrinsically ethical and that rupturing the bonds of relationality is therefore the worst thing we could ever do. Indeed, it is easy to see how her current ethical (Levinasian) vision bolsters the disempowering elements of her earlier (Foucaultian) theories of subjectivity and psychic life: now it is not merely impossible—but *ethically unacceptable*—to break our connection to what injures us. This is where my resistance to masochism kicks in, for though I understand that disentangling ourselves from debilitating patterns of power is difficult, I do not think that it is impossible; likewise, because I do not share Butler's view that self-assertion is invariably evil, I believe that there are times when severing relational bonds is absolutely the best thing to do.

Severing a devastating relational bond is one way in which the subject courts the real as a seat of antisocial energy—one way in which the subject "chooses" its freedom over the suffocating entanglements of traumatizing relationality. This can be difficult to do because we live in a culture that worships the virtues of sociality in a fairly habitual manner, so that opting out of relationality tends to be pathologized even in cases when it is the least pathological course of action (we are supposed to "talk though" our problems rather than to walk out on our loved ones). That Butler's relational ethics, along with her rejection of the concept of the real, uncritically mirrors this mentality says something about the normative assumptions that seep into her theory—a topic I will revisit later. But let us also recall that—as I argued at the end of the previous chapter—Butler balks at the real in part because she dislikes the idea that there might be a "formal" limit to subjectivity (or subjection) that is not socially and historically conditioned. In essence, she believes that the concept of constitutive, foundational lack (which is one way to read the function of the real) undermines our ability to comprehend the socially and historically specific ways in which individuals are rendered lacking: traumatized, wounded, injured, and so on. As she states, "If the subject always meets its limit in the selfsame place, then the subject is fundamentally exterior to the history in which it finds itself: there is no historicity to the subject, its limits, its articulability" ("RU" 13). She further notes, "I agree with the notion that every subject emerges on the condition of foreclosure, but do not share the conviction that these foreclosures are prior to the social" ("CU" 140), adding that, in Lacan, the trauma that inaugurated the subject is "prior to any and all social and historical reality" ("CU" 141). But Lacan says no such thing. The trauma that inaugurates the subject-of-lack is caused by an encounter with the signifier and—as I have already emphasized—this encounter always takes specific social and historical forms; the collective norms that the signifier carries are always going to have a socially and historically specific content. Lacan's point about the real is merely that such norms never have a complete hold over us, and that the ethical act is a vehicle through which the undomesticated energies of the real spill into the symbolic realm (which constantly tries—but always to some extent fails—to contain them). This is why it is a misreading of Lacan to accuse him of relying on a static conception of the symbolic order.

The stakes of this misreading become obvious when Butler asserts that Žižek—and by implication, Lacan—posits "a transcultural structure of social reality that presupposes a sociality based in fictive and idealized kinship positions that presume the heterosexual family as constituting the defining social bond for all humans" ("CU" 141–2). As I have admitted, I also find Žižek's anachronistic approach to feminist and queer theory exasperating, but in this instance I have to defend him by pointing out that heteronormative "sociality based in fictive and idealized kinship positions" is not Žižek's private invention but rather the edifice that has historically governed the collective reality of many, perhaps most, societies, and certainly of Western societies. Nor is this heteronormative sociality what Lacan advocated. Lacan never claimed that this type of sociality was the only way, or the most desirable way, to organize societies but merely that it was how heteropatriarchal societies had been organized. Like Freud, Lacan understood that the process of becoming an intelligible member of the symbolic order usually meant a degree of compliance with its heteropatriarchal edicts—a point that seems similar to Butler's own observations about social subjection—which is precisely one reason he thought that subject formation was unnecessarily coercive. This is why, as we will discover in the next chapter, the aim of Lacanian clinical practice was to free the subject from hegemonic blueprints of desire so that it could pursue alternative psychic trajectories. Along related lines, Lacan repeatedly stressed that the authority of the phallus in a phallocentric world was purely spectral, that "man" as the possessor of the phallus was by necessity an imposter. This seems like a far cry from endorsing the "fictive and idealized kinship positions" of heteropatriarchy.

Moreover, I would say that there is something rather reductive about the idea that any admission of constitutive dispossession (foundational lack or deprivation) precludes an analysis of more socially and historically specific dispossessions (lacks or deprivations). I concede that an exclusive attention to the former might detract attention from the latter—a danger I have often noted in my previous work. But I do not see any reason to judge the matter as an either/or game: surely the notion that there might be an inherent limit to the symbolic coherence of the subject (the real) in no way negates the fact that specific subjects can be limited (wounded) in highly specific (socially and historically unique) ways. There is, in other words, nothing that prevents us from theorizing both types of dispossession—to the extent that they can be separated at all—simultaneously. Butler assumes that admitting the real as a meaningful theoretical category implies that we understand "opposition" apolitically, as "a vain effort to displace a founding limit that is structural in status" ("RS" 13). Yet no one—not even

Žižek—is arguing this. There is nothing about the concept of the real that keeps us from engaging in socially and historically specific political struggles. In addition, Butler's denial of constitutive lack leads to a theoretical dead end that seems entirely incompatible with her otherwise antihumanist slant: the possibility that there might exist a subject in the world who is fully present to itself—an entirely nonalienated subject who does not experience any limits to its sovereignty and self-sufficiency. That such a subject *does* in fact find its way into Butlerian theory may explain some key components of this theory, such as the idea that we are "dispossessed" by the other. This idea seems to imply that before our "dispossession" by the other there was full self-possession, a place where our being was still completely our own. I agree that others often dispossess us in various ways. But Butler's assertion that the self-other relationship is *intrinsically* dispossessing—rather than, say, enriching—suggests that there is some originary wholeness that the other's presence interrupts (recall that *interruption* is exactly the term Butler uses to describe the intrusion of the other into the space of the self.) But if the self is always already relational to begin with, what exactly is it that is being interrupted? Some sort of a core self that has not been riven by constitutive lack?

9

Despite all these disagreements, Butler cannot always maintain the distance between her theories and those of Lacanians. For instance, Butler's commentary on Levinas's notion of messianic justice and Walter Benjamin's notion of divine violence contains elements that echo basic Lacanian insights regarding the act (and therefore, indirectly, the real). To be sure, Butler expresses some doubts about the kind of unwavering "decision" that the act calls for: "Decision cannot finally be the ground for the struggle for non-violence. Decision fortifies the deciding 'I,' sometimes at the expense of relationality itself."[25] Butler's rejection of "decision" as the foundation of politics therefore relies on the same logic as her rejection of everything that hints at autonomy, namely that it could increase the arrogance of the self by downplaying its relational (and hence precarious) constitution. "Maybe the 'act' in its singularity and heroism is overrated," Butler contends: "It loses sight of the iterable process in which a critical intervention is needed, and it can become the very means by which the 'subject' is produced at the expense of a relational social ontology" (*FW* 184). Butler here privileges her iterative, incremental political approach over the singularity and heroism of the act, and by implication, over the subject that this act brings into being. Moreover, she seems to presume that the act produces the subject at the expense of other subjects, or at the very least at the expense of the ethical obligations that arise from its social ontology. Yet this is not necessarily the case: it may be that the subject, in committing the act, sacrifices itself for the sake of an other (as Antigone does). Butler is nothing but consistent in her suspicion that the subject might be too ego-driven and self-promoting and thus in need of being humbled. But, as I have argued all along, there is something overly simplistic about her attempt to construct a new definition of the subject purely out of the materials that were left out of the traditional definition, so that instead of being autonomous, the subject—at least the good subject—is now completely devoid of autonomy. Perhaps even more problematically, Butler's disdain for the singularity and heroism of the act—its "individualism," as it were—causes her to advocate *not acting* as a preferable political option: "So the problem is not really about how the subject should act, but about what a refusal to act might look like when it issues from the apprehension of a generalized condition of precariousness" (*FW* 183). "Not to act," she concludes, is "a way of comporting oneself so as to break with the closed circle of reflexivity, a way of ceding to the ties that bind and unbind, a way of registering and demanding equality affectively" (*FW* 184). Equality, here, seems to be the reward for not acting.

Yet Butler also, almost despite herself, celebrates something akin to the act in her discussion of Levinas and Benjamin, which is why I think that she comes closer to the Lacanian perspective than she is willing to acknowledge. Žižek has repeatedly—and I think legitimately—claimed Benjaminian divine violence as a theoretical cousin to the Lacanian act,[26] and Butler's adoption of the same allegory implies that their visions have, in spite of the strong objections of both, converged, now displaying a great deal of overlap. Or perhaps it would be more accurate to say that Butler's reading of Levinas and Benjamin brings her to the vicinity of Badiou's truth-event. For instance, in relation to Levinas's notion of messianic justice, Butler proposes that the subject's unconditional responsibility for the other constitutes the kind of messianic summons that cannot be resisted and that jolts the subject outside the sequence of time. This means, among other things, that, like Badiou's event, ethical action must be undertaken *now*, in the moment, without hesitation, without deliberation. It is, as Butler stresses, "an indisputable assignation," an assignation that "comes from a modality other than historical time, constituting its very anteriority."[27] Butler elaborates:

> One is called upon to respond ethically, and this call is the effective action of the messianic upon human life. . . .The messianic is thus not only an experience of waiting and of suffering but also an unwilled and infinite receptivity to the commandment that makes responsibility for the other coextensive with the self. Indeed, responsibility for the other constitutes the ek-static structure of the self, the fact that I am called outside of myself and that this relation to an alterity defines me essentially. (*PW* 40–1)

Predictably, the messianic call, for Levinas, leaps forth from the face. Furthermore, as we discovered in Chapter 1, Levinas believes that even though justice—as opposed to ethics—is compelled to take some distance from the face, ultimately it needs to refer back to the face, back to ethics. That is, even justice cannot afford to forget the call of the face:

> It awaits the voices that will recall, to the judgments of the judges and statesmen, the human face dissimulated beneath the identities of citizens. Perhaps these are the "prophetic voices." . . . There is something heard in the cries that rise up from the interstices of politics and that, independently of official authority, defend the "rights of man"; sometimes in the songs of the poets; sometimes simply in the press or in the public forum of the liberal states, in which freedom of expression is ranked as the first freedom and justice is always a revision of justice and the expectation of a better justice. (*EN* 196)

Levinas here, once again, reminds us that justice must continually strive to perfect itself so as to better live up to the ideals of ethics. Only in this way, he suggests, can we ensure that the "resources of charity" do not disappear "beneath the political structure of institutions"; it is only in this way that we can safeguard "a religious breath or a prophetic spirit in man" (*EN* 203).

These statements express the kind of faith in the press and the public forum of liberal states that Butler might not share. And they also steer us into the realm of explicitly religious discourse: not Derridean "messianism without a messiah,"[28] Lacanian acts, or Badiouan events, but actual "prophetic voices." But even this should not obscure the fact that Levinas's core message here is more or less identical to that of Žižek and Badiou: there *is* a way to demolish the hegemony of the social order, to interrupt the progression of history, and therefore to experience something genuinely transformative. Like the Lacanian-Žižekian act and Badiou's event, the Levinasian exodus from the "normal" state of things, the messianic insistence on reaching beneath the formalities of justice to the ethics of the face-to-face encounter, ruptures the symbolic coordinates of the subject's being, for the prophetic voices that remind the subject of its ethical accountability throw it off-kilter: "In the very structure of prophecy, a temporality is opened up, breaking with the 'rigor' of being" (*EN* 115). Prophecy—here the vehicle of ethics—therefore shatters being. More specifically, it shatters the subject's intellectual conceits: "'Subservience of an obedience preceding the hearing of the order'—is this just insanity and an absurd anachronism? Is it not rather the description of the paradoxical modality of inspiration, breaking precisely with the intellectualism of knowing, and in obedience to absolute order, outlining the very diachrony of the future?" (*EN* 151). Even here, Levinas seizes the opportunity to take a stab at the rational subject of metaphysics—a subject for whom "*I think* would preserve the last word" (*EN* 152). The ethical ushers the subject beyond "the intellectualism of knowing" to a realm of inspiration and unqualified obedience. Responsibility to the other, Levinas specifies, "is ordered, goodness pulling the self away from its irresistible return to self, pulling the self away from the unconditional perseverance of the entity in its being" (*EN* 152). In other words, ethics is an assault on the perseverance of being, on the subject's instinct for self-preservation, which is why Levinas characterizes it as "a breach made by humanness in the barbarism of being" (*EN* 187). "The human," he concludes, "makes it possible for a *beyond-being* to take on meaning" (*EN* 211).

10

Butler connects this Levinasian ethical vision with Benjamin's divine violence. Benjamin understood divine violence as the kind of anarchic violence that counters the (often invisible) violence of dominant power structures by a vehement (highly visible) insurrection. Divine violence, in other words, honors an ethical demand to override an oppressive law, state, or regime; if "legal" violence is the type of violence that regimes commit, divine violence refuses an uncritical allegiance to unjust institutions, obeying, instead—as Levinasian messianism does—the more primordial call of ethics. Benjamin's divine violence materializes in what Butler calls "provisional criminality" (PW 92): in revolutionary uprisings, general strikes, and other forms of revolt, which break the bonds of accountability that usually keep subjects faithful to coercive regimes. Perhaps most important, Benjamin, like Levinas, resorts to the notion of the "messianic" as a liberatory force, in this case as a force that rescues the oppressed from historical oblivion. As Butler explains:

> On one reading . . . the messianic puts an end to time and constitutes "a cessation of happening." . . . But, on another reading, some forgotten set of histories, those that belong to the history of the oppressed, flashes up and makes a sudden claim. On the first reading, the point is to stop history as we know it, to go on strike against the current temporal regime, and even not to act. But, on the second reading, a certain reconfiguration or reconstellation of present time takes place in which the forgotten history of the oppressed may well enter into or through the strait gate. We might even say that the memory explodes into the present and that someone called a historian, someone whose practice is remembrance, seems to be crucial to this inauguration of "now-time." The historian is not a messiah, and yet something of the messianic emerges here, perhaps as the time of an emergency brake pulled on history, but also by virtue of something flashing up or shooting through that calls for urgent attention. (PW 103–4)

The messianic not only arrests the march of history but also reconfigures it by creating an opening for what has been suppressed and forgotten: the experiences of those who have been downtrodden.

Memory, Butler argues, "is one of the few weapons available to those against whom the tide of history has turned" (*PW* 111). The messianic intervention of divine violence recovers past experiences of suffering, thereby forcing us to confront that suffering; through it, "'sparks' from another time . . . striate the present," so that the present is transformed into what Benjamin calls "now-time" (*PW* 92). As a result, the history of the oppressed "emerges in a flash, even as a sign of danger, breaking through or interrupting the continuum of history that goes under the name of progress" (*PW* 100). If the very notion of progress requires the denial of the history of oppression, the messianic resurrects this history in sudden flares. As Butler states, "It is memory that takes momentary shape as a form of light, recalling the kabbalistic *sephirot*, those scattered and quasi-angelic illuminations that break up both the suspect continuity of the present along with the amnesia and expulsion it ritually and seamlessly performs" (*PW* 106). In this sense, Benjaminian remembrance functions as the inverse of the history of the victors: it is not a matter of recounting history but rather of puncturing its official constellation, of interrupting its seamless continuity. As Benjamin explains: "The true picture of the past flits by. The past can be seized only as an image which flashes up at the instant when it can be recognized and is never seen again"; the present is, as it were, "shot through with chips of Messianic time."[29]

The theological tone of both Levinas and Benjamin is somewhat startling in the context of progressive criticism, and I cannot help but suspect that one reason—though undoubtedly not the only reason—Butler is drawn to it is that it offers her yet another way to deny the possibility that the subject might possess a degree of agency. After all, prophetic voices, messianic messages, divine violence, and kabbalistic, angelic illuminations strip the subject of self-determination even more effectively than any theory of social subjection ever could; if Butler, in her earlier work, was interested in the deconstruction of subjectivity, she now seems invested in a quasi-religious capitulation of being. Indeed, I find it telling that when Butler—after more than two decades of theorizing incremental social change—finally moves onto more revolutionary terrain, she does so through the mystifications of theology. Though there is no question that Žižek's theory of the act and Badiou's theory of the event also contain strong theological undercurrents, these remain relatively muted in part because agency is so important to Žižek and Badiou that they are not willing to allow God—or God's messianic, inspirational message—to swallow the subject's autonomy. Butler, in turn, finds agency so intolerable that she seems willing to go to more or less any lengths to invent a subject who has been purified of this unbecoming trait. One almost gets the impression that self-assertion, for her, constitutes a kind of original sin, so that the fact that her flight from Enlightenment rationality— initially expressed through an allegiance to poststructuralism—ends in a retreat to a messianic ethics may actually make some sort of sense. Unfortunately, this makes me wonder whether those who have accused poststructuralism of being apolitical might actually be onto something. I have always resisted this interpretation of poststructuralism because I have deemed its deconstruction of subjectivity—including its deconstruction of the meaning of gender and sexuality—to be profoundly political. But the fact that Butler finds it so easy to swap the vocabulary of poststructuralism for the vocabulary of messianism gives me pause.

I am not saying that Levinasian messianism and Benjaminian divine violence are not interesting ways to theorize revolutionary politics. And I do not deny that the Lacanian real can also be read theologically, as is clear, for example, from Lacan's notorious account of feminine jouissance and mysticism.[30] But I have always thought that Lacan was interested in explaining psychoanalytically what previous worldviews had understood theologically: his concept of the real was, in some ways, meant to capture the psychoanalytic resonances of the kinds of transcendent, sublime experiences ("hitting the real") that had previously been interpreted in religious terms. Furthermore, the jouissance of the real, for Lacan, was one way to talk about the death drive and the repetition compulsion, and therefore immune to the kind of false hope of redemption that theology has throughout the ages offered to the believer. There might have been a trace of God in the real but he was definitely not winning. Butler, in contrast, appears invested in reinjecting religious meaning into secular critical theory, implying that God has a role to play in the liberation of humankind. She might claim that critical theory's secularism was always more apparent than real—an argument I have already touched on and that I will return to in Chapter 5—but her Levinasian tendency to conflate ethics and theology has gotten so pronounced that it has become more and more difficult, for me at least, to trust that her vision retains space for progressive perspectives that regard religion with a degree of (well-justified) suspicion. To express the matter bluntly, I no longer know whether Butler is telling me to revere the other even when this other persecutes me because this is what God wants me to do or because she genuinely believes—independently of what God wants—that this is the right thing to do.

4

In search of defiant subjects: Rebellion in Lacan and Marcuse

It is because we know better than those who went before how to recognize the nature of desire . . . that a reconsideration of ethics is possible, that a form of ethical judgment is possible, of a kind that gives this question the force of a Last Judgment: Have you acted in conformity with the desire that is in you? . . . I propose then that, from an analytic point of view, the only thing of which one can be guilty is of having given ground relative to one's desire.

JACQUES LACAN[1]

1

In the last chapter, I argued that Lacan's model of the ethical act—particularly as it has been developed by Žižek and Badiou—offers a stronger account of agency than Butler's theories of reperformance, resignification, and reiteration do. And even though Butler's recent analyses of Levinasian messianic justice and Benjaminian divine violence gesture toward a posture of defiance akin to the Lacanian act, they remain shrouded in the kind of theological rhetoric that divests the subject of agency even more drastically than Butler's earlier theories of social subjection. If these earlier theories portrayed the subject as irrevocably caught up in the tentacles of disciplinary power as well as psychically attached to this power, Butler's turn to religion gives us a subject carried by a messianic summons that cannot be resisted; the subject who "acts" yields to a calling that originates outside of itself, in some quasi-divine register, with the consequence that it becomes a mere inert vehicle for a higher cause. This is why Butler's theological musings, though superficially closer to Žižek and Badiou than anything else she has written, cannot ultimately be conflated with either the Lacanian-Žižekian act or the Badiouan event. Not only do the latter call for the kind of subjective "decision" that Butler cannot allow into her theoretical apparatus, but they presuppose that the command that the subject obeys is an internal rather than an external (let alone a prophetic) one. Though the inspiration of Badiou's event, for example, can have external causes—such as the sudden revelation of an amorous link, a scientific truth, an artistic beauty, or a political justice—the subject is always in the final analysis responsible for its actions (rather than, say, an instrument of God's will). One might sum up the matter as follows: if Butler's messianic messages strip the subject of autonomy, thereby completing Butler's long-standing mission of emptying the subject of every trace of sovereignty, Badiou's subject of the event—like the Lacanian-Žižekian subject of the act—comes into being as an entity of autonomy (and even of freedom) because it is willing to honor its inner directive even at the risk of losing its social (let alone theological) viability.

Lacan theorized this inner directive in terms of desire specifically, which is why—as the quotation that opens this chapter conveys—the question of whether or not we have acted in conformity with our desire constitutes, for him, a kind of Last Judgment. This allows me to express the distinction between the Lacanian position—which Žižek and Badiou endorse—and the Levinasian-Butlerian one even more clearly: if Lacan believed that we are guilty when we give ground on our desire, the Levinasian-Butlerian approach implies that we are guilty when we act on this desire. Because the Levinasian-Butlerian paradigm elevates the other over the subject, any affirmation of the subject's desire—even its desire for sheer survival—is by definition a violation of ethics. And, unfortunately, I do not think that it is a coincidence that this has always been the message of monotheistic religion. Lacan, in contrast, had something quite different in mind when he developed his ethics of psychoanalysis: the ethics of not ceding on one's desire. As we have learned, in the Lacanian act—which is perhaps the most extreme manifestation of the subject's refusal to give ground on its desire—the subject plunges into the jouissance of the real in order to liberate itself from the repressive dictates of the symbolic order, including the latter's theological prohibitions against desire. The autonomy that the act grants is therefore not a matter of fortifying one's symbolic identity but rather of pursuing the truth of one's desire, sometimes to the point of allowing this desire to disintegrate into self-shattering jouissance. Simply put, in the act, the subject is willing to sacrifice its entire being for its desire (which always, ultimately, tends toward jouissance[2]), which is precisely why the act may appear a little deranged from the perspective of the symbolic establishment.

Here is Žižek's explanation of the act:

> In a situation of the forced choice, the subject makes the "crazy", impossible choice of, in a way, *striking at himself*, at what is most precious to himself. This act, far from amounting to a case of impotent aggressivity turned on oneself, rather changes the co-ordinates of the situation in which the subject finds himself: by cutting himself loose from the precious object through whose possession the enemy kept him in check, the subject gains the space of free action. Is not such a radical gesture of "striking at oneself" constitutive of subjectivity as such? Did not Lacan himself accomplish a similar act of "shooting at himself" when, in 1979, he dissolved the *École freudienne de Paris*, his *agalma*, his own organization, the very space of his collective life? Yet he was well aware that only such a "self-destructive" act could clear the terrain for a new beginning.[3]

In this instance, Žižek is drawing his examples from movies, which is why they are quite extreme, such as Kevin Spacey killing his wife and daughter in *The Usual Suspects* so as to be at liberty to pursue the members of the gang who held them at gunpoint.

But Žižek's observation about Lacan dissolving his own cherished psychoanalytic association in order to start from scratch points to real-life possibilities for the act, such as walking out on a job rather than enduring one more day of harassment by one's superiors (even when doing so puts one in financial jeopardy), or walking out on a lover who keeps causing pain (even when doing so destroys one's sense of security). The individual who commits the act, as it were, strikes at himself, at the very core of his social viability, in order to liberate himself from blows directed at him from the outside world; he cuts his social ties in order to gain the freedom (autonomy) to proceed differently from what is expected of him. I have already emphasized that the Butlerian relational approach implies that severing social bonds is intrinsically unethical; the Lacanian-Žižekian approach, in contrast, tells us to do exactly this when we feel that this action will release us from what oppresses us; it encourages us to surrender what is most precious to us—most important for our self-definition (our job, our lover, etc.)—if this means freeing ourselves from an intolerable situation and making room for a new beginning of some kind.

Let me restate the major differences between the Levinasian and Lacanian visions as follows: if for Levinas, ethics is a matter of honoring the other, for Lacan it is a matter of honoring one's own desire; if Levinas privileges the other's well-being over the subject's self-serving interests, Lacan privileges the subject's desire over everything else, including its relationships with others; if Last Judgment, for Levinas, can be found in the face that carries the imprint of God, Last Judgment, for Lacan, can be found in the "fundamental fantasy"—the fantasy that operates on the level of jouissance (the real)—that carries the truth of the subject's desire beyond its symbolic identity. Lacan's vision is also radically different from our loosely Kantian everyday understanding of ethics, which implies that ethics is a matter of rationally choosing between right and wrong, just and unjust, actions, and that ethical conduct therefore requires our ability to cast aside our idiosyncratic, irrational inclinations. From this perspective, there is virtually nothing that seems further from ethical virtue than acting in conformity with our desire. Indeed, placing Lacan in dialogue with Levinas and Kant reveals that Levinas and Kant might not be as incompatible with each other as they usually appear, that beneath their seemingly divergent paradigms resides an important point of agreement, namely the idea that ethics is the antithesis of desire. For Lacan, in turn, ethics is a matter of pursuing the truth of desire even when this means violating sociocultural norms of proper behavior.

No wonder, then, that Lacanian ethics can come across as individualistic or even selfish—a fact that my graduate students (at least those who have escaped Žižek's spell) remind me of on a regular basis. Surely there are many other things besides having compromised on our desire that we could feel guilty about. And what if our desire is hurtful to others? What if it clashes with the desires of others, generating the kinds of power struggles that end violently? And how are we supposed to know what our desire is in the first place? Isn't one of the main insights of psychoanalysis that we are frequently utterly alienated from our desire?

I think that it is impossible to conjure away such reservations about Lacanian ethics, which is why I am going to let them stand until the next chapter, where I offer a critique of the fact that Lacanian ethics, like its Levinasian-Butlerian counterpart, operates wholly without normative content. Essentially, I will illustrate that the aversion to *a priori* ethical principles that characterizes all the approaches I have examined in this book is not theoretically (or practically) viable, that we need such principles even as we continue the project of deconstructing the arrogant subject of Enlightenment rationalism. In this chapter, however, I would like to assess Lacanian ethics in its own terms in order to explain why it holds a great deal of political value, particularly as an opening to fundamental personal and social change. To accomplish this goal, I will relate Lacan's vision, first, to Herbert Marcuse's neo-Marxist critique of the biopolitical fashioning of obedient subjects under capitalism and, second, to recent feminist and queer theoretical attempts to conceptualize what it might mean to opt out of the dominant heteropatriarchal system in search of alternative modalities of being. We will discover that all of these approaches— Lacan, Marcuse, and recent feminist and queer theory—call for what Butler has found so difficult to envision: the subject's ability to take enough critical distance from the dominant social order to be able to dissociate itself from at least some of the demands of this order. All of them, in short, assume that the subject is, under certain circumstances, entirely capable of breaking its psychic attachment to its own subjection.

2

Lacan's ethics is not an ethics of moderation, which is one reason he explicitly positions it in opposition to both Aristotle and Kant. Lacan maintains that Aristotle's "middle path"—an ethical model based on "modesty," "temperateness," and "the cleaning up of desire"—is "wholly founded on an order that is no doubt a tidied-up, ideal order," adding that Aristotle's "morality is the morality of the master, created for the virtues of the master and linked to the order of powers" (*EP* 314–15). Lacan qualifies this statement by conceding that one should not always be contemptuous of the order of powers—that he is not speaking as an anarchist—but his overall argument is that hegemonic power is essentially hostile to desire:

> What is Alexander's proclamation when he arrived in Persepolis or Hitler's when he arrived in Paris? The preamble isn't important: "I have come to liberate you from this or that." The essential point is "Carry on working. Work must go on." Which, of course, means: "Let it be clear to everyone that this is on no account the moment to express the least surge of desire." The morality of power, of the service of goods, is as follows: "As far as desires are concerned, come back later. Make them wait." (*EP* 315)

Lacan's main disagreement with Aristotelian morality is that, insofar as this morality upholds the master's "service of goods," it enacts a similar suppression of desire, tolerating only its sublimated, socially useful manifestations. The Kantian categorical imperative ("Act in such a way that the maxim of your action may be accepted as a universal maxim") is equally problematic for Lacan, who translates it into the idea that you should never act "except in such a way that your action may be programmed" (*EP* 76–7). That is, the categorical imperative, in Lacan's view, dictates that you should invariably do whatever the mainstream morality of the big Other has conditioned you to do. Kant might have taken offense to this interpretation of his ethics, but the relevant point for our purposes is the vehemence with which Lacan juxtaposes the ethics of psychoanalysis with the conventional morality of the Other (the master's "service of goods"). Lacan's ethics is grounded in desire because he believes that desire is one of the few effective levers we have against the master's supremacy; if the big Other seeks to secure its authority by forcing (or enticing) us to accept the parameters of its desire, then the only way to oppose it is to activate frequencies of desire that retain a degree of autonomy from this (hegemonic) desire.

This way of looking at things immediately introduces a host of complications, for if we have learned anything from recent decades of theorizing (from the Frankfurt School to Althusser, Foucault, and Butler), it is that it is virtually impossible to dissociate our desire from the collective social order; insofar as we have been interpellated into a specific sociosymbolic edifice, our desire has been shaped to reflect the desires of this edifice. For instance, one of the triumphs of capitalism has been to translate the master's "service of goods"— the master's demand that "work must go on"—into "a way of life" that many of us have internalized to such an extent that we do not even think to question it. This is precisely the problem that Marcuse diagnoses in *Eros and Civilization*, pointing out that contemporary Western society is organized around a very particular version of the Freudian reality principle: "the performance principle." Productivity, Marcuse notes, is one of the most sacrosanct values of modern culture in the sense that it "expresses perhaps more than any other the existential attitude in industrial civilization"; it permeates the very definition of the subject, so that man "is evaluated according to his ability to make, augment, and improve socially useful things."[4] More broadly speaking, the performance principle dictates that we strive for ever higher levels of productivity; that we take it for granted that efficiency is not only a social good but also a personal virtue; that we understand that progress cannot be made without a degree of pain (or at least boredom); that we are willing to accept the idea that pleasure, gratification, and moments of happiness belong to the realm of leisure rather than of work; and that we are consequently willing to delay our satisfaction until our work for the day is done.

Marcuse concedes that those who are privileged enough to work in creative professions—artists, writers, artisans, inventors, professors, and (presumably) psychoanalysts, among others—may experience enclaves of satisfaction within their working lives. But for the majority of people performing various forms of "alienated labor," such as routine office work or tending the assembly line, there is a strict division of affective registers between work (pain) and leisure (pleasure). As Marcuse states, "Labor time, which is the largest part of the individual's life time, is painful time, for alienated labor is absence of gratification, negation of the pleasure principle" (*EC* 45). Yet even alienated workers do not usually interrogate the value of productivity and good performance. Moreover, their leisure hours function primarily as a means of buttressing the productivity and good performance of their working hours. This is why passive forms of entertainment—what Marcuse's Frankfurt School colleague Adorno associated with "the culture industry"[5]— have become so dominant in late capitalist consumer society. That "leisure" is often epitomized by the remote control of the television set in the privacy of one's living room is symptomatic of the fact that the high levels of activity demanded by the performance principle can only be sustained (replenished) by stretches of absolute passivity. Add to this that productivity has reached such a high level in Western societies that the workers themselves— unlike Marx's more deprived workers—reap some of the benefits of the production process in the form of consumer comforts and commodities, and we have a situation where the desires of even the least privileged tend to coincide quite seamlessly with the desires of the big Other. In this sense, nothing stifles the revolutionary impulse more effectively than the ideal of easy living (and the advertising industry that beautifies this ideal). Indeed, even those who fall short of this ideal live in its shadow in the sense that they keep hoping that they might one day be able to attain it.

Lauren Berlant characterizes this predicament as one of "cruel optimism": the stubborn, irrational belief that social arrangements and ways of life that hurt us will eventually pay off and make us happy. Berlant specifies that "a relation of cruel optimism" exists when something we desire is in reality an obstacle to our flourishing.[6] That is, cruel optimism entails the fantasy that our relentless efforts (say, our good performance) will bring us the love, intimacy, success, security, harmony, financial reward, or the so-called "good life" we crave even when they are extremely unlikely to do so. Berlant explains, for instance, that the economically disadvantaged may at times form optimistic attachments to the very power structures that oppress them, so that a poor person might support a conservative political agenda even when it is clear that this agenda will never help him or her overcome poverty. Or the daughter of working-class parents who has watched her parents toil without reward for two decades might still place a great deal of faith in the ideals of hard work and social mobility, hoping against hope that the American dream will one day rescue her even if it did not rescue her parents. As Butler has also suggested, such an optimistic attachment to potentially wounding modalities of life tends to arise from the desire to feel normal: we want to feel like we are a part of something familiar, like we "belong" to—and are recognized by—the world in which we live, with the result that we go along with the expectations that render this world comprehensible to us. In Berlant's terms, our investment in the notion of "a dependable life," "a life that does not have to keep being reinvented" (CO 170), can be so strong that we remain wedded to specific fantasies of satisfaction even after they have repeatedly disappointed us. We, in short, endorse forms of life that are not in the least bit good for us, coming, as it were, "to misrecognize the bad life as a good one" (CO 174).

Marcuse's argument about the performance principle is similar in the sense that he recognizes that workers often come to desire this principle even though it is predicated on a severe repression of their libidinal impulses:

> The restrictions imposed upon the libido appear as the more rational, the more universal they become, the more they permeate the whole of society. They operate on the individual as external objective laws and as an internalized force: the societal authority is absorbed into the "conscience" and into the unconscious of the individual and works as his own desire, morality, and fulfillment. In the "normal" development, the individual lives his repression "freely" as his own life: he desires what he is supposed to desire. (EC 46)

Most important for our purposes, Marcuse emphasizes that the repression demanded by the performance principle far exceeds the parameters of the kind of repression that Freud saw as the foundation of civilization. While social existence always requires a degree of libidinal repression, what we are witnessing in modern Western society is what Marcuse calls "surplus-repression": the kind of repression that meets the demands of a society organized by the unequal distribution of resources. "Within the total structure of the repressed personality," Marcuse explains, "surplus-repression is that portion which is the result of specific societal conditions sustained in the specific interest of domination. . . . The distinction is equivalent to that between the biological and the historical sources of human suffering" (*EC* 87–8). Surplus-repression is thus a historically specific form of suffering that is added, for the benefit of those who hold social power, to the mutilation of the drives demanded by "civilized" life as such. And because our desires have become so neatly aligned with what Lacan calls the "order of powers" (or the "service of goods"), we willingly participate in this arrangement, earnestly believing that it serves our most fundamental needs.

3

Lacan understood all of this perfectly well, which makes it all the more noteworthy that he conceptualized ethics in terms of the subject's unwillingness to give ground on its desire. Lacan knew that it is extremely difficult to differentiate the subject's desire from the desire of the big Other, yet his ethics demands precisely the capacity to do so. This is why Lacanian ethics offers such a powerful point of contrast to Butler's conviction that there is no way to break the subject's psychic attachment to hegemonic power. Lacan admits that such a rupture is hard to accomplish, but he insists that it is the task of psychoanalysis as a clinical practice—as a practice of ethics specifically—to produce the kind of subject who might be able to carry out such a feat of defiance. The ethical act that I have discussed is a radical example of this capacity, but we should not underestimate the importance of the moment when the analysand, perhaps after years of analysis, finally manages to say *Enough!* to whoever or whatever is causing her to suffer. If the goal of Lacanian analysis is to enable the analysand to dissociate herself from the desire of the big Other, or from the desire of those who, in her life, embody this desire, it is because this is the only way for her to shatter her (cruelly) optimistic allegiance to power structures that oppress her. There may still be an enormous distance between such tiny acts of individual defiance and revolutionary politics, yet there is arguably also a conceptual link between the analysand who is able to utter her *Enough!* with a degree of conviction and the politicized subject who utters the same *Enough!* in the context of collective social mobilization. That is, collective social mobilization relies on subjects who have the ability to stick to their desire in the face of the demand that they capitulate to the desire of the big Other.

I will return to this connection between individual and collective acts of defiance toward the end of this chapter. But first I want to explore in greater detail how, from a Lacanian perspective, it might be possible to talk about desire as something that can be dissociated from the master's morality. Let me restate the problematic I outlined above in the form of a question: if subjectivity is a function of being interpellated into the symbolic order, then how can we even begin to conceptualize forms of desire that have not been completely overrun by the desire of the big Other? This is where I find Marcuse helpful, for his analysis of surplus-repression implies that if we were able to somehow peel off this excess of repression, we would be left with what Lacan calls the truth of desire: the kind of desire that has certainly come into existence as a result of repression, but not as a result of the expectations of the performance principle. Indeed, though Lacan does not share Marcuse's neo-Marxist platform, he in many ways operates with a similar distinction between repression and surplus-repression: though he understands that there is no such thing as desire divorced from its social environment, he believes that there are degrees of freedom and unfreedom, that some desires are more primary than the desires driven by the performance principle. Such primary desires—desires that touch the subject's fundamental fantasy—reach toward the rebellious real rather than the conformist symbolic, which is why the subject's capacity to animate them is essential for its ability to defy the hegemonic decrees of the latter. Or, to express the matter slightly differently, the idea that the truth of desire might lurk beneath the performance principle explains why one of the objectives of Lacanian analysis is to allow the subject to break its allegiance to this principle. This, essentially, is what the subject who utters a passionate *Enough!* to its job, to its lover, or to any other key component of its life does, for such an *Enough!* signifies the subject's unwillingness to keep "performing" in the way that it has been conditioned to.

On the one hand, Lacan—like Marcuse—believes that a degree of repression is necessary for the emergence of social subjectivity. This is how he arrives at his well-known story about subject formation: we all start out as presymbolic creatures, dwelling in the realm of the bodily real (jouissance); our first inkling of identity takes place during the mirror stage which gives rise to both narcissistic self-regard (the grandiose ego) and self-alienation (the misrecognition of the self as more coherent and omnipotent than it actually is); finally, the signifier interpellates us into the symbolic order, thereby producing subjectivity as a site of meaning production and intersubjective capacity. According to this model, we sacrifice jouissance for the signifier, unmediated pleasure for the capacity to desire. We will henceforth experience ourselves as fundamentally lacking. But, in return, we gain the ability to wield the signifier, sometimes even in highly creative and rewarding ways. And we also gain the capacity to be interested in the world around us, including the people who populate this world; we gain the ability to desire, and sometimes even love, others. So, all in all, we come off quite well in the sense that what we gain is arguably more valuable than what we lose, and this is all the more the case given that we have not actually lost anything to begin with, that our unconscious conviction that we were once whole and completely satisfied is a misleading fantasy that in no way reflects the rather terrifying realities of jouissance.

On the other hand, Lacan—again like Marcuse—recognizes that the symbolic order is repressive beyond the demands of subject formation, that it includes forms of violence that exceed the ubiquitous violence of the signifier. And, as I have emphasized, even the violence of the signifier is not equally distributed, so that some of us are much more vulnerable to its injurious effects than others (consider, for instance, hate speech). Lacan does not necessarily talk about the unequal distribution of resources in the manner in which Marcuse does, but there is no doubt that his analysis of symbolic law as the Law of the Father points to a historically specific, deeply heteropatriarchal and hierarchical organization of social life. This is why I think that Butler is mistaken in accusing Lacan of presenting an ahistorical version of the symbolic order. In point of fact, one reason I have taken a detour through Marcuse is to illustrate the obvious ways in which Lacan's portraiture of the symbolic mirrors that of Marcuse's explicitly historical account: what Marcuse calls "the performance principle," Lacan calls the "service of goods." Both thinkers identify the underpinnings of a social order dominated by the ideal of productivity—an ideal that is, moreover, placed in direct opposition to the pleasure principle. Both emphasize that the dominant morality of this symbolic—what Lacan calls "the morality of the master"—measures the merit of lives based on largely pragmatic criteria. And both acknowledge that the model citizen of this symbolic is a subject who shows up at work reliably every morning, performs its duties with a degree of diligence, does not let its desires get the better of its productivity, and seeks satisfaction ("enjoys") in moderate, socially sanctioned ways. "Part of the world has resolutely turned in the direction of the service of goods," Lacan writes, "thereby rejecting everything that has to do with the relationship of man to desire" (*EP* 318). This, he adds, "is what is known as the postrevolutionary perspective" (*EP* 318). In other words, the service of goods reflects the mindset of the utilitarian subject who has deemed revolutionary change to be unrealistic.

Lacan is here referring to the kind of depoliticization that is arguably the hallmark of Western subjectivity under late capitalism. Lacan's point is by no means, as Butler seems to presume, that a different kind of symbolic is intrinsically impossible but rather that the configuration of subjectivity that Western modernity has produced—a subjectivity that has been subjected to a particular form of surplus-repression (the performance principle, the service of goods)—makes it virtually impossible for us to entertain the idea that the symbolic could be organized differently, that it could be centered around a different version of the reality principle.

Marcuse remarks that one reason the performance principle is so powerful is that it has managed to convince us that all alternatives to it are either utopian or otherwise unpalatable. Yet, for Marcuse, the very fact that this principle has been so successful also points to the possibility of transcending it. As he states:

> The very progress of civilization under the performance principle has attained a level of productivity at which the social demands upon instinctual energy to be spent in alienated labor could be considerably reduced. Consequently, the continued repressive organization of the instincts seems to be necessitated less by the "struggle for existence" than by the interest in prolonging this struggle—by the interest in domination. (*EC* 129–30)

This is to say that there is really nothing besides social power that keeps us invested in the notion that our welfare demands relentless toil. The performance principle has outlived its usefulness in the sense that our collective productivity these days surpasses what is necessary for the provision of food, clothing, housing, and other basic amenities. The fact that these amenities have not yet reached all corners of the world, or even all corners of our own society (the homeless, inner city dwellers, etc.), is a function of domination (the unequal distribution of resources) rather than of any deficiencies of productivity. As a result, in Marcuse's view, all we would need to do to bring about a more "non-repressive civilization" (*EC* 134) would be to refuse the parameters of the current symbolic; even something as simple as reducing the length of the working day would immediately realign our priorities, perhaps even impacting the very organization of our psychic lives. Our standard of living might drop somewhat, but we might also learn to assess the value of our lives according to other, less performance-oriented, measurements.

4

Psychoanalysis, particularly Lacanian analysis, does not have a normative goal; it does not seek to tell us how we should desire but merely to explore the idiosyncratic contours of our desire. But this does not change the fact that Lacan, at least as a theorist, was exasperated by people's inability to make their way out of the maze of the master's morality, including its performance principle; he was frustrated by individuals who were so out of touch with the truth of their desire that they were willing to sacrifice this desire for the sake of social conformity and that they were, furthermore, willing to do so to the point of self-betrayal. As he explains:

> What I call "giving ground relative to one's desire" is always accompanied in the destiny of the subject by some betrayal—you will observe it in every case and should note its importance. Either the subject betrays his own way, betrays himself, and the result is significant for him, or, more simply, he tolerates the fact that someone with whom he has more or less vowed to do something betrays his hope and doesn't do for him what their pact entailed. (*EP* 321)

Such a betrayal invariably results in the reassertion of the status quo, sending the subject back to the service of goods, what Lacan in this context calls "the common path" (*EP* 321). And given that desire, for Lacan, is "the metonymy of our being" (*EP* 321), betraying it in this way leads to the kind of psychic death that extinguishes the subject's sense of agency. To use Lacan's wording, "Doing things in the name of the good, and even more in the name of the good of the other, is something that is far from protecting us not only from guilt but also from all kinds of inner catastrophes" (*EP* 319).

It is precisely such inner catastrophes that Lacanian clinical practice was designed to counter, though it may be Julia Kristeva—rather than Lacan himself—who has most clearly developed this interpretation of analytic work. Kristeva depicts psychoanalysis as a means of restoring the subject's psychic aliveness, as an explicit revolt against the numbing impact of what she calls "the society of the spectacle."[7] This society of the spectacle—of technology, image, and speed—shares many parallels with Adorno's "culture industry": a flattened surface of the life world, a constriction of psychic space, a dearth of critical thought, the worship of efficiency over intellectual curiosity, and the incapacity to revolt. Against this backdrop, psychoanalysis—along with art, writing, and some forms of religious experience—offers, for Kristeva, a gateway to revolt, a way of resurrecting "the life of the mind" (a phrase Kristeva borrows from Hannah Arendt) through ongoing questioning, interrogation, and psychic recreation. "Freud founded psychoanalysis as an invitation to anamnesis in the goal of a rebirth, that is, a psychical restructuring," Kristeva writes: "Through a narrative of free association and in the regenerative revolt against the old law (familial taboos, superego, ideals, oedipal or narcissistic limits, etc.) comes the singular autonomy of each, as well as a renewed link with the other" (*IR* 8). In the context of my overall argument in this chapter, it is worth stressing that it is "the desire of the subject" that, in Kristeva's view, reserves a place "for initiative, autonomy" (*IR* 11). This is in part because the "Freudian journey into the *night of desire* was followed by attention to the *capacity to think*: never one without the other."[8] In other words, the exploration of desire, in psychoanalysis, is akin to the critical (or at least curious) movement of thought—the very movement that Arendt also saw as vital to the life of the mind. This is why psychoanalysis has, Kristeva asserts, "the (unique?) privilege today of accompanying the emergence of new capacities of thinking/representing/thinking, beyond the frequent and increasingly noticeable disasters of psychosomatic space—capacities that are so many new bodies and new lives" (*HF* 41–2).

Kristeva therefore draws the same link between desire and autonomy (in this instance, the capacity for critical thought) as Lacan does. Furthermore, to translate Kristeva's point into Marcuse's terminology, one might say that psychoanalysis, at least the kind of analysis that refuses to uphold social adaptation as a therapeutic goal, presents the possibility of sidestepping, or at the very least diminishing, the effects of surplus-repression. This, in turn, creates space for the truth of the subject's desire in the Lacanian sense. This does not mean that repression as such is defeated. Quite the contrary, as I will shortly demonstrate, the truth of the subject's desire is inextricable from the primary (constitutive) repression that accompanies subject formation. But, as I have already suggested, the lifting of surplus-repression renders the imprint of primary repression more clearly discernable, for when surplus-repression is removed, what remains are the always highly singular outlines of primary repression. And if Lacan—like Marcuse—sought to remove surplus-repression, it was because he understood that it was on the level of primary repression (the fundamental fantasy) that one could find the most basic building blocks of the subject's psychic destiny; primary repression was the layer of psychic life that expressed something essential about the distinctive ways in which the pleasure principle, in the subject's life, had become bound up with the repetition compulsion. This is why Lacan states:

> If analysis has a meaning, desire is nothing other than that which supports an unconscious theme, the very articulation of that which roots us in a particular destiny, and that destiny demands insistently that the debt be paid, and desire keeps coming back, keeps returning, and situates us once again in a given track, the track of something that is specifically our business. (*EP* 319)

According to Lacan, analysis aims to enable us to understand something about the eccentric specificity (or truth) of our most fundamental desire as well as about the track of destiny that this desire carves out for us (and that is therefore "specifically our business"). If it is indeed the case, as I have conceded, that most of us tend to be alienated from our desire, Lacanian analysis strives to undo this alienation by familiarizing us with the truth of this desire. This process entails, among other things, recognizing that the destiny we owe to this desire can never be definitively overcome, that the debt of desire can never be fully redeemed (for how are we to compensate the signifier for having brought us into being as subjects of desire?). Our destiny—which might initially coincide quite seamlessly with our repetition compulsion—consists of recurring efforts to pay off this debt, which is why it keeps ushering us to the same track of desire, the same nexus of psychic conundrums, our unconscious hope being that if we wear out the track of our desire by incessant reiteration, one day we might be able to absolve ourselves of our debt. But since we cannot, the only thing to be done is to "own" our destiny even as we might seek to mitigate its more painful dimensions. That is, the only way to arrive at the kind of psychic rebirth Kristeva is talking about is to take full responsibility for our (unconsciously generated) destiny. In the ethical act, our impulse is to embrace this destiny wholesale regardless of consequences. (This is one way to understand what it means to plunge into the jouissance of the real.) In analysis, the exploration of our destiny is more gradual, more self-reflexive. But in both cases, the point is not to obliterate our foundational destiny (or fundamental fantasies) but merely to elaborate it in more satisfying directions, away from the incapacitating effects of the repetition compulsion and toward the rewards of subjective autonomy. And, if we are to achieve this goal, nothing is more important than staying faithful to the truth of desire that, on the most elementary level, determines our destiny.

5

Let me try to unpack this more carefully. The track of desire Lacan is referring to must be understood in relation to what he, following Freud, calls *das Ding* (the Thing). As I noted above, within Lacan's theory of subject formation, the intrusion of the signifier into the bodily real gives rise to a sense of loss. This loss crystallizes around the fantasy of the Thing as the original (non)object sacrificed at the altar of the signifier. In concrete terms, the Thing connotes the body of the mother; in more global, even "existential," terms, it connotes the promise of the kind of primordial plenitude—unmitigated jouissance—that we all yearn for but can never attain in any permanent sense. Moreover, the Lacanian Thing replicates the dichotomous nature of the Kantian sublime object as one that elicits both awe and terror. As much as we want the Thing, coming too close to it is terrorizing for the simple reason that we are constitutionally not designed to endure unmediated jouissance (except, perhaps, in fleeting orgasmic moments). This is why Lacan emphasizes that we are always forced to approach the Thing obliquely, through the various objects of desire (*objets a*) that we use to compensate for its absence. The Thing, Lacan writes, is "found at the most as something missed. One doesn't find it, but only its pleasurable associations" (*EP* 52). "If the Thing were not fundamentally veiled," he continues, "we wouldn't be in the kind of relationship to it that obliges us, as the whole of psychic life is obliged, to encircle it or bypass it in order to conceive it" (*EP* 118). This process of encircling or bypassing the Thing—the distinctive track of desire we can never fully renounce—is governed by the pleasure principle, but quite often it takes the form of the tortured meanderings of the repetition compulsion, which is why Lacan maintains that our relationship to the Thing leads us to our "choice of neurosis" (*EP* 54): it establishes the always somewhat pathological ways in which we relate to our objects of desire.

Undoubtedly, one of the objectives of Lacanian analysis—like perhaps of any kind of analysis—is to loosen the grip of the repetition compulsion (so that a more satisfying destiny might become possible). But Lacan is equally interested in the more creative side of the Thing's power to usher us to a singular (unique and inimitable) track of desire. This singularity arises from the fact that even though the loss of the Thing is a universal precondition of social subjectivity, each of us relates to this loss in a manner that is wholly peculiar to us. More specifically, every *objet a* that we stuff into the void left by the Thing is, as Lacan puts it, "refound" (*EP* 118) in the sense that it always reflects something about our singular experience of the Thing as a site of melancholy yearning. This is why there tends to be a degree of consistency to our desire: we regularly find ourselves drawn to particular kinds of objects because these objects seem to resurrect some of the Thing's aura for us. Such consistency, taken to an extreme, is what the repetition compulsion is all about. But it is also—and here we have reached the gist of my argument—at the core of the truth of desire that Lacan deems so necessary for the ethics of psychoanalysis, for the distinguishing feature of such truth is, precisely, its (obstinately consistent) singularity. The ethics of psychoanalysis "works" to the degree that it is able to conjure up this singularity, that it is able to revive forms of desire that owe their existence to primary repression (the loss of the Thing) rather than to surplus-repression (social domination), for only such forms of desire have the power to resist the hegemonic desire of the big Other. Or, to state the matter more directly, if surplus-repression generates generic desires (such as the performance principle or the service of goods), primary repression generates matchless desires (our specific track of desire), which is why the latter represent an ethical force that we can only betray by betraying something essential about our very being.

I am well aware that this line of argumentation only works if one is willing to accept the basic distinction between primary repression and surplus-repression that I have borrowed from Marcuse. This distinction is easy to challenge in the sense that, as I have admitted, the social codes that bring the subject into existence as a culturally intelligible entity can never be entirely divorced from hegemonic power. Yet there are still more or less oppressive ways of being interpellated into the cultural order, which is precisely why Marcuse holds open the possibility of a nonrepressive civilization. As someone who has experienced first-hand the difference between Scandinavian and North American norms of gender and sexuality—particularly as these pertain to femininity and female sexuality—I am willing to entertain the notion that although subject formation always entails repression, this repression is existentially and epistemologically different from the kind of surplus-repression that supports "the morality of the master."[9] As a matter of fact, if we completely close up the gap between (primary) repression and surplus-repression, we automatically conjure away any possibility of agency or individual resistance. Though this has been the direction that much of recent theorizing, including that of Butler, has taken, I do not think that it represents an accurate reading of Lacan who, as I have attempted to illustrate, was strongly invested in the idea that analysis was a means of driving a wedge between the desire of the Other and the truth of the subject's desire. And if the Thing is where he went looking for the latter, it is because the Thing's echo connects us to an elemental realm of desire that, like a hidden subterranean stream, runs underneath the kinds of desires cultivated by the master's morality.

6

This is why the echo of the Thing that we discover in the objects of our desire introduces a code of ethics that is drastically different from the moral code that dictates the outlines of socially conformist modes of desire. As Lacan clarifies, "There is another register of morality that takes its direction from that which is to be found on the level of *das Ding*; it is the register that makes the subject hesitate when he is on the point of bearing false witness against *das Ding*, that is to say, the place of desire" (*EP* 109–10). This is an ethics that is not dictated by the instrumentalist imperatives of the service of goods but rather assesses the value of things—as well as of the ethical actions related to those things—on the basis of their proximity (or loyalty) to the Thing. The object that comes the closest (or remains the most loyal) to the Thing is, ethically speaking, more important than one that is merely useful. This does not mean that we have the right to expect our objects to capture the Thing's aura with complete precision. But it does imply that the objects that most powerfully emit this aura are also the ones that most readily engage our passion. Concretely speaking, whenever the Thing's echo resounds strongly enough in the object we have selected, it overshadows the social voices telling us that we have made a bad choice. For example, those around us may attempt to convince us that we have fallen in love with a person of the "wrong" age, race, gender, ethnicity, religion, social class, or educational level. Consider homophobia: at the present moment, the American cultural order is trying to convince us that love between two men or two women is not only an assault on traditional values but on God himself. This is a formidable obstacle to overcome. The miraculous thing about the Thing's echo is that it gives us the courage to fight the fight, so to speak. It is robust enough to trump the warnings and cajolings of the social order, making it possible for us to desire in counterhegemonic ways.

Think of it this way: the vast machinery of our commercial culture works overtime to eclipse the Thing's aura. We are bombarded from all sides by objects—enticing lures—that are deliberately manufactured to shine brightly enough to distract us; in the society of the spectacle, nothing is easier than losing track of the truth of our desire. Against this backdrop, insisting on this truth becomes an ethical stance, making it possible for us to appreciate the preciousness of what we may be culturally encouraged to shun, ignore, or trivialize. As Kaja Silverman proposes, the constellation of desire that surrounds the Thing allows us to bring into visibility objects that the social order strives to render invisible; it introduces the possibility of idealizing something other than what the service of goods programs us to idealize.[10] When we, to borrow Lacan's famous phrase, raise a mundane object to "the dignity of the Thing" (*EP* 112), we infuse it with the Thing's nobility, brilliance, and incomparable worth, thereby signaling that, as far as our desire is concerned, only *this* object will do; we, in short, deem the object in question irreplaceable. To the extent that we are able to do this, that we are able to insist on the truth of our desire, we might be said to have inherited some of Antigone's insubordination. And to the extent that we are able to hold our ground in the face of the culture industry—to the extent that we are able to resist being seduced by sparkly decoys—we are kept from becoming a mere cog in the commercial machine. This, in turn, offers some protection against the impression that the world is a lackluster place where nothing can rouse our passions or move us in any meaningful manner; to the degree that the Thing's echo makes mundane objects reverberate with an exceptional dignity, it fends off the kind of complacency that strips the world of all ideals, all higher aspirations. But this only works if we are able to recognize the highly specific timbre of this echo in the first place, which is why Lacan is so adamant that psychoanalysis should help us revere the truth of our desire even when it would be easier to capitulate to the desire of the Other; it is why he asserts that there is nothing that is, ethically speaking, more important than not ceding on our desire.

Lacan suggests that our faithfulness to the Thing's echo to some degree safeguards us against the nihilistic tendency to think that nothing we do makes a difference, that no matter how much we strive to create space for new values, new patterns of appreciation, the social establishment will always get the better of us. And, like Marcuse, he is interested in the idea that psychoanalysis, potentially at least, provides a place for a fruitful exploration of the connection between so-called deviant desires— desires that, precisely, respect the Thing's echo—and the subject's capacity for defiance. This is not to say that psychoanalysis is the only way to understand this connection. For example, social movements such as feminism, antiracism, anticolonialism, and other political struggles often also galvanize "deviant" desires in the service of defiant acts of rebellion. The British suffragettes who were imprisoned and force-fed through tubes crammed down their throats, the supporters of the Civil Rights movement, the populations who took up arms to liberate themselves from colonial rule, and the antiwar protesters willing to endure police brutality during the Vietnam era all had one thing in common: they were no longer willing to give ground on their desire in order to please the big Other. Similar acts of insurgence are currently erupting around the world, particularly in opposition to global capitalism and Western imperialism. To argue that psychoanalysis is responsible for such acts would be ludicrous. Yet Lacan's ethics of psychoanalysis as an ethics of fidelity to one's desire provides one way to grasp something about the psychic processes through which individuals come to possess the capacity for rebellion. This capacity, in turn, is a necessary component of political action; the individual's ability to take a degree of distance from social power may not, by itself, be enough to generate political action, but it is a necessary element of such action.

7

It would be possible to counter the argument I have been developing about personal and political defiance by positing that such defiance is precisely what neoliberal capitalism expects from us. After all, what does the individualistic ethos of our society teach us if not that we are supposed to rebel, "fight the man," chart our own path, and find our "true calling"? In this sense, we are trained to be defiant subjects—swaggering mavericks—from the moment we are born. Yet there is a crucial difference between such socially prescribed rebelliousness and the Lacanian notion of defiance I have been explicating, and this difference is what Žižek is getting at when he tells us that the genuinely defiant subject is willing to strike at itself, at what it holds most dear in the world, for the sake of its cause (or because it is desperate for change).[11] The rebelliousness promoted by neoliberal capitalism does not undermine our viability as productive (and consuming) subjects; we may be encouraged to be insubordinate in various ways but only to the extent that this insubordination remains compatible with the performance principle. The Lacanian *No!* or *Enough!*, in contrast, opens to a negativity (death drive) beyond this principle, which is precisely why it—at least temporarily—destroys the subject's social viability. My general point here, however, is not that we should all commit social suicide but merely that a kernel of such antihegemonic negativity (a trace of the death drive, as it were) can probably be found in more or less any "authentic" act of defiance.

A less drastic way of expressing the matter is to say that, as opposed to the rebellious "individual" of neoliberal capitalism, the genuinely defiant subject is willing to endure a degree of discomfort for the sake of its convictions (or desires). In this context, it is useful to consider Sara Ahmed's argument that political consciousness (and, eventually, political action) often takes the form of being able to resist the dominant "happiness scripts" of our society.[12] Such resistance is not easy, for happiness is more or less an unquestioned value in our culture: something that everyone is supposed to want. In addition, our society's happiness scripts—such as the performance principle—direct us to a very particular vision of the good life; we are taught to believe that specific kinds of objects, and specific kinds of aspirations, are essential for such a life. As Ahmed asserts, "There is no doubt that the affective repertoire of happiness gives us images of a certain kind of life, a life that has certain things and does certain things" (*PH* 90). This process, according to Ahmed, "blocks other possible worlds, as a blockage that makes possibles impossible, such that possibles are lost before they can be lived, experienced, or imagined" (*PH* 165). That is, a large array of life paths are deemed either undesirable or untenable before they even become possibilities, before we even get a chance to imagine what it would be like to pursue them. And sadly, we are often not in the least bit aware of what it is that we are giving up. Ahmed explains that it is not only social prohibitions ("don't do that") that lead to such personal sacrifices but, equally importantly, the affirmations we receive ("yes, that's good"). As a matter of fact, the latter are more difficult to resist because it is harder to see them as tools of social conditioning. With prohibitions, we usually have some inclination that our desire is being disciplined, that we are told to desire in conformist ways; with affirmations, in contrast, it is harder to see the machinery of disciplining at work—it is harder to understand that we are getting an education in how to desire.

As Ahmed states, "We can hear the 'no' in part as it asks us to stop doing something. It might be harder to hear the 'yes words' . . . because the words seem to 'go along' with or affirm what we are already doing" (*PH* 48).

The problem with dominant happiness scripts is therefore that they, like Berlant's cruel optimism, render us overly patient with our plight. Because they present a specific version of happiness as the goal, or telos, of life, they induce us to chase this version even though we might be very unlikely to ever attain it (or even though it might not actually make us happy in the end). As Ahmed maintains, the ideal of happiness

> might be how waiting for something can acquire a sense of meaning or purpose and can thus be endured, as it points toward something. The failure to achieve happiness in the present can even extend one's investment in a certain path of action: if the more one waits, the more one gives up, then *the more one waits, the harder it is to give up*. The more one persists unhappily on a path of happiness, the harder it is to give up on that path. Unhappiness can thus be what makes happiness harder to give up. (*PH* 236)

Indeed, our commitment to dominant happiness scripts can be so strong that when a given script does not deliver what it promises, when it makes us unhappy rather than happy, we do not think of questioning the script itself (say, the performance principle) but instead assume that somehow we have failed to live out the script correctly. In other words, when we have been invested in the notion that a certain kind of life is the happy life, it can be very difficult for us to admit that this life has not made us happy; it can be difficult to admit that our faith in a specific happiness script has led us astray. As Ahmed explains:

> It is hard labor just to recognize sadness and disappointment, when you are living a life that is meant to be happy but just isn't, which is meant to be full, but feels empty. It is difficult to give up an idea of one's life, when one has lived a life according to that idea. To recognize loss can mean to be willing to experience an intensification of the sadness that hopefulness postpones. (*PH* 75)

Against this backdrop, the defiant subject is someone who is able and willing to turn away from the promise of happiness (as conceptualized by the normative order). Ahmed presents four figures of rebellion—the feminist killjoy, the unhappy queer, the melancholy migrant, and the radical revolutionary—whose capacity to resist the happiness scripts of the social establishment depends on their ability to desire differently. For instance, in the context of the feminist killjoy, Ahmed revisits Betty Friedan's unsatisfied suburban housewife as a figure whose political consciousness was directly linked to her recognition that the truth of her desire deviated from the happiness script she was being asked to accept. We all know that this figure has been problematized—taken to task for the white middle-class privilege she represents—and Ahmed does not ignore these complexities. But ultimately she is interested in the fact that this woman, who had been taught to desire the comforts of heteropatriarchal domesticity, came to see that what was supposed to make her happy made her despondent. For many, this was the spark of feminist consciousness. From this perspective, Ahmed explains, "Feminist genealogies can be described as genealogies of women who not only do not place their hopes for happiness in the right things but who speak out about their unhappiness with the very obligation to be made happy by such things. The history of feminism is thus a history of making trouble" (*PH* 59–60). The feminist killjoy, Ahmed muses, is a woman who kills the joy of others because—and here the parallels between the insights of Lacan and Ahmed leap at us—she refuses to desire in the manner that others would like her to desire. Feminists, Ahmed concludes, kill joy because they "disturb the very fantasy that happiness can be found in certain places": "it is not just that feminists might not be happily affected by the objects that are supposed to cause happiness but that their failure to be happy is read as sabotaging the happiness of others" (*PH* 66).

Ironically, feminism itself is not immune to the same dynamic, so that the so-called "angry black woman" (*PH* 67) kills the joy of white feminists by refusing to accept the trope of feminist sisterhood as a trope of happiness. Along related lines, Ahmed analyzes the figure of the unhappy queer not as one that embodies the wretchedness of queer subjects but as one that makes *others* unhappy because he or she refuses to desire in the expected way. In other words, the unhappy queer may be perfectly happy in his or her own life—a life that may

be filled with various forms of satisfaction—but what makes him
or her a political irritant is the fact that his or her happiness renders
normative subjects unhappy, frequently to the point that they seek
to convince this queer subject that, deep down, he or she cannot
really be happy. "Even the happy queer might become unhappy at
this point" (*PH* 94), Ahmed notes, for "the unhappy queer is here
the queer who is judged to be unhappy" (*PH* 93). Likewise, the
melancholy migrant—the immigrant who is unable to discard his
attachment to lost modalities of life—frustrates those who would
(for example) like to align the pursuit of happiness with the pursuit
of the American dream, so that it is incomprehensible to them why
anyone who has been lucky enough to get a foothold in this dream
is not perfectly happy, why such a person might have desires other
than those condoned by this dream. Finally, the revolutionary is
obviously a figure who refuses to bring her desire in line with the
desire of the collective order. This is one way to understand what
I have tried to express in this chapter from a specifically Lacanian
perspective, namely that social change demands subjects who are
able to mobilize behind desires other than those of the big Other.
In Ahmed's words:

> It is no accident that revolutionary consciousness means feeling
> at odds with the world, or feeling that the world is odd. You
> become estranged from the world as it has been given: the world
> of good habits and manners, which promises your comfort in
> return for obedience and good will. As a structure of feeling,
> alienation is an intense burning presence. (*PH* 168)

Ahmed specifies that deviating from dominant happiness scripts
does not necessarily mean that we discard the ideal of a meaningful
life; it merely means that we conceptualize such a life differently.
As she states, "If we do not assume that happiness is what we must
defend, if we start questioning the happiness we are defending, then
we can ask other questions about life, about what we want from life,
or what we want life to become. Possibilities have to be recognized
as possibilities to become possible" (*PH* 218). In Marcuse's terms,
questioning dominant happiness scripts might turn the possibility
of a less repressive reality principle into a real possibility. In Lacan's
terms, it might lead to the surfacing of hitherto repressed desires,
and perhaps even to new ways of living out our destiny (our specific

track of desire). In a certain sense, one could argue that Lacan's attempt to empower the analysand to remain loyal to the truth of her desire is a form of consciousness raising. To be sure, the analyst does not necessarily actively (or deliberately) "raise" the analysand's consciousness by calling attention to, say, social injustice; the process is usually much more subtle than this. Yet analysis and consciousness raising share the same impulse of self-reflexivity: both rely on the idea that the subject possesses the capacity to become more discerning about the causes of its unhappiness as well as about the ways in which it might be able to stand up to those who contribute to this unhappiness. Imagine, for instance, the relief of a woman who is finally able to say *Enough!* to the patriarchal Name of the Father—and perhaps even to the actual father who, for her, represents that Name. What is so powerful about Lacan's ethics of psychoanalysis as an antidote to the master's morality is that it asks, quite simply, that we cease to care about what the big Other wants—that we reject the legitimacy of the Other's desire so as to make room for the truth of our own.

8

Ahmed pays particular attention to our society's tendency to privilege heterosexual marriage as the pinnacle of happiness: "Marriage [is] defined as 'the best of all possible worlds' as it maximizes happiness. The argument is simple: if you are married, then we can predict that you are more likely to be happier than if you are not married. The finding is also a recommendation: get married and you will be happier!" (*PH* 6). The matter is worth examining in some detail because marriage is one of the most efficient means of disciplining desire—and perhaps even of stifling the truth of this desire—that our society has invented. Not only Marcuse, but also Foucault,[13] viewed marriage as a biopolitical tool that allows social power to penetrate the most intimate recesses of our being. Most people in our society believe that their decision to marry is a "choice." But from a biopolitical perspective, it is the result of a powerful edifice of cultural conditioning that presents marriage as the most reasonable and rewarding way to organize our private lives. Needless to say, persuading people to marry is a tremendously effective way of generating a population that acts in a relatively predictable, relatively responsible manner. And it is also an effective way of producing citizens whose emotional lives mirror the collective needs of our society. Every society has a stake in producing the kinds of personalities, the kinds of character types, that suit its socioeconomic purposes, and marriage has always been a means of molding such characters, of creating psychological structures that reflect the normative codes of our culture, including its economic imperatives (the performance principle, the service of goods).

Antonio Gramsci observed that Henry Ford was among those who recognized the socioeconomic benefits of marriage. When Ford updated the technology of his car factories in the 1920s—shifting to an assembly line process that hugely increased his workers' productivity (while arguably eroding the quality of the hours they spent at work)—he capitalized on the link between marriage and (presumed) productivity by demanding proof of marital status as a precondition of higher wages. He even had a cadre of investigators who conducted spot checks at workers' homes to verify that their domestic arrangements were what they had reported. This is because he understood that stable domestic arrangements tended to produce more stable, and therefore more efficient, workers. As Gramsci states:

> The new industrialism wants monogamy: it wants the man as worker not to squander his nervous energies in the disorderly and stimulating pursuit of occasional sexual satisfaction. The employee who goes to work after a night of 'excess' is no good for his work. The exaltation of passion cannot be reconciled with the timed movements of productive motions connected with the most perfected automatism.[14]

In this sense, the precision of industrial labor benefits from an ideology of family values; from the perspective of capitalism, it is better that you are married, no matter how miserably, than that you cruise night clubs until 4 am, ending up at the conveyor belt (or desk) at 8 am hung-over and bleary-eyed.

One might say that in the context of the performance principle, sexuality outside of marriage is a "useless" pleasure: beyond reproductive goals it does not "lead" to anything. As Marcuse explains, in "a repressive order, which enforces the equation between normal, socially useful, and good, the manifestations of pleasure for its own sake must appear as *fleurs du mal*" (*EC* 50). It is hence not surprising that our society strives, much like Henry Ford did, to promote monogamous marriage as the optimal sexual arrangement. The degree of our conditioning is evident in the fact that many of us are willing to diligently "work at" our marriages even when they make us utterly wretched. As Laura Kipnis remarks in her scathing critique of marriage in *Against Love*, the notion that marriage takes hard work has become so widely accepted that it is these days almost impossible to talk about marriage without immediately conjuring up the language of mines, factories, sweatshops, and chain gangs. "Yes, we all know that Good Marriages Take Work," Kipnis quips: "we've been well tutored in the catechism of labor-intensive intimacy."[15] As a consequence, we work at getting along, at not getting on each other's nerves, at doing what we are supposed to do, at not doing what we are not supposed to do, and so on. We spend countless hours negotiating, adjusting, and resolving our "issues," frequently even paying therapists to play umpire to our domestic dramas. And even though we may have moments of yearning for something different, we frequently do not act on these yearnings because—and this is an excellent example of Ahmed's observation that the longer we persist "unhappily on a path of happiness, the harder it is to give up on that path"—we have already invested so much of ourselves in our marriage that we cannot bear the thought of losing it all. So we work even harder. We even work at sex. As Kipnis poignantly asks, "When did sex get to be so boring? When did it turn into this thing you're supposed to 'work at'" (*AL* 5–6).

From a certain point of view, when we have to work at sex, let alone love, something has already gone wrong. Yet our society elevates this type of labor-intensive relationality—relationality that feels like an endless boot camp—over less permanent affairs, and this is the case regardless of how vitalizing or uplifting these affairs might be. One of the incredible feats of our social order is that it has made "working for love" sound admirable—as the "noble," "mature," or "grown-up" thing to do. Consequently, people frequently stay in marriages that they experience as deadening, suffocating, frustrating, and sometimes even frightening; they meekly put up with the fact that the very alliance that was supposed to usher them to the heart of the good life is making them miserable. Sniping, sarcasm, bickering, resentment, the silent treatment, and other forms of psychological warfare seem to be among the standard devices of this mode of relationality, which is why Kipnis argues that it is difficult to imagine "a modern middle-class marriage not syncopated by rage" (AL 35). The social glorification of marriage, in short, cannot obscure the fact that, as Kipnis puts it, "toxic levels of everyday dissatisfaction, boredom, unhappiness, and not-enoughness are the functional norms in millions of lives and marriages" (AL 190).

Faithful to Foucault's analysis of marriage as an instrument of biopolitical manipulation, Kipnis stresses that the ideology of romantic love that underpins our vision of married life is one way in which social norms colonize the depths of our interiority, in fact shaping our very understanding of what this interiority consists of in the first place:

> Has any despot's rule ever so successfully infiltrated every crevice of a population's being, into its movements and gestures, penetrated its very soul? In fact it creates the modern notion of a soul—one which experiences itself as empty without love. Saying "no" to love isn't just heresy, it's tragedy: for our sort the failure to achieve what is most essentially human. And not just tragic, but abnormal. (AL 26)

Kipnis further observes that domesticity—the form of love promoted by our society—is the concrete mechanism by which our ideal of love is enforced: "Imagine the most efficient kind of social control possible. It wouldn't be a soldier on every corner—too expensive, too crass. Wouldn't the most elegant means of producing acquiescence be to somehow transplant those social controls so seamlessly into the guise of individual needs that the difference between them dissolved?" (AL 39). Foucault already argued that societies invent institutions such as factories, schools, prisons, and asylums to guarantee that people can be disciplined into predictable routines, which is why they tend to regulate both mobility and timetables (forcing people's lives to conform to enclosed spaces and the ticking of the clock). Against this backdrop, Kipnis asks: "What current social institution is more enclosed than modern domesticity? What offers greater regulation of movement and time, or more precise surveillance of body and thought to a greater number of individuals?" (AL 93). The answer to this rhetorical question is, of course, that there is no modern institution that tames people more effectively than marriage.

9

Is there, then, no force capable of thwarting the process of interpellation that seeks to convince us that heteronormative marriage represents the cradle of happiness? There is: the unruliness of the kind of desire that escapes surplus-repression—that is, the unruliness of what Lacan calls the truth of desire. Our society may try to tell us that the durability of our marriage is its own reward—and even a sign of our moral fiber—but even this narrative cannot always stifle our awareness that marriage as a long-term social arrangement tends to war against the realities of human desire. Social critics, Marcuse included, have long argued that desire—eros in its unshackled form—is one of the most antisocial forces under the sun in the sense that desire is not in the least bit interested in the feasibility of the cultural order; among other things, it could not care less about tax breaks, joint bank accounts, or our children's education. When it overflows the restrictions that are designed to contain it, it wreaks havoc with everything that is organized and well established about our lives. And its force is often so overwhelming that we are willing to risk just about everything for a moment's satisfaction, as is proven by politicians, celebrities, and other persons of social prominence who routinely tarnish their reputations by having affairs. This is to say that there is always a limit to the degree of renunciation our desire is capable of tolerating; there is only so much dissatisfaction it is willing to endure.

I have underscored that cruel optimism can cause us to wait indefinitely for whatever it is that we think will give us satisfaction. Within this framework, what makes desire such a rebellious force is that it refuses to wait: it wants satisfaction *now*. It causes us to lose our patience, jolting us to a new life because we are no longer willing to stay sheepishly devoted to the old one. In this sense, the flip side of a new desire is an alienation from previous forms of life. As we learned from Ahmed, alienation is frequently the precondition of our ability to reject the dominant happiness scripts of our society, for it forces us to recognize just how limiting such scripts can be; it causes us to become aware of how much we have given up in order to conform to the master's morality (the performance principle, the service of goods). Desire and alienation cannot therefore be easily disentangled: new desires generate alienation and alienation generates new desires. What has previously been unintelligible may become intelligible so that we are no longer stuck in scenarios that render possibles impossible but rather—to return to Badiou's wording—make impossibles possible. In this sense, it is in the nature of desire—as it is in the nature of the Lacanian-Žižekian act and the Badiouan event—to be transformative. It connects us to disclaimed dimensions of ourselves—dimensions that we have had to suppress to sustain the life that we have been living. Such disclaimed dimensions may have for the most part stayed invisible, but they are never fully annihilated. And when the right occasion arises, they start to clamor for recognition; they remind us of the alternative life that we could have lived—and that we might still be able to live. We may not always act on our new information, our new inclinations. But neither can we pretend that this information, these inclinations, are not now a clandestine element of our lives. Most likely, they will lie in wait for the next opening, the next time our desire is unexpectedly stirred. And the more we strive to repress them, the more momentum they are likely to gather.

Desire, in this sense, functions as a kind of utopian inkling that things could be otherwise—that we are not forever beholden to the modalities of life that we have inherited. Furthermore, once this inkling escapes the confines of the individual psyche, once it becomes a communal, collective matter, it can fuel political movements, as we just discovered in the context of the history of feminism. A more contemporary example can be found in queer theory which, like 1960s' feminism, possesses a great deal of curiosity about happiness scripts other than the marriage script. I have already noted that gay marriage—which supporters view as an essential civil right and opponents view as a betrayal of queer politics—has become a hugely divisive issue within the LBGTQ community (see Chapter 3). From a queer theoretical perspective, gays and lesbians who agitate for marriage rights are caught up in the tentacles of cruel optimism, deluded in their hope that the heteronormative, patriarchal, and state-controlled institution of marriage will make up for the legacies of gay and lesbian abjection. Though many queer critics of marriage recognize that there are situations where marriage rights are practically desirable, as for instance when one's access to social benefits or one's partner's hospital bed depends on these rights, they see gay marriage as a narrow political agenda that merely reproduces the core values of neoliberal capitalism, including its privileging of one relational modality (marriage) over all others. Social benefits should be granted to everyone regardless of relationship status, such critics argue.

But queer theory's critique of neoliberal capitalism is more comprehensive than its critique of marriage specifically, which is, incidentally, why I wish that Žižek read the field instead of blindly complaining about its "identitarian" tendencies: it offers extensive analyses of the kind of ethics of defiance—of stubbornly pursuing the truth of one's desire regardless of social consequences—that Žižek celebrates. Indeed, though queer theory does not invariably embrace psychoanalysis, the analogies between some of its reflections and Lacanian theory are striking, and this is nowhere more evident than in queer theoretical attempts to conceptualize what I have come to call an ethics of opting out.[16] "Opting out"—refusing to play the game, checking out of the system, defying the cultural status quo, or inventing an alternative set of rules—has always been one of the principal ambitions of queer theory and, as is the case in Lacanian theory, it carries a specifically ethical meaning. One might even say that, like Lacan, queer theory is often less interested in what comes after one opts out of the system than it is in the ethical valences of the act of opting out itself; it is interested in the ethical implications of refusing to participate, of choosing not to care, of simply turning away, or of insolently valorizing what the system devalorizes.

Some examples are in order here. Perhaps the most well known is Lee Edelman's explicitly Lacanian *No Future: Queer Theory and the Death Drive*.[17] In this text, Edelman utters a resounding *No!* to all fantasies of a better future, to the kinds of fantasies of progress that are upheld by both the neoliberal capitalist order and the mainstream gay and lesbian movement. Edelman claims that such fantasies—which imply that one day things will be better—merely obscure the fact that the day we are waiting for will never come. Edelman's antidote to this state of things— Edelman's version of the ethics of opting out—is to propose that queers should stop chasing a more hospitable future and, instead, embrace the negativity (the death drive) that dominant culture routinely bestows upon them by casting them as death-driven, AIDS-ridden, self-hating, and dangerous to the social order. That is, instead of fighting the damaging stereotypes that heteronormative culture imposes on queers, queers should accept the negative force of these stereotypes, thereby, as it were, raising the middle finger at the establishment.

Along related lines, Tim Dean, in *Unlimited Intimacy*, analyzes bareback sex—which sometimes includes the semi-intentional wish to contract HIV—as a way of subverting the idea that all of us want to lead long, healthy, balanced, and reasonable lives. Dean maintains that our culture is so health-obsessed that we are constantly barraged by advice on how to increase our longevity. We are told that we can keep illness at bay through a meticulous management of our bodies: the avoidance of risk factors such as smoking, drinking, and sexual promiscuity, along with the promotion of a balanced diet and regular exercise, is supposed to prolong our lives. To a degree, this is obviously true. But it is also a way to moralize illness, to cast judgment on those who fail to adhere to the right regimen. Ultimately, what we are dealing with is a regulation of pleasure—a process of medicalization that tells us which kinds of pleasures are acceptable and which are not (so that eating organic food is an acceptable pleasure but anonymous, unprotected sex is not). Not only does this place the full responsibility for our well-being in our own hands (thereby absolving the collective order of any accountability), but it makes us so paranoid about doing the right thing that instead of living our lives, we waste our energies on relentlessly worrying about the dangers that might await around the corner. Barebackers, Dean posits, are saying *No!* to this way of going about the project of living, choosing instead to accept risk as an intrinsic (and even desirable) component of human existence.[18]

A less extreme example of the queer ethics of opting out can be found in Heather Love's *Feeling Backward*, where Love urges us to consider the political potential of "bad feelings," such as shame, sadness, depression, abjection, bitterness, hopelessness, and disappointment.[19] Such feelings are usually seen as politically "useless" in the sense that, unlike more "dignified" sentiments, such as anger or outrage, they are not easy to translate into collective action. Indeed, as I argued in Chapter 2, this is one of my reservations about Butler's valorization of grief as a basis of ethics. Yet Love finds much to honor in her queer archive of bad feelings, advocating the act of taking an unflinching look at this archive so as to resist the ethos of robust cheerfulness that characterizes mainstream culture, including the mainstream gay and lesbian movement. Love is in fact intensely critical of the gay and lesbian movement's attempts to translate a shame-filled past—a pre-Stonewall past—into a triumphant future by simply just discarding what was excruciating about this past; she is critical of the attempt to translate shame into (gay) pride. Essentially, Love tells us that our efforts to transcend the pain of the past will never be entirely successful, that no matter how much we try to suppress the traumatizing aspects of gay, lesbian, and queer histories, these aspects will always find their way into our present. For instance, she analyzes the image of the melancholy lesbian who never gets the girl in traditional Western literary depictions of same-sex love, suggesting that the present-day young lesbians who do not have any trouble getting the girl are still, in some ways, living in the shadow of this historical figure whose romantic endeavors were always tinged by suffering. Though Love does not use psychoanalysis in her discussion, her basic insight is deeply psychoanalytic, namely that the past will always be a part of the present and that our attempts to deny this reality will only make this past more powerful. This is why tarrying with queer abjection, for Love, becomes an ethical choice, a way of opting out of the normative system, particularly the injunction to be happy that is such a major part of the neoliberal capitalist story of what the good life is supposed to entail.

10

My final example is in some ways the most obvious, namely Judith (now Jack) Halberstam's *The Queer Art of Failure*, where Halberstam promotes failure in its various forms—from stupidity (and ignorance) to forgetfulness to unemployment to slacking off to self-cutting—as a countercultural practice that rescues queers (and other marginalized subjects) from the cultural injunction to succeed.[20] Halberstam's argument foregrounds a theme I already alluded to in the context of Marcuse: the wish to escape the emphasis on success, achievement, self-improvement, and self-actualization that represents the trademark of capitalist consumer culture. This culture asks us not only to work hard but also to tirelessly, and narcissistically, work on ourselves: to attain ever higher levels of accomplishment, to perfect our bodies and résumés alike, to optimize the functioning of our minds, and to cultivate well-oiled relationships devoid of emotional messiness. One of the strengths of Halberstam's argument is to highlight our complicity with this system and to offer some tools for starting to think about how our failures to live up to its expectations might serve as a form of rebellion, of opting out of the rat race. As Halberstam states, "We might read *failure*, for example, as a refusal of mastery, a critique of the intuitive connections within capitalism between success and profit.... Let's leave success and its achievements to the Republicans, to the corporate managers of the world, to the winners of reality TV shows, to married couples, to SUV drivers" (*QF* 11–12; 120).

Halberstam thus counters the neoliberal capitalist emphasis on success narratives by narratives of utter failure. Yet her/his text also raises some questions about who can afford to "opt out" in the ways s/he advocates. My sense is that the vast majority of those who "fail"—underperform in school, cannot secure employment, work at jobs that no one associates with success, or cut themselves in a desperate effort to bypass dominant beauty ideals, for instance— do so not out of choice but because they, precisely, feel like they do *not* have a choice. That is, Halberstam's effort to subvert the performance principle of white middle-class society may carry its own (unintended) white middle-class bias in the sense that the kinds of failures s/he lauds might only become possible once one has already succeeded.

For example, at the beginning of her/his text, Halberstam proudly announces that s/he has never been able to become fluent in a foreign language. But who can afford such a failure? Certainly not immigrants who move to the United States from non-English-speaking countries. And who can become a university professor without passing her exams, as Halberstam claims s/he was able to do? Indeed, who can write a book about failure that becomes an enormous academic success? And what about Halberstam's conviction that there is something politically subversive about praising ignorance? Is ignorance not already at the core of the all-American complacency about the rest of the world that allows the US government to run over other nations without its population raising a protest? The valorization of ignorance—the notion that intelligence (or thoughtfulness) is inherently elitist and therefore contrary to American democratic values—may already be so endemic in mainstream American culture that turning it into a trope of resistance might end up bolstering the very system that one is trying to undermine.

Halberstam's analysis thus highlights a problem I have already called attention to in the context of Žižek and Badiou: the difficulty of distinguishing between authentic acts of defiance and inauthentic simulacra of such acts. Halberstam is not influenced by Lacanian theory specifically, but it is telling that the obstacle s/he runs into is the same that Žižek and Badiou encounter in their attempts to develop an explicitly Lacanian understanding of ethics, namely that this ethics is wholly devoid of normative considerations, so that one act of defiance is just as good as another, irrespective of the "content" of the act in question. Indeed, parts of Halberstam's text give the impression that antinormativity has, for her/him, become a default ethical stance to such an extent that the only thing that matters is the ever-elusive quest for the next radical edge I have identified as one of the shortcomings of contemporary theory. For instance, at one point in her/his argument, Halberstam aligns feminism—or what s/he calls "shadow feminism"—with masochism, passivity, sacrifice, feminine quietness, "pain and hurt," and the practice of self-cutting, maintaining that "cutting is a feminist aesthetic proper to the project of female unbecoming" (*QF* 135). The context of Halberstam's discussion makes it clear that this is an attempt to provide a progressive alternative to liberal feminist notions of agency and sovereignty. But it also feels that some line has been crossed here so that sounding radical truly *is* more important than the substance of what is being said: call me a "liberal," but it seems to me that if the new definition of feminism tells women to cut themselves and bleed all over the sidewalk—as a character in a novel that Halberstam lauds as an illustration of "shadow feminism" does—then patriarchy really has won. And what makes things even more troublesome is that it is obvious from Halberstam's rhetorical choices that her/his own position in relation to this argument about "female unbecoming" is that of a detached observer: whatever Halberstam's own modality of "unbecoming" might be, it is definitely not a matter of feminine masochism, passivity, and self-sacrifice.

In the next chapter, I will address the obstacle of trying to devise an ethics without normative content more systematically. Here I merely wish to conclude by saying that even though I do not agree with all aspects of Halberstam's argument, it—along with much of the rest of recent queer theory—illustrates, in a tangible way, the connection between deviant desires and defiance that I have sought to develop in this chapter, clarifying, among other things, why this connection offers a stronger model for resistance than the Butlerian model of subversive reperformance, why politics is not always a matter of negotiating with power but rather of rejecting the worldview that this power represents. Butler might object that there is no such thing as desire that has not been shaped by collective norms. As she writes:

> The norm does not simply enter into the life of sexuality, as if norm and sexuality were separable: the norm is sexualized and sexualizing, and sexuality is itself constituted, though not determined, on its basis. The body must enter into the theorization of norm and fantasy, since it is the site where the desire for the norm takes shape, and the norm cultivates desire and fantasy in the service of its own naturalization.[21]

But what I have attempted to demonstrate is that Butler's way of envisioning the relationship between desire and normativity overlooks the possibility that beneath the level of culturally compliant desire, there might exist a strain of unruly desire that has to some extent—never entirely but to some extent—evaded social conditioning and that can therefore energize both our personal and political acts of rebellion.

I am not arguing that our desires—or our fantasies—can be fully dissociated from the desires—or fantasies—of our collective environment. Indeed, in proposing—as I just did—that women's desire to cut themselves is a patriarchal desire, I have conceded the opposite. Yet, like Lacan and Marcuse, I think that there is a distinction between the kinds of desires that respond to the performance principle (or the service of goods) and the kinds of desires that respond to the loss of the Thing (as an experience in the real). Likewise, I believe that there is a distinction between mass-generated fantasies and the singular cadence of what Lacan calls the "fundamental fantasy" (again, fantasy in the real). As a matter of fact, I might be more persuaded by Halberstam's analysis of the rebellious valences of female self-cutting if it were not such an entirely predictable response to women's oppression. Though there is admittedly something visceral about self-cutting that seems to be of the order of Lacanian jouissance, the fact that so many women do it—and that they sometimes showcase their mutilated bodies in their Internet profiles—implies that it may be a part of the female performance principle of contemporary Western society: women are "performing" a version of feminine abjection that is, on some level, expected from them (and that is, in part at least, supposed to result from the "disappointments" of feminism).

My larger point is that the moment we relinquish the distinction between desires generated by the performance principle (the service of goods) and desires generated by the loss of the Thing, we lose the capacity to imagine agency, which is exactly the weakness of Butler's paradigm. In part because Butler does not want to acknowledge the Lacanian real as a valid theoretical concept, she is unable to envision a dimension of subjectivity that might elude total capture by hegemonic sociality. I understand her reluctance because there is always the danger that the notion of an asocial bodily real might slide into the notion that biology is destiny. But this is not at all what Lacan suggests. Quite the opposite, he implies that the real offers a way out of—always fleetingly, always incompletely—the destiny that our society tries to impose on us, and this includes our "biological" (gendered, sexed, racialized, etc.) destiny. As I have explained in this chapter, the only destiny that the real guides us into is the wholly idiosyncratic destiny that arises from our fundamental fantasy (or repetition compulsion), and this destiny is much more likely to disregard, say, normative categories of gender and sexuality than it is to promote them. This is why I think that it would be a mistake to read Lacanian ethics as apolitical. If anything, this ethics is in some ways more radical than our conventional understanding of ethics for, as I have shown, it explicitly raises the possibility not only of individual transformation but also of social change. This does not mean that it is devoid of limitations, as has already become clear, and as will become more clear in the next chapter. But it does offer a productive counterargument to Butler's contention that every desire is hopelessly caught up in the meshes of hegemonic power. While no one is saying that desire is wholly independent of such power, Lacan, Marcuse, some feminists, and many queer theorists are saying that our desires can, and often do, open to undomesticated realms of experience.

5

Beyond the impasses: The need for normative limits

It is a mistake to assume that our only options are either to hold on to the dangerous illusion of genuine context transcendence—an illusion whose danger is evident from the fact that it has so often been used to justify the colonizing of those others who are perceived to be less morally or politically enlightened than "we" are—or to accept a radically contextualist form of relativism. Instead . . . we can rely on the normative ideals of universal respect and egalitarian reciprocity in making normative judgments while at the same time acknowledging that these are ideals that are rooted in the context of late Western modernity.

AMY ALLEN[1]

1

In my assessment of Levinasian and Lacanian ethics, as well as of the attempts of Butler, Žižek, and Badiou to expand on the insights of Levinas and Lacan, I have repeatedly come up against the same shortcoming, namely that these ethical approaches function wholly without normative content, shunning all *a priori* ethical principles. If Enlightenment universalism relied on what Allen describes as "the dangerous illusion of genuine context transcendence"—if it falsely assumed that it could devise the kinds of moral codes that would be applicable in every time, place, and situation—the postmetaphysical ethical models I have considered have tended to swing to the opposite extreme of trying to operate entirely without normative ideals. To be sure, the Levinasian respect for the other represents an ideal of the highest order, but its flip side is the utter incapacity to place any restrictions on the behavior of this other; as far as Levinasian ethics goes, the other, quite literally, cannot do wrong. Lacan, in turn, elevates antinormativity to an ethical virtue without much consideration for the question of how we should treat others; the truth of our desire, for Lacan, seems more important than the intersubjective repercussions of our conduct. More generally speaking, it seems to me that we cannot discard *a priori* norms without generating insurmountable problems, including the radical relativism that Allen also warns us against. One solution would be to distinguish between ethics and justice, as Levinas does, and to argue that ethics has no space for the kinds of normative assumptions that justice presupposes, but this seems too facile in the sense that it is hard to imagine a justice completely divorced from ethics and vice versa. Indeed, in the absence of overlap between the two, it is difficult to avoid the problem of inconsistency that Butler runs into when she, in the context of the Israel-Palestine conflict, introduces codes of justice derived from Enlightenment cosmopolitanism into her otherwise Levinasian ethical vision.

I recently had a vivid reminder of this problem, which seems to emerge whenever real-life questions of justice intrude into otherwise purely theoretical discussions, in my queer theory graduate seminar. We had read text after text performing the by now more or less obligatory poststructuralist gesture of attacking "normativity" in its various manifestations—hegemonic power, neoliberalism, biopolitics, language, the state, and the legal system, among other things—when a student who had been notably quiet in earlier discussions tentatively raised his hand and asked, "If a man is raped by another man, don't you think that we need the courts to address the issue?" This student was headed to law school rather than a doctoral program, and his question made me realize that, on some level, progressive intellectuals in my field are able to engage in a quasi-habitual disparagement of *a priori* norms—as well as of the kinds of rights-based political movements that are trying to make these norms more inclusive—because they know that there are others (lawyers, activists, academic "liberals," and so on) who will keep defending these norms.

By this I do not mean that I believe that our current *a priori* norms are beyond reproach. For instance, I agree with those who have pointed out that neoliberal capitalism—which has the capacity to reduce politics and justice alike to market rationality—has damaged the principles of democracy. And I agree that rights-based approaches alone will not solve the underlying problems of socioeconomic inequality, racism, sexism, and so on. At the same time, I am not persuaded that rights-based approaches—and the *a priori* norms that sustain such approaches—are intrinsically less political than (or even antithetical to) progressive politics, as some of their critics seem to assume.[2] Historically, they have been such an important starting point for social justice (the women's vote, the Civil Rights movement, reproductive rights, immigrant rights, etc.) that I wonder how those critical of them would react if we started losing some of our basic "rights." To put the matter slightly differently, though I agree with those—Žižek among them—who agitate for more far-reaching social change than that offered by legal reform, I also find the customary dichotomy between rights-based approaches and "radical"—more fundamentally transformative— approaches somewhat counterproductive in the sense that both seem sorely needed. For example, it is difficult to envision genuine economic justice for women around the globe without the support of equal rights legislation. Considerations such as this are one reason I am not convinced that the flight from *a priori* norms that characterizes posthumanist theory—including the theories I have discussed in this book—augments our capacity to arrive at a more just world.

In more abstract terms, I would say that one of the major limitations of posthumanist (anti-Enlightenment) theory is that it places so much emphasis on deconstructing normativity that it tends to forget that while there certainly are normative limits we need to criticize and transgress, there are others we might need to endorse and refine. As Dominick LaCapra explains with his characteristic prudence, there are some normative limits "you might want to place in question, some you may want to reform, and others you may want to test critically and perhaps validate."[3] In other words, not all normative limits are diabolical: there are some that are by far the best (and perhaps even the only) way to check the abuses of power. I am in fact willing to go as far as to argue—and here I return to some of the concerns of Chapter 3—that there may even be times when it is necessary not to respect the difference of those who refuse to respect differences. I know that this idea is routinely used as an excuse for questionable state violence; and, in the global context, it often serves as a façade for Western imperialism. But I would say that such instances represent a misuse of normative limits rather than an argument for their dismantling. There are times when we need to make decisions about right and wrong, and to act accordingly. Whether we are talking about a man aiming his gun at Norwegian youth, or about a dictator aiming his genocidal rage at segments of his own population, we need *a priori* principles— normative limits—and the fact that we might never be able to fully agree on their parameters does not diminish the urgency of our desperate need for them.

2

Though I understand the reasons for the posthumanist attempt to deny this reality—though I am aware of the violence that has historically accompanied normativization in its various forms— I have come to recognize that this denial can lead to problems that are arguably equally detrimental. Consider Badiou's situation-specific ethics. The core idea of this ethics is the same as in Laclau's theory of hegemonization: any given social situation can potentially, albeit unpredictably, produce a generic truth that everyone comes to recognize as valid. Such a truth-event is capable of unifying disparate political entities behind a shared cause. It arises from the idiosyncratic logic of the situation at hand yet, once in place, it applies to everyone without fail. This offers an alternative to liberal democratic models such as Habermasian discourse ethics by replacing the ideal of a negotiated consensus by the ideal of a spontaneous revelation (of truth, of justice, of commitment). Yet, as I have illustrated, Badiou gives us no way to distinguish between productive truth-events and unproductive—even reactionary—simulacra of such events. And he also gives us no way to ensure that the ethical principle that emerges from a given situation is able to transcend the power differentials of that situation; he gives us no way to address the possibility that some people will find it easier than others to "name" the void of the situation and thus also the parameters of the ethics that this void is supposed to generate. This possibility is clear to anyone who teaches large university lecture courses: even when a class is predominantly female, men tend to dominate the question and answer period by an overwhelming majority. So whatever "common"—to use Hardt and Negri's term—is being created in the classroom is being created between the professor and the male students. Indeed, let us not forget that, as I emphasized in Chapter 3, this was one of the main failings of the classical Marxist approach that Badiou promotes: it defined the void (or "cause") of politics from the perspective of white men to such an extent that other voids (or "causes") became invisible.

Habermasian discourse ethics is of course plagued by the same problem in the sense that it is difficult to ensure that everyone gets to participate equally in the process of negotiating a consensus; it is difficult to ensure that the Habermasian ideal speech situation— which is supposed to guarantee that everyone affected by the issue at hand has an equal opportunity to participate in the conversation regarding this issue and that it is "the force of the better argument" rather than brute (or hidden) force that decides the outcome—actually delivers what it promises. For example, Habermas's supporters and opponents alike have called attention to the rationalist biases of his model, noting that the form of communication it presupposes is not universally accessible (or even desirable).[4] Butler's assessment is fairly typical:

> Although the procedural method purports to make no substantive claims about what human beings are, it does implicitly call upon a certain rational capacity, and attributes to that rational capacity an inherent relation to universalizability. . . . Thus the procedural approach presupposes the priority of such a rationality, and also presupposes the suspect character of ostensibly non-rational features of human conduct in the domain of politics.[5]

Seyla Benhabib, who is otherwise much more sympathetic to the Habermasian approach than Butler, has likewise criticized its rationalist slant. However, rather than rejecting discourse ethics altogether, Benhabib has made an effort to transcend the cognitive communication style favored by Habermas's original formulation, proposing that the ideal speech situation should in principle be open to a variety of alternative styles, including more emotionally charged and embodied ones, and that when it excludes such alternatives, it betrays its own democratic ideas.[6] Other feminist philosophers who, in various ways, have taken up the Habermasian model—such as Nancy Fraser—have staged comparable critiques, thereby reconceptualizing the foundations of discourse ethics in a more genuinely egalitarian direction.

I do not here wish to revisit the details of these critiques of Habermas, which I mostly agree with, but merely to point out that the problem of power discrepancies may be even more pronounced in Badiou's paradigm, where the event is supposed to produce a generic truth without any of the checks and balances of democratic deliberation. Though the event, like the Lacanian act, can be a private revelation—one of Badiou's examples is the amorous event as an experience of unconditional love—its ethical valences are most clearly discernible in the context of collective situations where participants are supposed to arrive at a shared truth through a miraculous galvanization of their passions. Ethics becomes a matter of the kind of leap of faith—the kind of inspired moment of certainty (and even of madness)—that does not recognize any grounding principle external to itself. What matters is the strength of conviction and the capacity to rally others behind this conviction, with the consequence that those with charismatic or forceful personalities are likely to overpower more reticent ones. The heat of the truth-event, in other words, favors those who do not hesitate to dominate. It may be true that the resolutions that result from a democratic process are no more objective than those that are extracted from a specific situation through the irruption of the event, but at least they have the advantage of being open to challenge. And while it is undoubtedly true that *a priori* norms that sustain unjust social systems are oppressive, so are, potentially at least, ethical decisions based on spur-of-the-moment evaluations that carry a mystical, quasi-theological force.

I understand why Badiou does not want to determine the content of good and evil *a priori*, ahead of the specific necessities of a given situation, for in his view, this effectively precludes the possibility of any genuinely new, surprising, or unprecedented perspectives. Jamieson Webster explains the matter beautifully when she claims that Badiou's ethical vision—what she describes as an "ethics of *that which is not yet in being*"—can be likened to the position of the analyst who does not seek to fix the truth of the analysand's desire ahead of time but rather waits for this truth to reveal itself through the gradual exploration of the unconscious.[7] As Webster specifies, the ideal ethical actor, in Badiou's sense, would aspire to the stance of the analyst as someone who chooses to be "without memory" (*LD* 108), who starts from scratch with every new patient, without assuming that the desire of a new patient has anything to do with the desire of her previous patients. Badiou's situation-specific ethics, Webster claims, demands a similar clean slate, a similar lack of *a priori* judgments.

I can see how, conceptually, this comparison is seductive. But using the analyst's position to explain Badiou's ethics also reveals the limitations of this ethics. It may make sense for the analyst to be "without memory," but this posture would be disastrous in relation to historical events such as American slavery, the Holocaust, Vietnam, Cambodia, Yugoslavia, Congo, Sudan, or Syria (to name just a few of the most obvious examples). The impulse to let sociopolitical atrocities fall into oblivion, or even to deliberately hide them, is already so strong that the aspiration to be "without memory" in relation to them hardly seems like the appropriate response. Furthermore, in the clinical encounter, there is time and space to linger in the specificity of desire. In contrast, in the domain of world politics, being able to act swiftly—on the basis of predetermined codes of conduct—is sometimes the only way to prevent violence from escalating. Saying that we should approach ethics with the same attitude of unknowingness and refusal of precedent as the analyst takes in relation to each new patient is a bit like saying that, the next time Jews start being rounded up and shipped off to undisclosed locations, we should assume that the past can teach us nothing and that we need to consequently enter into a lengthy process of seeing how things will unfold. I am sure that this is not what Webster—or even Badiou—means to suggest. But it is a matter worth contemplating. What, in Badiou's model, is to guarantee that an ethics that arises from a particular situation does not serve the interests of those who happen to be powerful in that situation? It seems to me that an *a priori* set of ethical principles would have a much better chance of handling this dilemma successfully.

3

Badiou's attempt to replace rational (or quasi-rational) democratic deliberation by the largely irrational energy of the event is merely one among many examples of the lengths that anti-Enlightenment theory goes to in its critique of reason. My response to this critique is more or less the same as my response to the critique of *a priori* norms: I understand the motivations for it but also think that it is sometimes taken to such absurd extremes that it becomes a mere rhetorical exercise—an empty quest for the next radical "edge" in critical thought—without any concrete applicability; truth be told, attacks on reason performed by high-powered academics who have spent much of their careers trying to outreason each other often seem intellectually dishonest to me. I agree that rationality is not the defining ingredient of human beings; as a psychoanalytic thinker, I am aware of both the limits of rationality and the potential brutality of ethical models that overvalorize our rational agency. I am, among other things, well versed in arguments about the masculinist and imperialist ("civilizational") hubris of traditional Western models of rationality. Yet I also think that it is futile to pretend that rationality does not play an important part in human life, and particularly in ethics.

This is why I appreciate Allen's observation that there is a big difference between categorically rejecting reason on the one hand and trying to reenvision it along less tyrannical lines on the other. Speaking of Foucault in particular, Allen maintains that it is a mistake to assume, as those who fixate on Foucault's analysis of madness tend to do, that Foucault wanted to do away with reason, for he thought that "nothing would be more sterile."[8] Foucault was not interested in destroying reason but rather in historicizing it by examining how it had been constructed at various points in time, how it had been connected to power, and how it had been deployed to meet specific sociopolitical goals. There is no question that this project entailed a critique of the failings of Enlightenment reason. But it also left open the possibility of alternative—less repressive, less objectionable—forms of reason; reason, for Foucault, was always contaminated by its context, but this, far from negating its value, was what made the reconceptualization of reason feasible in the first place. As Foucault explains, "If critical thought itself has a function—and, even more specifically, if philosophy has a function within critical thought—it is precisely to accept this sort of spiral, this sort of revolving door of rationality that refers us to its necessity, to its indispensability, and, at the same time, to its intrinsic dangers."[9]

Reason is impure, and often dangerous, but it is also indispensable. And sometimes it is even empowering. As Allen remarks, even though feminists have been at the forefront of criticizing the abuses of reason, they have frequently also found it enabling because it has allowed them to mount their intricate critiques of normativity, including, somewhat ironically, reason's patriarchal underpinnings.[10] In this sense, the impurity of reason—its socially and historically contingent nature—does not automatically render it useless. Undeniably, this impurity means that reason is never devoid of bias, which is why it must be diligently questioned; we are right to ask how our dominant models of rationality have been implicated in various relations of power. But this does not mean that we can (or should try to) replace rationality with something else, such as the uncritical celebration of relationality that characterizes the Levinasian-Butlerian ethical approach. Relationality is an important—and fascinating—part of human life, but so is rationality, with the result that when we use the trope of relationality to *exclude* (or vilify) rationality, we cannot help but impoverish our understanding of this life. Furthermore, even though relationality sounds benevolent, it is no more pure, no more devoid of power struggles, than rationality; relationality sounds nice because it makes us sound nice—altruistic rather than selfish—yet it can be hugely toxic. This is precisely why, as I have argued, the Lacanian act (severing social ties, walking away from intimate bonds) is often the best antidote to oppressive relationality. Along related lines, there is no intrinsic reason to associate rationality with individualism, as posthumanist critics, Butler included, tend to do: the possession of rational capacities does not automatically render us callous to the lot of others or incapable of responding to their needs; sometimes it might even make us better at navigating the complexities of relationships.

In this context, it is worth emphasizing that whatever the rationalist failings of the Habermasian ideal of deliberative democratic process, Habermas himself appears to recognize the impurity of reason when he writes, "There is no pure reason that might don linguistic clothing only in the second place. Reason is by its very nature incarnated in contexts of communicative action and in structures of the lifeworld."[11] There is a great deal of disagreement among Habermasians regarding the extent to which Habermas manages to transcend a metaphysical notion of rationality, but what interests me here is that he seems to acknowledge that the ideal speech situation is a regulative ideal rather than an empirical fact: like Derrida's democracy to come, it is something we can aspire toward but will always fail to reach. Yet our failure is perhaps not quite as inevitable (and therefore paralyzing) as it is in relation to the Levinasian demand that we revere the faces of those who persecute us or in relation to the related Derridean demand that we forgive the unforgivable. Because it is empirically possible to assess various speech situations—to look at who is included and who is excluded, who dominates and who remains silent, and so on—the ideal makes it possible to distinguish between speech situations that approximate it and others that do not. This, in turn, means that situations where the socially powerful control the outcome—as they could easily do in Badiou's model, for instance—are automatically deemed invalid. One could of course squabble endlessly about how these judgments are made, yet it is also the case that, on a very basic level, it is probably not that difficult to arrive at a reasonable evaluation: if I see that men speak more than women, that whites speak more than blacks, that some participants pressure others to agree with their views, or that one communication style—say, an aggressively rationalist one—overwhelms other styles, I will immediately deem the speech situation defective. And if I fail to do so, then I have not understood—or refuse to respect—the rules of the game, which makes me ineligible for the democratic process to begin with. From this perspective, a sexist or racist speech situation, for example, would not pass the test.

Though no actual speech situation is perfect, the Habermasian approach offers a nugget of insight that the ethical models I have outlined in this book lack and that I think is essential for our ability to overcome some of the impasses of these models: the possibility of *a priori* norms that are binding *without being metaphysically grounded*. One of the main reasons that the anti-Enlightenment thinkers I have discussed reject *a priori* norms is that they assume that such norms are irreversibly rooted in the Enlightenment metaphysical tradition. Again, there is considerable disagreement, even among Habermas's followers, about the degree to which Habermas himself might still be stuck in this tradition. But his feminist interlocutors, among others, have shown that *a priori* ethical principles do not necessarily need to be anchored in metaphysical conjectures about right and wrong but can, rather, be brought into existence through a continuous and open-ended communicative process. That is, *a priori* norms can be context-transcending (universally valid) without being fixed for all times to come; they can be normatively compelling while at the same time being amenable to revision. Perhaps one could say that if Badiou approaches every situation as a clean slate, Habermasian feminists approach situations as being governed by *a priori* norms that are operative *for the time being*, until they are replaced by new (or at least modified) ones.

To state the matter more concretely, Habermasian universality must accommodate the ongoing articulation of what Benhabib calls "democratic iterations." Benhabib borrows the term *iteration* from Derrida, which may account for the fact that, despite her long-standing disputes with Butler, her understanding of it is close to that of Butler: "In the process of repeating a term or a concept, we never simply produce a replica of the original usage and its intended meanings: rather, every repetition is a form of variation."[12] For this reason, democratic iterations allow meaning to travel from one context—say, one culture—to another in a flexible manner, so that universalization is not a matter of one context—say, Western societies—imposing its views on others but rather an (always temporary) agreement reached through a complex give and take between different contexts. Needless to say, the universal that is constructed in this manner is only legitimate if everyone—each "particularity"—concerned has had an equal opportunity to participate in its formulation. As I have conceded, this can be difficult to accomplish in practice, particularly in today's world of global power imbalances, but as an ideal it holds a great deal of promise. Commenting on the tension between the universal and the particular, Benhabib observes, "The point is not to deny this tension by embracing only one or another of these moral alternatives but to negotiate their interdependence, by resituating and reiterating the universal in concrete contexts."[13] Such "interactive universalism" depends on processes of translation (say, between different cultures) because, as Benhabib specifies, a universalization always requires "local contextualization, interpretation, and vernacularization by self-governing peoples" (*DA* 118). On this view, universalism is not a static metaphysical notion but rather something that is constructed contextually, in changing, and often conflicting, cultural and cross-cultural settings.

4

After the collapse of metaphysical justifications for universality, we do not have any choice but to admit that the version of universality we conjure into existence—and the *a priori* norms that support this universality—inevitably arises in a particular context: it is historically and culturally specific even as it strives to transcend this specificity. But—and my point here mirrors the argument I made about rationality above—this does not mean that our universalism is intrinsically worthless; while the loss of metaphysical foundations for our normative systems complicates their claim to universality, it does not automatically invalidate them. This is exactly what Allen is getting at in the passage I quoted at the beginning of this chapter: we make a mistake if we assume that our only options are either the delusion of being able to transcend our context into a realm of "pure" universality or a descent into "anything-goes" relativism. More specifically, Allen argues that we can profess the universal validity of some of our principles—such as the principles of equality, reciprocity, or mutual respect—as long as we remain aware that these principles are derived from the historical and cultural resources of Western modernity. In this manner, Allen advocates what she calls "principled contextualism": we may take our norms "to be universal and context transcendent, as long as we recognize that the notions of universalizability and context transcendence are themselves situated in the context of late Western modernity" (*PS* 180). An important part of this recognition is the admission that "it may turn out from some future vantage point that our normative ideals are themselves, in some ways that we have yet to realize, pernicious and oppressive" (*PS* 180). That is, we need to be "more historically self-conscious and modest about the status of our normative principles" (*PS* 180); among other things, we need to be open to the possibility that our principles can be contested. Yet this does not imply that "we are incapable of making normative judgments in light of such principles" (*PS* 180).

Allen is looking for a way out of nihilistic relativism by proposing that our awareness that we must continuously interrogate our ethical principles does not mean that these principles are devoid of all value. Nor does our recognition that our principles cannot be divorced from their context mean that we cannot claim that they are capable of transcending their context; that is, our principles can be context-transcending without being context-neutral. This, as we saw in Chapter 2, is Butler's argument in *Parting Ways*, even if she ends up backpedaling on the universalist implications of her approach.[14] More important for our present purposes, this is how Allen arrives at the "historical a priori" I have referred to in passing. As Allen explains, "The historical specificity of our a priori categories, their rootedness in historically variable social and linguistic practices and institutions" (*PS* 31–2) does not cancel the power of these categories to order our existence. However, if we want others to be convinced by our *a priori* ideals, we need to persuade them through a democratic process. If the Enlightenment resorted to aggression to spread its views, the Habermasian democratic method, according to Allen, relies on more collectively formed public opinions. Allen's point is akin to the one Benhabib makes through her notion of "democratic iterations": rather than the solitary Kantian subject trying to figure out in the abstract what everyone might conceivably agree on, the Habermasian approach offers a model where social agents collaborate with each other to forge a perspective that everyone can agree on. This junction of compatible views, then, becomes the current "historical a priori," the current version of the universal.

Any given "historical a priori" can obviously take hegemonic forms. I grant, as does Allen, that we need to remain vigilant about the constitutive exclusions that *a priori* norms often imply. Yet the merits of a normative system that is brought into being through a continuous democratic process—a process that can accommodate the tensions of rethinking, refinement, and renegotiation—also seem considerable. Borrowing from Fraser, one could say that the historical *a priori* is always open to reframing. Such reframing happens, for instance, when individuals or groups who have been excluded from a given ethical frame demand admission to it, thereby automatically altering the parameters of the frame. Proposing that "misframing" may be "the defining injustice of a globalizing age," Fraser advocates—echoing Butler's observations about the necessity of revising the frames of perception that eliminate some populations from the status of the fully human—"an enlarged, transnational sense of who counts as one's fellow subjects of justice."[15] This implies that when the frame shifts—say, from a national to a transnational one—so does the historical *a priori*: an *a priori* that was formulated in a given national context might not be appropriate for a transnational one. There must thus be a period of readjustment, but this does not imply the neutralization of the *a priori*—as some cultural relativists might assume—but merely its reconfiguration. Or, to restate the larger argument I have tried to articulate, the concept of the historical *a priori* requires that we admit that an *a priori* principle can be normatively meaningful even as it is open to alteration; the *a priori*—as I noted above—holds *until* it is deemed somehow flawed or unjust. In Fraser's words, "The result would be a grammar of justice that incorporates an orientation to closure necessary for political argument, but that treats every closure as *provisional*—subject to question, possible suspension, and thus to reopening" (*SJ* 72).

The model Fraser advocates hence treats every ethical closure as provisional. Fraser calls this model "reflexive justice," specifying that it scrambles the opposition between the Habermasian democratic model on the one hand and the more poststructuralist, Marxist, and skeptical model (which she calls "agonistic")—the model that dominates contemporary progressive criticism—on the other. If the first of these is sometimes accused of being excessively normalizing, the second—which is essentially the model I have been analyzing in this book (with the exception of Levinas)—is, as Fraser puts it, "often seen as irresponsibly reveling in abnormality" (*SJ* 73). Against this backdrop, the advantage of Fraser's model is the following:

> Like agonistic models, reflexive justice valorizes the moment of opening, which breaches the exclusions of normal justice, embracing claimants the latter has silenced and disclosing injustices the latter has occluded—all of which it holds essential for contesting injustice. Like discourse ethics, however, reflexive

justice also valorizes the moment of closure, which enables political argument, collective decision-making, and public action—all of which it deems indispensable for remedying injustice. (*SJ* 73–4)

In this manner, Fraser declares the standard opposition between the Habermasians and the agonists to be a false one, for it is possible to admit the best insights of both by acknowledging the value of both opening (contestation) and closure (binding norms that enable ethical and political decisions). Such an approach rejects relativism, enabling normative judgments and political interventions, but without thereby locking the content of such judgments and interventions into a fixed, immutable definition.

All of this of course implies that there is one norm that stands above every other: what Fraser calls "the overarching normative principle of *parity of participation*" (*SJ* 60). On this view, Fraser explains, "Overcoming injustice means dismantling institutionalized obstacles that prevent some people from participating on a par with others, as full partners in social interaction" (*SJ* 60). In other words, for Fraser's paradigm to function, one needs a base-level faith in the democratic process even as one acknowledges that it is always going to fall short of its own ideals. Like Levinasian justice, which knows that it will never be able to live up to the demands of ethics, concrete democratic formations are invariably guilty, humiliated by their failures, but this cannot, for the Habermasians at least, discourage us to the point that we stop trying to improve them. As Benhabib explains:

As with any normative model, one can always point to prevailing conditions of inequality, hierarchy, exploitation and domination, and prove that "this may be true in theory but not so in practice" (Kant). The answer to this ancient conflict between norm and reality is simply to say that if all were as it ought to be in the world, there would be no need to build normative models, either. The fact that a normative model does not correspond to reality is no reason to dismiss it, for the need for normativity arises precisely because humans measure the reality they inhabit in the light of principles and promises that transcend this reality. The relevant question therefore is: Does a given normative model enable us to analyze and distill the rational principles of existing practices and institutions in such a fashion that we can then use these rational reconstructions as critical guidelines for measuring really existing democracies?[16]

Allen sums up the matter by noting that though imbalances of power are important for Habermasian critical theory to grapple with, the solution to this "can only be more discourse or debate" (*PS* 18). This continued faith in the perfectibility of the democratic process is what distinguishes the Habermasian feminists I have cited in this chapter from the thinkers—perhaps, again, with the exception of Levinas—I have discussed in earlier chapters of this book. The latter thinkers, as well as those aligned with these thinkers, would in fact ridicule the Habermasian stance for its naïve inability to recognize how power corrupts the democratic process, how, for example, neoliberalism and global capitalism have torn democracy into shreds. As Wendy Brown explains, "This is a political condition in which the substance of many of the significant features of constitutional and representative democracy have been gutted, jettisoned, or end-run, even as they continue to be promulgated ideologically, served as a foil and shield for their undoing and for the doing of death elsewhere."[17] Indeed, what good can the ideal of participatory parity do in the context of biopolitical and other invisible forces of power that constitute us as compliant subjects well before we understand the basic principles of such parity? If our psychic lives, including our unconscious desires, fantasies, and motivations, are shaped by hegemonic power, then participatory parity seems like a mere stop-gap measure—something that makes us feel slightly better about being nothing but the obedient marionettes of power.

5

To some degree I agree with such pessimism about the Habermasian democratic process. But I am not convinced that the alternative approaches I have analyzed in this book necessarily fare any better in terms of being capable of addressing the problem of power. I have already explained my reservations about the ability of Žižek and Badiou to do so. Butler may at first glance seem more competent in this regard, given that the critique of disciplinary power has always been central to her theory. Yet, as I have demonstrated, I am not reassured by her assertion that opposing power is a matter of negotiating with it. Nor am I persuaded by the haphazardness of her understanding of resistance—a haphazardness that arises from her rejection of agency. Take her assertion that the Benjaminian messianic rupture of divine violence—outlined in Chapter 3—offers the possibility of a political intervention based on *distraction*:

> Perhaps we need to be more distracted, as Baudelaire was said to be, in order to be available to the true picture of the past to which Benjamin refers. Perhaps, at some level that has implications for the political point I hope to bring out here, a certain disorientation opens us to the chance to wage a fight for the history of the oppressed.[18]

Butler here offers disorientation and chance—rather than action, choice, or decision—as a political strategy. As she adds, "We have to be provisional situationists, seizing the chance to fight when it appears" (*PW* 110).

This is not a new problem, for long before Butler's turn to ethics, she wrote, in relation to our tendency to identify with the power structures that subjugate us: "The very categories that are politically available for identification restrict in advance the play of hegemony, dissonance and rearticulation. It is not simply that a psyche invests in its oppression, but that the very terms that bring the subject into political viability orchestrate the trajectory of identification and become, *with luck, the site for a disidentificatory resistance.*"[19] I have already expressed my dissatisfaction with the idea that the psyche invariably "invests in its oppression," but in the present instance I want to call attention to Butler's reduction of resistance—here configured as a practice of disidentification—to a kind of lucky break from the generalized background of power. Allen has noted the same problem, arguing that luck is too flimsy a basis for political resistance, and pointing out, furthermore, that Butler's reluctance to theorize the social world as anything but hegemonic makes it difficult for her to envision the possibility of social solidarity, including nonsubordinating, nonstrategic forms of mutual recognition. As Allen asserts:

> Without a more fully developed and less ambivalent notion of recognition, Butler is left unable to explain the possibility of

collective or, ultimately, individual resistance. . . . Without an account of how the recognition of our commonality provides the basis for political community and collective resistance, Butler is left suggesting that the transformation from identification to disidentification, from signification to resignification, from subjectivation to a critical desubjectivation, is nothing more than a matter of luck. (*PS* 93)

Exactly. As complicated and potentially flawed as the democratic ideal of participatory parity may be, it still seems like a better basis for political action than dumb *luck*.

One of the stock objections to participatory parity, of course, is that it is a Western invention and therefore intrinsically imperialistic. Undeniably, as Allen's notion of "principled contextualism" suggests, it is important to acknowledge this possibility. Yet it is equally possible that the very belief that the ideal of participatory parity is a distinctively Western virtue is merely yet another example of Western superciliousness—which dictates that all good things must by definition be Western—for surely it would be easy enough to find examples of non-Western societies that, in various ways, respect this ideal (as do, for instance, many hunter-gatherer and tribal societies). In addition, as vehemently as progressive critics such as Butler, Žižek, and Badiou attack "liberalism," including Habermasian discourse ethics, the ideals that they end up promoting are usually ultimately not that different from the ideals that someone like Benhabib would endorse: freedom, equality, reciprocity, and democratic process. Indeed, my sense is that these fundamental Enlightenment ideals continue to constitute the silent background of much of progressive theorizing, that no matter how insistently poststructuralist or Marxist academics rail against the Enlightenment—while also disagreeing with each other—they still secretly hold onto its basic values: they merely add "radical" in front of these values, so that rather than speaking about, say, freedom, they speak about "radical" freedom.

By this I do not mean that there are not any genuine rifts between the Habermasians and the progressives. But even these are often not quite as pronounced as one might expect. Take the heated dispute about human rights. Because Habermasian critics such as Benhabib and Fraser continue to believe in the perfectibility of the democratic process, they have chosen to endorse the recent shift toward cosmopolitanism in debates about global justice. At the core of this shift is the realization that national boundaries often undermine global justice, and that the unit of ethical deliberation should therefore not be the citizen of a given nation-state but rather the individual as an equal member of a worldwide network of humanity. That is, the basic idea is that individuals should have fundamental rights—such as collectively agreed upon human rights—because of their humanity rather than because of the passport they happen to carry. As Benhabib explains, "Cosmopolitanism involves the recognition that human beings are moral persons equally entitled to legal protection in virtue of rights that accrue to them not as nationals, or members of an ethnic group, but as human beings as such" (DA 9). Many human rights agreements signed since World War II, she specifies, signal an eventual transition to a mode of international law "that binds and bends the will of sovereign nations" (AC 16). This idea—that transnational justice "binds and bends the will of sovereign nations"—is at the heart of cosmopolitanism, which seeks to curtail the authority of states so as to augment the well-being of individuals. While many progressive critics, including Žižek and Badiou, have jumped to the conclusion that this is merely a way to propagate a Western ethos of individualism around the globe, a more generous reading would see it as an effort to protect individuals who are vulnerable to oppression, displacement, and dispossession by states. In part because of globalization, which has, among other things, created an ever-escalating number of problems that transcend the purview of nation-states, there has been an acknowledgment that nationalisms and other forms of communitarianism (such as the quest for ethnic or religious purity) can only stand in the way of global justice.

This cosmopolitan vision bears a conceptual similarity to Žižek and Badiou's argument about every singularity being able to partake in the universal without the mediation of the particular (see Chapter 3), which makes it all the more interesting that Žižek and Badiou repeatedly condemn cosmopolitan human rights discourses as a ruse of global capitalism and Western imperialism. I am not saying that they do not have any cause for this, for there is no doubt that human rights discourses have frequently functioned as a smokescreen for Western economic, political, and military interests. Žižek and Badiou are right when they say that the rhetoric of tolerating "the other" that underpins human rights is hypocritical in that it falls apart the moment this other seems too radically different (again, see Chapter 3). And they are right to point out that human rights often lead to the fantasmatic division of the world into the passive, pathetic, and persecuted victims who reside outside the West and their Western saviors—who, moreover, become the fascinated spectators of the suffering of those less fortunate than themselves. But I do not think that Benhabib and Fraser would disagree with any of this (more on this below). Furthermore, there is also something rather crude about Žižek's claim that "the Marxist symptomal reading can convincingly demonstrate the particular content that gives the specific bourgeois ideological spin to the notion of human rights: 'universal human rights are in effect the right of white male property owners to exchange freely on the market, exploit workers and women, and exert political domination.'"[20]

This is certainly not how most academic supporters of human rights—let alone feminist supporters of women's equal rights—understand cosmopolitan justice. Among other things, even the most straightforwardly "liberal" of them seem aware of the problematic nature of global capitalism and Western imperialism. Benhabib, for instance, writes:

> We are confronted with the galloping spread to all corners of the world of "our" Western way of life which often, however, uses the shields of Western reason and Enlightenment to bring other peoples and cultures under the influence of an inegalitarian global capitalism, whose effects are manifestly neither rational nor humane. The legacy of Western rationalism has been used and abused in the service of institutions and practices that will not stand scrutiny by the very same reason that they claim to spread. (DA 59)

At the same time, Benhabib is unwilling to conflate human rights with the effort to bring the entire world under the umbrella of Western capitalism, pointing out that human rights cannot be reduced to norms protecting free market transactions. If anything, many international human rights covenants contain "provisions *against* the exploitative spread of market freedoms, in that they protect union and associational rights, rights of free speech, equal pay for equal work, and workers' health, social security, and retirement benefits. Global capitalism, which creates special free-trade zones, is often directly in violation of these human rights covenants" (*DA* 122). That is, if human rights can sometimes be used as a Trojan horse for capitalist interests, they can also be used to fight these interests, not the least because they seek to guarantee the basic freedoms that make collective resistance possible in the first place. Benhabib concludes that the critics of human rights norms ignore that such rights can empower "civil society actors who then become part of transnational networks of rights activism and hegemonic resistance" (*DA* 126). Along related lines, Fraser remarks that critics, such as Hardt and Negri, who see cosmopolitanism and human rights as nothing but a mask of neoliberal empire concentrate "exclusively on the dark side of the move beyond nation-state sovereignty" (*SJ* 37), thereby ignoring the various ways in which transcending the limits of nation-states could be beneficial to various global populations, including ones who do not have access to a nation-state.

What the vehement pitch of Marxist critics of human rights conceals is that the ideal of such rights has not emerged *only* as a prop for Western politico-economic domination. It has emerged, in part at least, from our prior experiences with various collective atrocities. I think it would be insincere to pretend that these atrocities are so drastically different from each other that they cannot support any *a priori*, universally applicable ethical principles. Benhabib and Fraser do not deny that cosmopolitanism can be abused through what Benhabib describes as "the ambivalences, contradictions, and treacherous double meanings of the current world situation, which often transform cosmopolitan intents into hegemonic nightmares" (*DA* 123). Neither do they deny that international laws have been unevenly applied, most egregiously in the context of the US-led war on terror.[21] But they resist the conclusion that international laws are merely an oppressive arm of Western imperialism. If anything, it is possible to argue that if we are horrified by the manner in which the United States has violated international laws, it is because we have these laws in the first place; if we recognize these violations as violations, it is because we still—on some level—believe in the values that international laws attempt, however precariously, to uphold. In this sense, attacking human rights legislation—legislation that has often been painstakingly constituted in increasingly transnational forums—will not make the world a less violent place; the effort to protect these rights more equitably might. This is why Benhabib argues for "a *cosmopolitanism without illusions*"

(*DA* 14): a cosmopolitanism that remains alert to the various ways in which it could be exploited. As she concludes:

> We need . . . to use the public law documents of our world and the legal advances in human rights covenants soberly, without too much utopian fanfare, to enable the growth of counter-hegemonic transnational movements, claiming rights across borders in a series of interlocking democratic iterations, and reinventions and reappropriations of valuable norms that have often been misunderstood and abused as they have been advanced. (*DA* 14–15)

Obviously, the West has never been able to live up to the ideals of the Enlightenment. Yet, as *ideals*—as normative goals—freedom, equality, reciprocity, and democratic process are hard to argue with. One of the mistakes that the Enlightenment made was to deny the sociohistorical specificity of these ideals. On the one hand, its relative success arose precisely from its ability to universalize its particularity beyond its narrow cultural parameters; that is, it succeeded in doing with its ideals what Butler attempts to do with the Jewish heritage, namely to translate a specific tradition into something that transcends the confines of this tradition. On the other hand, it undermined these very ideals by trying to violently impose them on the rest of the world (surely there is a deep irony in attempting to *force*, say, the ideal of "democratic process" on others). But such misuse does not mean that the ideals in question are intrinsically corrupt, which is precisely why even the most passionate critics of the Enlightenment tend to fall back on its definition of justice, as Butler does in the context of the Israel-Palestine conflict.

6

In Chapter 2, I pointed out that Butler's attempt to have it both ways—to denounce the Enlightenment while simultaneously using its resources—leads to conceptual contradictions that cannot easily be resolved. The matter is worth revisiting here in greater detail because it highlights my major disagreement with Butler, namely that her wholesale vilification of autonomy reaches the kinds of hyperbolic ideological heights that cannot be theoretically defended. Indeed, it is in part the predictability of Butler's stance on this issue that explains why I have been so critical of her in this book: that I always know ahead of time how the argument is going to go—autonomy, sovereignty, rationality, normative limits bad; antinormativity, no matter how far-fetched, good—makes me feel the same way I do when I am grading yet another graduate student paper that undertakes the task of "deconstructing" the humanist subject. In the latter instance, it takes all the pedagogical willpower I can conjure up to not write in the margin, "Didn't we already do this circa 1975?" In Butler's case, I suppose I would like some explanation for why the monotonous disparagement of autonomy and related concepts is so important to her.

This question is worth asking because the problematic of the subject—the question of the proper way to theorize the relationship between autonomy and subjection, agency and abjection, accountability and social determination—has been one of the most divisive issues of contemporary theory. I have already outlined my own position, which is that either-or solutions to this problematic are too one-dimensional, that if human beings are not entirely autonomous, they are not entirely subjected either, which is why we need to theorize both poles of the dichotomy simultaneously. This, refreshingly, is what Allen tries to do, which is one reason I have found her arguments so convincing. Allen explains that her goal "is to offer an analysis of power in all its depth and complexity, including an analysis of subjection that explicates how power works at the intrasubjective level to shape and constitute our very subjectivity, *and* an account of autonomy that captures the constituted subject's capacity for critical reflection and self-transformation, its capacity to be self-constituting" (*PS* 2–3). Without an account of subjection, Allen adds, critical theory cannot grasp "the real-world relations of power and subordination along lines of gender, race, and sexuality that it must illuminate if it is to be truly critical"; but without a satisfactory account of autonomy, critical theory "cannot envision possible paths of social transformation" (*PS* 3). This is why it is important to understand how we can be constituted by power yet capable of constituting ourselves, how we can be limited by our social context yet capable of critical reflection and self-transformation beyond this context.

Undoubtedly even our capacity for critical reflection and self-transformation is socially constituted, so that it would be possible to posit—with Žižek—that this capacity merely renders our subordination more livable. In Žižek's skeptical reading (and this is a possibility I touched on in Chapter 4), what the system *wants* is precisely that we rebel against it—that we strive for the kind of self-transformation that gives us the illusion of being able to distance ourselves from it—because, in the final analysis, our attempts to defy its power merely consolidate this power; as Žižek maintains, in one of his more Foucaultian moments, power thrives on our actions of disidentification because it "can reproduce itself only through some form of self-distance, by relying on the obscene disavowed rules and practices that are in conflict with its public norms."[22] Yet it is also the case—as Žižek himself repeatedly stresses—that without the capacity for critical reflection and self-transformation, our relationship to the big Other would be one of utter subjection.

It is this knotty relationship between autonomy and subjection that repeatedly derails the logic of Butler's efforts to think through the Israel-Palestine conflict. More specifically, as I started to suggest in Chapter 2, it is Butler's resistance to autonomy that causes her to deny that she is relying on neo-Kantian principles of liberal cosmopolitanism even though this is clearly the case. As a way of approaching this inconsistency, let us consider, first, the parts of Butler's argument where she makes no attempt to hide her allegiance to liberalism. A good example of this is her assertion that Israel fails to adhere to "classically liberal principles of citizenship that would forbid discrimination on the basis of race, religion, and ethnicity."[23] She further derides Israel for viewing classical liberalism as a threat "to the project of Zionism" (*PW* 32), and even as "a form of genocide" ("JZ" 76). As she explains:

> The classically liberal position—in particular, that the requirements for citizenship should not be based on race, religion, ethnicity—is subject to intense vilification. When an Israeli publicly remarks that he or she would like to live in a secular state, one that does not discriminate on the basis of religion, ethnicity, or race, it is common to hear that position (and person) decried as aiding and abetting the "destruction" of the Jewish state or committing treason. If a Palestinian (Israeli or not) espouses the same position, namely, that citizenship ought not to be determined by religious or ethnic membership, then that might be considered a "terrorist" act. How did it become historically possible for the

precepts of classical liberalism to be equated with terrorism and genocide in the beginning of the twenty-first century? (*PW* 32)

I find Butler's defense of classical liberalism here very interesting, given how different it is from the more Levinasian, relational perspective she otherwise promotes. I do not know whether Benhabib would endorse Butler's condemnation of Israel's policies, but I am fairly certain that she would endorse her sudden appreciation for the core values of classical liberalism.

Butler draws on Hannah Arendt (and Edward Said) to argue that "never again should there be a group of permanent refugees who are actively dispossessed of land and rights in order to shore up a state that bases itself on a religion, ethnicity, principles of national sameness, or race" (*PW* 110). Arendt notoriously maintained that everyone, regardless of nationality, ethnicity, religion, and so on, should have "the right to have rights."[24] As I noted above, this stance underpins the contemporary cosmopolitan view that it is the individual rather than the nation-state (or ethnic group or religion) that should be the unit to which certain basic rights are granted. In more concrete terms, because there has been a realization that states and other collectivities often function in oppressive ways (e.g., by barring some of their populations from basic civil rights, as does Israel in relation to Palestinians, and as do many religious communities in relation to women), there has been an attempt to shift the emphasis from collectivities to individuals as equal holders of rights—as beings of equal worth, dignity, and protection. Butler supports this view when she maintains, in the context of Israel specifically, that "an ethical and political alliance . . . can be achieved only by living to the side of one's nationalism, making the border into the center of the analysis, and allowing for a decentering of a nationalist ethos" (*PW* 50). While she shies away from a categorical condemnation of nationalism—insisting that "the nationalism of a militarized nation-state" and "the nationalism of those who have never known a state" are two different things (*PW* 50)—she, like cosmopolitan thinkers, recognizes that there is something about the particularism of nationalism that thwarts our aspirations for global justice. As she maintains, we need to be able to break from communitarian discourses "that cannot furnish sufficient resources for living in a world of social plurality or establishing a basis for cohabitation across religious and cultural difference" (*PW* 9).

Butler's endorsement of cosmopolitan human rights is in fact quite unequivocal: "Whether or not we continue to enforce a universal conception of human rights at moments of outrage and incomprehension, precisely when we think that others have taken themselves out of the human community as we know it, is a test of our very humanity."[25] Like Benhabib and Fraser, Butler does not believe that it is up to the Western world to unilaterally dictate what human rights should consist of. Instead, true to her earlier theoretical aspirations, she asks us to rethink the very question of what it means to be human; asserting that "human rights law has yet to understand the full meaning of the human," she proposes that the current task of this law is to "reconceive the human when it finds that its putative universality does not have universal reach" (PL 91). I wholeheartedly agree with these points, but what I find less credible is Butler's effort to illustrate that her allegiance to the ideals of freedom, equality, reciprocity, and democratic process arises from Levinasian ethics rather than from Kantian cosmopolitanism.

Butler makes a valiant effort to show that her cosmopolitanism is not the same as that of Kant by positing that it is precarity rather than the integrity of the sovereign self that is the basis for equal rights. This argument is perhaps the clearest example of the dynamic I alluded to at the end of Chapter 1, namely Butler's attempt to apply Levinasian ethics to questions of justice, including geopolitical justice. Butler draws a parallel between the Levinasian idea that we are responsible for the other who "interrupts" our ontology and the Arendtian idea that none of us has the right to choose with whom we share the world, so that, like the Levinasian other, those with whom we cohabit the earth are "given to us, prior to choice" (PW 125). This is an excellent explanation for why we are responsible for even those who challenge our identity and cultural belonging, but I am not entirely convinced by Butler's efforts to sidestep Arendt's Kantian heritage—the fact that Arendt's cosmopolitan stance of sharing the world beyond national boundaries was explicitly indebted to Kant—by emphasizing the similarities between Arendt's vision and that of Levinas. Moreover, I am not even persuaded that precarity can be dissociated from the integrity of the "sovereign" self: Are we not precarious precisely when our integrity has in one way or another been violated? Is it not the case that those who argue for rights on the basis of integrity are, in a way, saying that humans should be protected against the kind of brutality that exploits their precarity (violates their always fragile integrity). Along related lines, when Butler posits that her ethics "seeks to diminish suffering universally"—indeed "seeks to recognize the sanctity of life, of all lives" (*PL* 104)—I wonder what the difference between sanctity and integrity might be. And I also wonder what the difference might be between Butler's ethics of precarity and the Kristevian revamped humanism that I discussed in Chapter 1 (and that Kristeva aptly sums up as follows: "liberty, equality, fraternity . . . and vulnerability").[26]

There are of course some grounds for Butler's efforts to align Arendt with Levinas rather than Kant, given that Arendt's vision of freedom, plurality, and political action is deeply intersubjective. Like Butler, Arendt saw human ontology through the lens of relationality, in terms of collective action and social belonging, and politics, for her, was a matter of world building. But it is hard to deny that Arendt also had some strongly Kantian leanings, including an appreciation for the categorical imperative. As Arendt writes: "Kant's moral philosophy is . . . closely bound up with man's faculty of judgment, which rules out blind obedience": "by using his 'practical reason' man found the principles that could and should be the principles of law."[27] Arendt uses this basic Kantian notion to condemn traditional, dogmatic forms of authority, including oppressive laws, and to advocate independent, critical thought as an antidote to such authority. Yet it is this Kantian element in Arendt that Butler, predictably enough, condemns: "One can surely see why there would be a Kantian reading of Arendt, one that concludes that plurality is a regulative ideal, that everyone has . . . rights, regardless of the cultural and linguistic differences by which anyone is characterized" (*PW* 126). Butler proceeds to suggest that such a "Kantian reading of Arendt" would be misguided, and this is, counterintuitively, the case even though the reading in question is virtually identical to Butler's own position—the position I have just delineated. Indeed, far from acknowledging the kinship between Arendt's Kantian vision and her own, Butler accuses Arendt of "a strange sort of Eurocentrism, and an identification of what is best in German culture with Kant's philosophy" (*PW* 141). As much as I try to sympathize with Butler's resistance to Kant, there is something incongruous about criticizing Kant for having come up with the very set of ideas Butler herself promotes. Is it really the case that all the ideas of an Enlightenment thinker are automatically unacceptable just because he happens to be an Enlightenment thinker? If the ideas are good, and identical to your own, is it really so terrible that Kant happened to think of them first?

7

Once again, it is not Butler's ideas that I find objectionable but rather her attempt to convince us that they have nothing to do with the ideals of the Enlightenment—ideals that Arendt still to some extent adheres to. Likewise, Butler's efforts to inject a heftier dose of Levinasian relationality into Arendt's philosophy than this philosophy might be able to accommodate result in assertions that seem largely untenable, such as the following:

> In Arendt the dialogue that is thinking has a performative and allocutory dimension that underscores the centrality of free self-constitution in her view. If free self-constitution is an action, however, it must be done on the basis of some set of prior social relations. No one constitutes him or herself in a social vacuum. Although this precept is sometimes strained by what Arendt occasionally says about the solitary character of thinking, sometimes it is not, especially when thinking is understood as speaking. . . . To think is not necessarily to think about oneself, but rather to think with oneself (invoking oneself as company and so using the plural "we") and to sustain a dialogue with oneself (maintaining a mode of address and, implicitly, addressability). (PW 169)

I find this reading somewhat strained, given that Arendt consistently suggests that solitude is necessary for thought and that there is even something about the incessant sociality of modern culture that drowns out our capacity to think. Moreover, even if the thinker converses with herself—even if she refers to herself as a "we" (and I admit that I would be worried if I suddenly started doing this)—surely this is not the same thing as sociality in the usual intersubjective sense. More generally speaking, even if it is true, as Butler claims, that "sociality precedes and enables what is called thinking," I am not certain that sociality constitutes the crux of thinking; in other words, the fact that thinking, like speaking, draws on language that is socially generated does not necessarily mean that, as Butler asserts, "sociality becomes an animating trace in any and all thinking any one of us might do" (*PW* 173). Or, more precisely, this is such an abstract, all-encompassing definition of "sociality" that the concept loses all meaningfulness; according to this classification, absolutely everything about human life is social. This of course is Butler's point when she maintains that solitariness is, in the final analysis, "a social relation" (*PW* 173).

It feels to me that Butler is here theorizing away an important distinction between solitude and sociality. In Chapter 2, I criticized Butler's tendency to confuse our social ontology—the fact that we owe our existence to others—with the idea that we are responsible for each and every other regardless of how this other treats us. Something similar is going on in the present context in the sense that Butler's analysis of primary sociality makes it impossible for her to acknowledge the value of more asocial frequencies of life, such as solitude. As a matter of fact, while I, generally speaking, appreciate Butler's relational model, there are times—this being a perfect example—when she lapses into the kind of fetishization of sociality that demonizes all solitary endeavors, all attempts to find an enclave of calm outside the social, as if these somehow eroded our basic humanity. What exactly is wrong with solitude—or even with asociality? And is Butler not overreaching here to produce an effect of primary sociality that is more Levinasian than Arendtian? Butler is, as it were, trying to force the private into the public realm even though Arendt was notoriously averse to the overproximity of others that often characterizes public life. This overproximity, for Arendt, was one of the causes of totalitarianism, of the tendency of the undifferentiated social mass to cancel out critical thought, which is precisely why Arendt sought to protect the privacy of thought against the totalitarian elements of sociality. That Butler is unwilling to acknowledge this central component of Arendt's philosophy is an indication of what happens when autonomy—and related concepts such as solitude—becomes unthinkable. Or, to state the matter slightly differently, given how strongly Butler's earlier work focused on the hegemonic aspects of sociality, it is difficult to understand why sociality is now, for her, such an unmitigated good. What has happened to Butler's capacity to see the violent, hurtful, and banal aspects of sociality?

But perhaps we are not dealing with a blindness to the brutality of sociality but with a bifurcation of the concept of sociality. It seems that, for Butler, the sociality of the collective symbolic order (the big Other) is hegemonic and ruthless but the sociality of what she calls "the plurality" is invariably beyond reproach. But this merely highlights the failings of categorical either-or types of thinking, for it is possible to argue, as I did in Chapter 4, that the symbolic, while certainly being hegemonic, also enables us in various ways—for instance by granting us access to a language that allows us to communicate with others. Conversely, there are times when the so-called "plural" is hugely oppressive and wounding; there are instances where "community," even a "pluralistic" one, is just about the most violent entity conceivable. Furthermore, it seems to me that "plurality," for Arendt, was a matter of the equality of singular individuals rather than of the kind of primary sociality that Levinas explores. Butler writes, attacking Arendt's more "individualistic" tendencies: "I think the recourse to the sovereign mind, its faculty of judgment, its individual exercise of freedom, is in some quite strong tension with the idea of cohabitation that seems to follow . . . [from Arendt's] explicit reflections on plurality" (*PW* 177). But I would say that there is no tension, no contradiction, because, for Arendt, plurality is composed of quasi-sovereign individuals who possess the capacity for critical thought rather than of people whose autonomy and freedom have been completely conjured away by their social ontology.

More generally speaking, Butler's critique of Arendt illustrates the tendency of her relational model to congeal into a rigid definition of the human. As much as Butler tries to argue that, say, Habermasian discourse ethics is too close to Enlightenment assumptions about human ontology, such as the primacy of reason, her own relational model relies on an even more robust definition of ontology—one that literally excludes from the realm of the human everything that is not appropriately social. If Kantian-Arendtian cosmopolitanism suggests that everyone has the right to have basic rights on the basis of their membership in the global community, Butler seems to assume that human beings have the right to have such rights *because of their specific (social, relational, and vulnerable) ontology*. This is precisely why—as I argued in Chapter 2—I am not convinced by her assertion that, unlike Lacan, she makes no assumptions about "fundamental structures of being," for what actually happens is that she excludes the "asocial" Lacanian real from her definition of the human because her relational ontology, *her* theory of "fundamental structures of being," cannot accommodate anything that is not thoroughly social; she merely supplants an account of "being" that allows for bits of asociality (the real) by one that does not. From this viewpoint, one could even argue that Butler's response to the loss of metaphysical underpinnings for our ethical principles takes a form that is much more reliant on ontological assumptions than, for instance, Benhabib's "interactive universalism"; that is, one could argue that Butler posits a more fixed foundation for ethics than the Habermasian ideal of participatory parity, which—at least in its feminist formulation—allows for a diversity of communicative styles.

8

Nor am I reassured by the fact that Butler's resistance to Enlightenment rationalism seems to have ushered her into the folds of religious irrationalism. There is no need here to revisit the arguments I made in Chapter 3, but it is worth pointing out that one of the main conceptual tensions of *Parting Ways* is that even though Butler endorses the rights-based discourse of secular, postnational cosmopolitanism—and even though she accuses Israel of religious nationalism—she simultaneously turns to theology as a theoretical resource. In part this can be explained by the distinction she draws between the theocratic state of Israel (bad) and the Jewish intellectual heritage (good). When it comes to opposing the former, secularism (even classical liberalism) is needed; but when it comes to the latter, secularism is largely irrelevant. This division may have some intellectual viability. Nor do I deny that religion can be a fascinating topic of study, particularly in relation to the complex ways by which it has historically shaped cultural life around the world. But Butler's turn to religion goes further than this: in contexts other than Israel, she seems eager to carve out a space for religion within the political sphere in ways that directly contradict her statements about Israel's theocratic tyranny. As a matter of fact, she seems quite willing to overlook the oppressive legacies of monotheistic religions in order to join the powerful chorus of Western intellectuals who have recently been calling for a more prominent place for religion in public life.

This call has some understandable causes, such as anxieties about being branded Islamophobic. As I acknowledged in Chapter 1, in the context of the current global environment, which pits Western "enlightened" secularism against "irrational" Islam, anyone who comes down on the side of secularism may seem to automatically be anti-Islam. Furthermore, if one believes—as Butler does—that Western secularism is merely a version of Christianity, then the very distinction between (enlightened) secularism and (irrational) religion is designed to privilege Christianity. Add to this fears about coming across as elitist—of straying too far from the religious concerns of "common folk"—and one can see why progressive critics are suddenly bending over backward to apologize for their (former) secular ways. But if this is the way we are going, perhaps we should also attempt to resuscitate patriarchy, given that it—rather than feminism—tends to be the way of the "common folk."

Ironically, it is Cornel West—a far more overtly religious thinker than Butler—who reminds us that "the dominant forms of religion are well-adjusted to greed and fear and bigotry. Hence well-adjusted to the indifference of the status quo toward poor and working people."[28] West, a bit like Levinas and Benjamin, finds in prophetic religion—the kind of religion that mobilizes people to fight injustice—an antidote to such greed, fear, and bigotry. This makes some sense to me. But what does not is that now that poststructuralism is behind us, religion seems to be the new academic religion of progressive thinkers such as Butler. Consider the following statement she makes regarding Derrida:

> One might discern in Derrida's idea of "dissemination" a certain *revenant* of messianic scattering. It is perhaps an instance of a religious term that translates into a textual meaning (and which, of course, always had something of a textual meaning), questions the possibility of return to hypothetical origins, and whose implicit signification of a kabbalistic scattering of divine light makes sense of Derrida's own move from dissemination in the early works to the messianic in the later works. (*PW* 13)

Are we to believe that even deconstruction has religious origins? Butler goes on to assure us that this is not what she means, but it is hard to fathom how her statement could result in any other conclusion. Another telling moment in Butler's argument comes when she claims, in relation to Said, that "although Said himself was a defender of secular ideals, he nevertheless understood the kind of convergence of histories and the proximities of exile that might make for a new ethos and politics" (PW 16). *Although? Nevertheless?* Since when have secular thinkers not been able to understand exile? Are we to believe that Said performed a superhuman feat of intellectual exertion in being able to theorize exile *despite* not being a religious thinker? Finally, consider Butler's chilling dismissal of Arendt's secularism: "Her secularism could only be understood in relation to the specific religiosity [Judaism] she rejected. In other words, her way of inhabiting Judaism was through her secularism" (PW 35). This statement implies that "genuine" secularism is impossible, that, again, secularism is merely religiosity (here, Judaism) by another name. Religion has become the origin of origins: the foundation that cannot be eluded even if it can be denounced.

Along similar lines, Butler takes issue with Étienne Balibar, who defends secularism by noting that cross-cultural processes of hybridization—that is, processes that transcend specific social and religious contexts—"form the material conditions for the development of translation processes among distant cultural universes."[29] Butler counters Balibar's view by stating that "if we refuse to sanctify the moment of translation as purely secular (and secularism does have its modes of self-sanctification), then it follows that religious significations are continued, disseminated, and transmuted on the occasion of translation" (PW 17). "If translation has a theological history," Butler asks, "does that theological history simply fall away when translation is positioned as the neutral arbiter of religious views? Indeed, what if translation is itself a religious value?" (PW 16). So now even translation is *intrinsically* religious? I suppose you can turn anything into a remnant of religion if you really try, but why would you want to? It seems to me that it would be equally possible to propose that absolutely everything about monotheistic religion derives from—represents a continuation, dissemination, and transmutation of—premonotheistic traditions. For instance, it would be possible to argue that Christianity resulted from the conversion of ancient Greek polytheistic mythologies, along with other pre-Christian sources, into the language of monotheism. Where one draws the line is an ideological, political decision rather than some sort of a God-given fact.

What is disturbing here is not so much Butler's appreciation for religion but the crowding out of the secular that accompanies her revival of religious themes. Suddenly there is no breathing space outside of religion—something that is a little difficult for an atheist such as myself to process. The implication is that my secularism is an elaborate ruse or self-deception. If in Butler's earlier theories, there was no outside of power, now there is no outside of religion. Either way, there is a love of subjection, but with the replacement of power by religion comes the strange notion that there is something laudatory about this subjection. Even though Butler has spent years criticizing Lacan's concept of the Law of the Father, she now seems to have no problem with God the Father. I admit that this is when Kant starts sounding like my best friend. Indeed, what I see happening in Butler's discourse is something that happens frequently in contemporary theory: in its eagerness to formulate the latest critical paradigm— to reach the ever-so-coveted radical edge I mentioned above—this theory tends to vilify the entity which immediately precedes the new paradigm *even when the entity in question is much less hegemonic than the one it once replaced.* In the present instance, because secularism is what immediately preceded the current moment of postsecularism, progressive critics are falling over each other to prove that it was a tremendous evil, perhaps even a bigger evil than the religious authority that it replaced. Yet from, say, a secular feminist perspective—which, I concede, is not the only valid feminist perspective—this seems like a hugely conservative curveball thrown into an otherwise progressive game. Again, by this I do not mean to suggest that there is no space for religion in intellectual analysis, even in progressive theory. But—and I suppose this has been my complaint throughout this book—I find the either-or logic which dictates that now that religion is "in," secularism has to be "out," fundamentally flawed. I am willing to entertain the (somewhat strained) idea that God the Father could be turned into a progressive trope. But I am not prepared to give up the advances represented by secularism— including the fact that I, as a woman, am free to have sex outside of matrimony—in order to venerate this trope.

9

When I started writing this book, I did not know that I would end up defending aspects of Enlightenment secularism, let alone *a priori* normative limits. My background in progressive critical theory predisposed me to be much more interested in antinormative critiques aimed at unearthing the covert functioning of disciplinary power. Completing this book certainly has not erased this interest. But the more I thought about ethics, the more convinced I became that the categorical rejection of *a priori* norms—even of the type of "historical a priori" that Allen advocates—that characterizes the postmetaphysical approaches I have analyzed is not only theoretically untenable but also practically unbearable. In this conviction, I found an unexpected ally in Žižek who, in the closing pages of *Less Than Nothing*, seems to gesture toward something similar when he admits—thereby notably deviating from his usual critical stance regarding human rights—that even though we must acknowledge that human rights discourses privilege Western individualistic values, we should not make the mistake of thinking that they are "*directly and only* capitalist ideological masks for domination and exploitation."[30] Indeed, Žižek asserts that this mistake would be even "more dangerous" (*LN* 1005) than the opposite one of accepting human rights as an instance of value-free universality. This is because, Žižek continues, "formal freedom"— which human rights, like other rights-based systems of justice, presumably aspire toward (even if they always fall short of this goal)—"is *the only form of appearance (or potential site) of actual freedom.*" In other words, freedom cannot become actual without the envelope of formal freedom, which is why Žižek concludes that "if one prematurely abolishes 'formal' freedom, one loses also (the potential of) actual freedom" (*LN* 1006).

These statements are somewhat difficult to reconcile with Žižek's overall Marxist-Lacanian stance—a stance that valorizes the radical negativity of the ethical act that I analyzed in the previous chapter. Yet they are compatible with Žižek's anti-Levinasian defense of the "coldness of justice" that we encountered in Chapter 2. Realizing this, and considering the arguments I have made in this book, I am forced to admit that the conceptual sliding I perceive in Žižek between the negativity of the ethical act and the impartial coldness of justice (or "formal freedom") is not very different from my own vacillation between the Lacanian act (Chapter 4) and cosmopolitan human rights (this chapter). It in fact seems obvious that both of these approaches—revolutionary and rights-based—are necessary for our capacity to think about ethics in the global arena. This is why I have stressed in my commentary on Butler that I am not bothered by the sudden resurgence of liberal values in her theory but merely by her unwillingness to own up to this resurgence. Žižek does not have much trouble avowing his more Kantian moments. Butler, in contrast, falls into the category of progressive thinkers who, as Žižek puts it, "improvise endlessly on the motif of impossible universality" (*LN* 831) at the same time as she, whenever this serves her purposes, falls back on this very universality. It is this aspect of her work that ruffles me.

Undoubtedly *a priori* norms are often problematic, as is obvious from the painful histories of oppression, exclusion, and marginalization that have accompanied them. But they have also been essential for overcoming such histories, for gaining the kinds of "rights" that have had far-reaching economic, cultural, symbolic, and ideological repercussions. This is why it seems injudicious to reject them across the board. Furthermore, I am not even certain that the rejection of *a priori* norms necessarily decenters the self in quite the way that Butler, among many others, appears to assume. Butler privileges Levinasian relational ethics over Kantian, Habermasian, and other Enlightenment-inspired approaches in part because the latter's respect for *a priori* norms, in her opinion, leads back to the rationalist, autonomous humanist subject, or at the very least to its contemporary avatar: the neoliberal capitalist subject. Yet arguably the effect of *a priori* norms is to render the subject secondary (rather than autonomous): the subject is expected to obey such norms regardless of its self-serving interests. The Kantian categorical imperative, for instance, starts from the premise that how the subject feels—whether it, for example, regards a given norm as a threat to its capacity to experience pleasure—is completely irrelevant to ethical deliberation. We all know that separating feeling from ethics is a tall order. But the relevant point here is that, from the Kantian perspective, the rejection of *a priori* norms comes across as too convenient, even self-centered and narcissistic, which is why it could easily be interpreted as a *symptom* of the very neoliberal capitalism that critics such as Butler denounce.

The self-absorbed neoliberal individual, who is used to an endless array of existential possibilities, and who does not like limitations on her freedom—including her freedom to buy everything that a decent department store makes available—may be perfectly happy with the idea that she should not be beholden to norms that might in some way thwart her ability to move about the world without restriction. From this viewpoint, one could argue that *a priori* norms war *against* the neoliberal capitalist ethos of unmitigated choice, that they, in a certain sense, "interrupt" the neoliberal subject (and its projects of self-actualization) just as effectively as the Levinasian-Butlerian other does by introducing within its being "alien" elements (norms) that it experiences as constraining. This is one reason I believe that *a priori* norms are not a completely preposterous alternative to the relativism that nibbles at the edges of contemporary progressive ethics and that, ironically enough, carries its own violence.

Let me add a final insight about *a priori* norms that may disrupt our usual lines of ideological allegiance, namely that Žižek's conceptualization of the Lacanian ethical act may tell us something useful about how to keep Allen's "historical a priori" from solidifying into an oppressive status quo. To grasp what I mean, it is necessary to understand a major distinction between Badiou's account of the truth-event on the hand and Žižek's account of the act on the other. As we have seen, the event and the act both reveal (are supposed to reveal) a "truth" of some kind. But the ontological status of this "truth" is quite different for these two thinkers: if the event, for Badiou, reveals a truth that can be named and incorporated into the new social order that (potentially, through the subject's fidelity to the event) emerges from the ashes of the event, Žižek insists that the truth that arises from the subject's act of negativity has no positive status but, rather, signifies the ultimate failure of meaning as such. That is, while Badiou views the void of the event as containing some sort of legitimate meaning, Žižek views it in a more strictly Lacanian vein, as the "real" of the situation, as an insurmountable impediment to the legitimatization of meaning. This is why Žižek consistently accuses Badiou of downplaying the negative, destructive force of the event: "This, then, is the ultimate difference between Badiou and Lacan: Badiou's starting point is an affirmative project and the fidelity to it; while, for Lacan, the primordial fact is that of negativity (ontologically, the impossibility of the One being One)" (*LN* 836). For Žižek, "naming" the event, as Badiou strives to do, merely establishes a new hegemony—one that seeks to suppress the disruptive force of negativity percolating beneath every social order (as it also percolates beneath every "coherent" subjectivity).

What can we make of this difference? Though Žižek would be unlikely to agree with Allen's broadly Habermasian approach, his

insistence that the negativity of the event should not be translated
into the positivity of meaning implies that negativity—understood
here as a space of irresolvable antagonism—creates an opening
within which the ongoing negotiation of *a priori* principles might
become possible; it offers one way to understand how the historical
a priori might remain genuinely historical—open to modification—
rather than solidifying into a static normative order. The difference
from Badiou may seem minimal, but it is important. If Badiou's
ethics is linked to naming the void that the event discloses, and
if this naming—as Žižek maintains—generates a new hegemony,
then the fact that some people might find it difficult to participate
in the process of naming the void results, as I argued above, in
their exclusion from the emerging ethical vision. In contrast, Žižek's
model, which refuses to name the void but rather sees it as what will
prevent any social order from attaining full legitimacy, allows for
continuous contestation over what the rules of the game, including
its ethical norms, should be; negativity as a site of pure antagonism
supports the kind of process of meaning production that never finds
a resting place but, instead, ceaselessly flows into new modalities
of making sense of the world. This, in turn, implies that new actors
may over time enter the stage—that no one is irrevocably excluded.
This does not mean that there are no *a priori* principles but merely
that such principles are being repeatedly reworked. The question of
how to sustain this type of antagonism over time is, of course, one
of the major challenges—perhaps *the* challenge—of democracy:
a task at which most existing democracies fail miserably. Because
antagonism of this kind cannot be divorced from volatility and
social disorder, most democracies seek to curtail it. But they can
only do so at the cost of true democracy.

10

I have demonstrated that the Levinasian and Lacanian ethical
approaches analyzed in this book are all preoccupied with the
other. This is hardly surprising, given that, for both Levinas and
Lacan, the other is constitutive of subjectivity, so that we are
not merely talking about how one subject relates to another but
about how the other is always already integrated into the very
ontological texture of the subject. In Lacan, there is no symbolic

subjectivity—no socially viable subject—that is not riven by
the Other (or by the multiple others that represent the Other).
In Levinas, likewise, the other is primary. The major difference,
as I have shown, is that Lacan is principally interested in how
the subject might be able to take a degree of critical distance
from the Other/other, whereas Levinas is interested in how the
subject can honor its debt to the other. That is, the Lacanian
Other/other tends to be hegemonic (even if it is also in some ways
enabling)—and therefore something to be resisted—whereas the
Levinasian other is elevated to such sacred heights that he or she
is inviolable. What I have come to realize in the course of writing
this book is that between these extremes there is a complex ethical
landscape that calls for a more nuanced arbitration, where it is not
sufficient to define the other as either primarily hegemonic or fully
sacrosanct. Levinas viewed this landscape as the responsibility of
justice rather than of ethics but, as I have attempted to illustrate,
I am not sure that this is a meaningful distinction. Does justice not
call for ethical deliberation? Does ethics not often entail decisions
about justice—decisions based on *a priori* principles?

It seems to me that our efforts to devise ethical paradigms that
exclude *a priori* norms (principles of justice) are intrinsically illusory
in the sense that such norms always—however discreetly—operate
in the background of ethics. For instance, Levinasian ethics, despite
its rejection of metaphysical principles, relies on religious principles
that are equally binding. Lacanian ethics, in turn, runs the risk of
turning antinormativity into a new norm. In this sense, the attempt
to disavow *a priori* norms merely ensures that hidden normative
assumptions make their way into our ethics without our being able
to acknowledge that this is the case, with the result that our so-called
nonnormative ethics is scarcely less normative than normative ethics;
its normativity merely takes different, less obvious, forms.

Thinking over the main interventions of this book, I guess
I would like Butler to admit that her ethics of precarity gestures
toward universalism. And I would like Badiou (and Žižek at those
moments when he aligns himself with Badiou's view that every
singularity should be able to directly participate in the universal) to
admit that his version of universalism can easily slide into a form of
particularism—a particularism that repeats many of the historical
failings of traditional Western universalism, including its equation
of the universal with straight white masculinity. In other words,

I think that, despite Butler's rejection of the label of universalism, her ethics is much more genuinely universal than the more overtly universalist paradigm of Badiou; as critical as I have been of Butler, I recognize that her relational ontology offers a powerful means to rethink ethical accountability in the global context. At the same time, her denigration of autonomy, as well as her suggestion that I should try to forgive those who harm me, leads her to masochistic extremes I cannot comfortably endorse. During my more skeptical moments, I suspect that such masochism is indicative of the guilt that many progressive Western academics feel in relation to the rest of the world; on some level, it is an attempt to become the "good" Western subject who knows what it means to suffer (and who is willing to suffer for the other).

I want to be careful here. I am not saying that Western subjects do not have good reasons to feel guilty about the global state of power imbalances—for obviously we do. But I think that rhetorical practices of self-flagellation are unlikely to help in any way, that—quite the contrary—they might actually impede our capacity to work toward global justice. As I suggested in Chapter 2, feeling bad can become an excuse for not doing a whole lot; or, more precisely, feeling bad can make us feel that we are doing something when in reality we are not (in this way, feeling, as it were, becomes our preferred way of "doing"). This explains why I tend to be apprehensive of the current trend in Western theory to turn "bad" feelings, such as despair, suffering, abjection, melancholia, and depression, into the "good" ("proper") feelings that we are supposed to experience as proof of our (ever-so-precarious) humanity. I have myself participated in this trend and certainly see the value of paying attention to the kinds of difficult feelings that have historically caused excruciating shame to some populations. For example, I am hugely appreciative of the efforts of critics such as Sara Ahmed, Lauren Berlant, Ann Cvetkovich, David Eng, and Heather Love to explore the queer theoretical archive of bad feelings I referred to in the previous chapter.[31] However, there is an important difference, in my mind, between such efforts—which focus on the historically specific agonies of marginalized individuals—and Butler's more comprehensive efforts to cast ethical subjectivity *as such* as a matter of a masochistic flight from autonomy. There is no doubt that I am drawn to *a priori* ethical norms in part because I want to believe that I have—to a degree at least—the semiautonomous capacity to make ethical choices and that, conversely, I can expect others to have a similar capacity so that when they mistreat me, I can hold them responsible rather than offer them my unqualified forbearance. That is, *a priori* norms make it impossible for both me and others to pretend that we do not understand the consequences of our actions; they make it impossible for us to hide beneath the cloak of relativistic impotence.

In this final chapter, I have drawn on Habermasian feminists because they seem capable of filling a major gap in the Levinasian and Lacanian models, namely the possibility of normative limits that are not metaphysically founded. That is, I have sought to illustrate that feminists such as Benhabib, Fraser, and Allen discredit the assumption that the Habermasian approach has nothing to offer to more radical theories, such as poststructuralist and Marxist ones. As a matter of fact, they even deconstruct the idea that what distinguishes Marxist and other progressive paradigms from the Habermasian one is the former's greater emphasis on economic justice, for Fraser and Allen are deeply invested in redistributive justice, and even Benhabib, as we have seen, condemns unbridled capitalist expansion. Add to this that even liberal advocates of globalization, such as Michael Held, are, these days, calling for greater economic parity,[32] and it appears that there is a loose consensus, among academics from vastly different intellectual traditions, that global capitalism is a monster of such gargantuan proportions that if we are to have a fighting chance of alleviating any of the world's problems, from hunger, poverty, forced migration, and ecological damage to ethnic and religious violence, this is the place to start. Žižek may be screaming from the top of his lungs that we have all given up on the class struggle. But my impression from surveying the literature is that everyone is so upset at global capitalism that even the liberals are sounding a little Marxist. This, to me, seems like an excellent starting point for a productive dialogue across critical approaches that are usually viewed as being mutually incompatible; it seems like an opening to intellectual exchanges that could potentially enrich the conceptual resources of everyone concerned.

NOTES

Preface

1 Judith Butler, Ernesto Laclau, and Slavoj Žižek, *Contingency, Hegemony, Universality: Contemporary Dialogues on the Left* (London: Verso, 2000).

2 Both poststructuralism and multiculturalism presuppose relativism to such an extent that the matter is not always explicitly stated. However, it tends to surface forcefully in instances, such as the debate about gender equality on the global scale, where cultural and religious customs clash with universalizing human rights discourses. For a recent influential analysis, see Saba Mahmood, *Politics of Piety: The Islamic Revival and the Feminist Subject* (Princeton: Princeton University Press, 2005). Within philosophy departments, debates about relativism and universalism, contextualism and context transcendence, tend to be articulated more formally than they are in the kind of progressive (posthumanist) theory that I will be focusing on in this book. For an effective overview of such philosophical debates, see Amy Allen, *The End of Progress: Critical Theory in Postcolonial Times* (New York: Columbia University Press, in press).

3 I should specify that my discomfort with this—which in part arises from purely personal considerations—started with Butler's *The Psychic Life of Power: Theories in Subjection* (Stanford: Stanford University Press, 1997). I did not have the same reaction to Butler's early work on feminism and queer theory, which still had a strongly agentic tone. On the latter, see *Gender Trouble: Feminism and the Subversion of Identity* (New York: Routledge, 1990) and *Bodies That Matter: On the Discursive Limits of "Sex"* (New York: Routledge, 1993).

4 In Chapter 4, we will see that Žižek does sometimes acknowledge the importance of *a priori* norms. Lacan's own position on the matter is also somewhat ambiguous.

5 Wendy Brown, *Edgework: Critical Essays on Knowledge and Politics* (Princeton: Princeton University Press, 2005), 80. Hereafter cited in the text as *EW*.

Chapter 1

1 Emmanuel Levinas, *Entre Nous: Thinking-of-the-Other*, trans. Michael B. Smith and Barbara Harshav (New York: Columbia University Press, 1998), 202. Hereafter cited in the text as *EN*.

2 See Luce Irigaray, *To Be Two*, trans. Monique M. Rhodes and Marco F. Cocito-Monoc (New York: Routledge, 2001); Jacques Derrida, *The Politics of Friendship*, trans. George Collins (New York: Verso, 2005); and Eric L. Santner, *On Creaturely Life: Rilke, Benjamin, Sebald* (Chicago: University of Chicago Press, 2006).

3 Emmanuel Levinas, *Difficult Freedom: Essays on Judaism*, trans. Seán Hand (Baltimore: Johns Hopkins University Press, 1990), 8. Hereafter cited in the text as *DF*.

4 Emmanuel Levinas, *Totality and Infinity: An Essay on Exteriority*, trans. Alphonso Lingis (Pittsburgh: Duquesne University Press, 1969), 194; 203. Hereafter cited in the text as *TI*.

5 Judith Butler, *Frames of War: When Is Life Grievable?* (New York: Verso, 2010), 170.

6 Julia Kristeva, *Hatred and Forgiveness*, trans. Jeanine Herman (New York: Columbia University Press, 2010), 28; 42. Hereafter cited in the text as *HF*.

7 Julia Kristeva, *This Incredible Need to Believe*, trans. Beverley Bie Brahic (New York: Columbia University Press, 2009), 29. Hereafter cited in the text as *NB*.

8 Carl Schmitt, *Political Theology: Four Chapters on the Concept of Sovereignty*, trans. George Schwab (Chicago: University of Chicago Press, 2005), 36.

9 Giorgio Agamben, *The Kingdom and the Glory: For a Theological Genealogy of Economy and Government*, trans. Lorenzo Chiesa (Stanford: Stanford University Press, 2011).

10 Judith Butler, "Is Judaism Zionism?," *The Power of Religion in the Public Sphere*, by Judith Butler, Jürgen Habermas, Charles Taylor, and Cornel West (New York: Columbia University Press, 2011), 71. Hereafter cited in the text as "JZ."

11 Kristeva offers a complex psychoanalytic explanation for the need to believe in higher ideals, tracing it back to Freud's "oceanic feeling," the imaginary father of prehistory, and the primordial loss of the Thing (*das Ding*).

12 Jasbir Puar, *Terrorist Assemblages: Homonationalism in Queer Times* (Durham: Duke University Press, 2007).

13 Quoted in Judith Butler, *Giving an Account of Oneself* (New York: Fordham University Press, 2005), 88–9.

14 Judith Butler, *Precarious Life: The Powers of Mourning and Violence* (New York: Verso, 2004), 140.

15 Slavoj Žižek, "Neighbors and Other Monsters: A Plea for Ethical Violence," *The Neighbor: Three Inquiries in Political Theology*, by Slavoj Žižek, Eric L. Santner, and Kenneth Reinhard (Chicago: University of Chicago Press, 2005), 160.

16 See, for instance, *The Summons of Love* (New York: Columbia University Press, 2011).

17 Besides the aforementioned texts by Kristeva, see Alenka Zupančič, *The Shortest Shadow: Nietzsche's Philosophy of the Two* (Cambridge, MA: MIT Press, 2003) and José Esteban Muñoz, *Cruising Utopia: The Then and There of Queer Futurity* (New York: New York University Press, 2010). See also my discussion of Zupančič in *The Singularity of Being: Lacan and the Immortal Within* (New York: Fordham University Press, 2012).

18 Jacques Derrida, *On Cosmopolitanism and Forgiveness*, trans. Mark Dooley and Michael Hughes (New York: Routledge, 2001), 31–2. Hereafter cited in the text as *CF*.

19 In this context, Derrida adds that the ideal of forgiving the unforgivable "must announce itself as impossibility itself" (*CF* 33). It represents "a madness of the impossible" (*CF* 45), an act that plunges "into the night of the unintelligible" (*CF* 49), at the same time as it contributes to the evolution of justice in the sense that it, like Levinasian ethics, inspires justice to become more just.

Chapter 2

1 Judith Butler, *Frames of War: When Is Life Grievable?* (New York: Verso, 2009), 2. Hereafter cited in the text as *FW*.

2 Judith Butler, *Precarious Life: The Powers of Mourning and Violence* (New York: Verso, 2004), 45. Hereafter cited in the text as *PL*.

3 Judith Butler, *Parting Ways: Jewishness and the Critique of Zionism* (New York: Columbia University Press, 2012), 6. Hereafter cited in the text as *PW*.

4 Judith Butler, *Giving an Account of Oneself* (New York: Fordham University Press, 2005), 100. Hereafter cited in the text as *GA*.

5   Consider, for example, Lee Edelman's argument in *No Future: Queer Theory and the Death Drive* (Durham: Duke University Press, 2004).

6   Wendy Brown, *Regulating Aversion: Tolerance in the Age of Identity and Empire* (Princeton: Princeton University Press, 2006).

7   Frantz Fanon, *The Wretched of the Earth*, trans. Constance Farrington (London: Penguin, 1961).

8   See Jessica Benjamin's *Like Subjects, Love Objects: Essays on Recognition and Sexual Difference* (New Haven: Yale University Press, 1995) and *Shadow of the Other: Intersubjectivity and Gender in Psychoanalysis* (New York: Routledge, 1998).

9   I am thinking of Butler's earlier theories of subjectivity as a form of social subjection. See, for instance, *The Psychic Life of Power: Theories in Subjection* (Stanford: Stanford University Press, 1997).

10 I develop this argument in greater detail in *The Call of Character* (New York: Columbia University Press, 2013).

11 Amy Allen, *The Politics of Our Selves: Power, Autonomy, and Gender in Contemporary Critical Theory* (New York: Columbia University Press, 2008), 35.

12 Hannah Arendt, *Eichmann in Jerusalem: A Report on the Banality of Evil* (New York: Penguin, 1994).

13 Jacques Derrida, *Specters of Marx: The State of the Debt, the Work of Mourning, and the New International*, trans. Peggy Kamuf (New York: Routledge, 2006), 74.

14 Along similar lines, Butler argues that it is because one historical trauma resonates with another, because "vocabularies articulated to relay one set of traumatic events enable the articulation of another," that it might become possible to "awake to a present that would learn from the Holocaust the necessity of opposing fascism, racism, state violence, and forcible detention" (*PW* 200). This would be a new way "*never* to forget, because it would not install the past as the present, but rather consult the past in order to conduct the comparative and reflective work that would allow us to derive principles of human conduct that would make good on the promise not to reiterate in any way the crimes of that historical time" (*PW* 201).

15 Seyla Benhabib, *The Claims of Culture: Equality and Diversity in the Global Era* (Princeton: Princeton University Press, 2002), 123.

16 Along related lines, Butler writes at the beginning of *Parting Ways*, "There are not only significant differences among Jews—secular, religious, historically constituted—but also active struggles within that community about the meaning of justice, equality, and the

critique of state violence and colonial subjugation" (2). If this were not the case, any critique of Israeli state violence would automatically be anti-Semitic, which is exactly the point of view Butler wants to oppose, given that her aim is to offer a *Jewish* critique of this violence.

17 Slavoj Žižek, "Holding the Place," *Contingency, Hegemony, Universality: Contemporary Dialogues on the Left*, by Judith Butler, Ernesto Laclau, and Slavoj Žižek (London: Verso, 2000), 310.

Chapter 3

1 Slavoj Žižek, "Neighbors and Other Monsters: A Plea for Ethical Violence," *The Neighbor: Three Inquiries in Political Theology*, by Slavoj Žižek, Eric L. Santner, and Kenneth Reinhard (Chicago: University of Chicago Press, 2005), 137. Hereafter cited in the text as *N*.

2 Alain Badiou, *Ethics: An Essay on the Understanding of Evil*, trans. Peter Hallward (London: Verso, 2001), 20. Hereafter cited in the text as *E*.

3 Note, for instance, that none of the most path-breaking thinkers in postcolonial studies—from Homi Bhabha to Edward Said to Gayatri Spivak—could possibly be accused of promoting an "identitarian" agenda. Likewise, prominent critics in ethnic studies, such as David Eng, Roderick Ferguson, and Paul Gilroy, have staged sustained critiques of identitarian agendas (without, at the same time, denying that identity categories continue to matter in the context of institutionalized forms of social inequality).

4 More specifically, Žižek argues that the other as *das Ding* (the Thing) exudes the kind of excess jouissance that challenges the subject's imaginary supports and precludes the possibility of symmetrical intersubjective dialogue. As Žižek states, "The neighbor (*Nebenmensch*) as the Thing means that, beneath the neighbor as my *semblant*, my mirror image, there always lurks the unfathomable abyss of radical Otherness, of a monstrous Thing that cannot be 'gentrified'" (*N* 143).

5 As Levinas puts it, "It is this presence for me of a being identical to itself that I call the presence of the face" (*Entre Nous: Thinking-of-the-Other*, trans. Michael B. Smith and Barbara Harshav [New York: Columbia University Press, 1998], 33; hereafter cited in the text as *EN*).

6 The classic text on this topic is Ernesto Laclau and Chantal Mouffe, *Hegemony and Socialist Strategy: Towards a Radical Democratic Politics* (London: Verso, 1985).

7 Michael Hardt and Antonio Negri, *Commonwealth* (Cambridge, MA: Harvard University Press, 2009).

8 Leo Bersani and Adam Phillips, *Intimacies* (Chicago: University of Chicago Press, 2008), 86.

9 Alain Badiou and Slavoj Žižek, *Philosophy in the Present*, trans. Peter Thomas and Alberto Toscano (Cambridge, UK: Polity Press, 2009), 72. Hereafter cited in the text as *PP*.

10 Slavoj Žižek, "Da Capo senza Fine," *Contingency, Hegemony, Universality: Contemporary Dialogues on the Left*, by Judith Butler, Ernesto Laclau, and Slavoj Žižek (London: Verso, 2000), 239. Hereafter cited in the text as "DC."

11 Žižek, for instance, argues that the "postmodern political series class-gender-race" overlooks the fact that, unlike the "particular struggles" of gender and race, class functions as the structuring principle of the social order as such ("Class Struggle or Postmodernism?," *Contingency, Hegemony, Universality: Contemporary Dialogues on the Left*, by Judith Butler, Ernesto Laclau, and Slavoj Žižek [London: Verso, 2000], 96; hereafter cited in the text as "CS").

12 Ernesto Laclau, "Structure, History and the Political," *Contingency, Hegemony, Universality: Contemporary Dialogues on the Left*, by Judith Butler, Ernesto Laclau, and Slavoj Žižek (London: Verso, 2000), 203. Hereafter cited in the text as "SHP."

13 See, for instance, Tim Dean, *Unlimited Intimacy: Reflections on the Subculture of Barebacking* (Chicago: University of Chicago Press, 2009); Lee Edelman, *No Future: Queer Theory and the Death Drive* (Durham: Duke University Press, 2004); David Eng, *The Feeling of Kinship: Queer Liberalism and the Racialization of Intimacy* (Durham: Duke University Press, 2010); Judith Halberstam, *The Queer Art of Failure* (Durham: Duke University Press, 2011); Lynne Huffer, *Mad for Foucault: Rethinking the Foundations of Queer Theory* (New York: Columbia University Press, 2010); Heather Love, *Feeling Backward: Loss and the Politics of Queer History* (Cambridge, MA: Harvard University Press, 2007); José Esteban Muñoz, *Cruising Utopia: The Then and There of Queer Futurity* (New York: New York University Press, 2010); Jasbir Puar, *Terrorist Assemblages: Homonationalism in Queer Times* (Durham: Duke University Press, 2007); and Michael Warner, *The Trouble with Normal: Sex, Politics, and the Ethics of a Queer Life* (New York: Free Press, 1999). I will return to some of these critics in Chapter 4.

14 Nancy Fraser, *Scales of Justice: Reimagining Political Space in a Globalizing World* (New York: Columbia University Press, 2010), 58. Hereafter cited in the text as *SJ*.

15 Ernesto Laclau, "Constructing Universality," *Contingency, Hegemony, Universality: Contemporary Dialogues on the Left*, by Judith Butler, Ernesto Laclau, and Slavoj Žižek (London: Verso, 2000), 290. Hereafter cited in the text as "CU."

16 Slavoj Žižek, "Holding the Place," *Contingency, Hegemony, Universality: Contemporary Dialogues on the Left*, by Judith Butler, Ernesto Laclau, and Slavoj Žižek (London: Verso, 2000), 326. Hereafter cited in the text as "HP."

17 Besides Žižek's "Neighbors and Other Monsters" (see note #1 of this chapter) and his contributions to *Contingency, Hegemony, Universality* (see notes #10, 11, and 16 of this chapter), consult, for instance, his *The Ticklish Subject: The Absent Centre of Political Ontology* (London: Verso, 2000).

18 Jacques Lacan, *The Seminar of Jacques Lacan, Book VII: The Ethics of Psychoanalysis*, trans. Dennis Porter (New York: Norton, 1992), 278.

19 Judith Butler, "Competing Universalities," *Contingency, Hegemony, Universality: Contemporary Dialogues on the Left*, by Judith Butler, Ernesto Laclau, and Slavoj Žižek (London: Verso, 2000), 151. Hereafter cited in the text as "CU."

20 Wendy Brown, *Edgework: Critical Essays on Knowledge and Politics* (Princeton: Princeton University Press, 2005), 111–12.

21 Nancy Fraser, "Pragmatism, Feminism, and the Linguistic Turn," *Feminist Contentions: A Philosophical Exchange*, by Seyla Benhabib, Judith Butler, Drucilla Cornell, and Nancy Fraser (New York: Routledge, 1995), 161–2.

22 Judith Butler, "Restaging the Universal: Hegemony and the Limits of Formalism," *Contingency, Hegemony, Universality: Contemporary Dialogues on the Left*, by Judith Butler, Ernesto Laclau, and Slavoj Žižek (London: Verso, 2000), 14; emphasis added. Hereafter cited in the text as "RU."

23 Judith Butler, "Dynamic Conclusions," *Contingency, Hegemony, Universality: Contemporary Dialogues on the Left*, by Judith Butler, Ernesto Laclau, and Slavoj Žižek (London: Verso, 2000), 277.

24 As Žižek explains, "Precisely because of this internality of the Real to the Symbolic, it *is* possible to touch the Real through the Symbolic": "this is what the Lacanian notion of the psychoanalytic *act* is about—the act as a gesture which, by definition, touches the dimension of some impossible Real" ("CS" 121).

25 Judith Butler, *Frames of War: When Is Life Grievable?* (New York: Verso, 2009), 183. Hereafter cited in the text as *FW*.

26 See, for example, Slavoj Žižek, *Violence* (New York: Picador, 2008).

27 Judith Butler, *Parting Ways: Jewishness and the Critique of Zionism* (New York: Columbia University Press, 2012), 40. Hereafter cited in the text as *PW*.

28 Jacques Derrida, *Specters of Marx: The State of the Debt, the Work of Mourning, and the New International*, trans. Peggy Kamuf (New York: Routledge, 2006).

29 Walter Benjamin, "Theses on the Philosophy of History," *Illuminations*, trans. Harry Zohn (New York: Schocken, 1969), 102–3.

30 Jacques Lacan, *The Seminar of Jacques Lacan, Book XX: On Feminine Sexuality, the Limits of Love and Knowledge*, trans. Bruce Fink (New York: Norton, 1999).

Chapter 4

1 Jacques Lacan, *The Seminar of Jacques Lacan, Book VII: The Ethics of Psychoanalysis*, trans. Dennis Porter (New York: Norton, 1992), 314, 319. Hereafter cited in the text as *EP*.

2 For an explanation of how this is the case, see Chapter 2 of my *The Singularity of Being: Lacan and the Immortal Within* (New York: Fordham University Press, 2012).

3 Slavoj Žižek, "Class Struggle or Postmodernism?," *Contingency, Hegemony, Universality: Contemporary Dialogues on the Left*, by Judith Butler, Ernesto Laclau, and Slavoj Žižek (London: Verso, 2000), 122–3.

4 Herbert Marcuse, *Eros and Civilization: A Philosophical Inquiry into Freud* (Boston: Beacon Press, 1955), 155. Hereafter cited in the text as *EC*.

5 Theodor Adorno and Max Horkheimer, *Dialectic of Enlightenment: Philosophical Fragments*, ed. Gunzelin Schmid Noerr, trans. Edmund Jephcott (Stanford: Stanford University Press, 2002).

6 Lauren Berlant, *Cruel Optimism* (Durham: Duke University Press, 2011), 1. Hereafter cited in the text as *CO*.

7 Julia Kristeva, *Intimate Revolt: The Powers and Limits of Psychoanalysis*, trans. Jeanine Herman (New York: Columbia University Press, 2002), 4. Hereafter cited in the text as *IR*.

8   Julia Kristeva, *Hatred and Forgiveness*, trans. Jeanine Herman (New York: Columbia University Press, 2010), 41. Hereafter cited in the text as *HF*.

9   What I am getting at here is the idea that because Scandinavian cultures place much less emphasis on normative codes of gender and sexuality than does North American culture, subject formation in these cultures does not entail the same degree of surplus-repression regarding these matters as does subject formation in North America. This is not to say that these cultures are, generally speaking, less repressive than North American culture. But when it comes to gender and sexuality, there is a noticeable difference, so that when I moved to the United States at the age of nineteen, I was genuinely startled by what, to me, seemed like a pathological obsession with the (presumed) differences between men and women. "Why does this matter to you so much?" "What difference can it possibly make?" I kept asking (and still do). The desperate cultural (or scientific) hunt for the "truth" about men and women, or about "male" and "female" sexuality, made absolutely no sense to me (and still does not).

10 Kaja Silverman, *World Spectators* (Stanford: Stanford University Press, 2000).

11 Žižek explains, among other things, that the ethical act arises from "a principle for which, in clear and sometimes ridiculous contrast to its vulnerability and limitations, the subject is ready to put everything at stake" (*Less Than Nothing: Hegel and the Shadow of Dialectical Materialism* [New York: Verso, 2012], 829).

12 Sara Ahmed, *The Promise of Happiness* (Durham: Duke University Press, 2010), 90. Hereafter cited in the text *PH*.

13 Michel Foucault, *The Birth of Biopolitics: Lectures at the Collège de France, 1978-1979*, trans. Graham Burchell (New York: Picador, 2010).

14 Antonio Gramsci, *Selections from the Prison Notebooks*, trans. and ed. Quintin Hoare and Geoffrey Nowell Smith (New York: International Publishers, 2012), 304–5.

15 Laura Kipnis, *Against Love: A Polemic* (New York: Vintage, 2003), 18. Hereafter cited in the text *AL*.

16 My next book project is tentatively entitled *The Impasses of Justice: Feminism, Queer Theory, and the Ethics of Opting Out*.

17 Lee Edelman, *No Future: Queer Theory and the Death Drive* (Durham: Duke University Press, 2004).

18 Tim Dean, *Unlimited Intimacy: Reflections on the Subculture of Barebacking* (Chicago: University of Chicago Press, 2009).

19	Heather Love, *Feeling Backward: Loss and the Politics of Queer History* (Cambridge, MA: Harvard University Press, 2007).

20	Judith Halberstam, *The Queer Art of Failure* (Durham: Duke University Press, 2011). Hereafter cited in the text as *QF*.

21	Judith Butler, "Competing Universalities," *Contingency, Hegemony, Universality: Contemporary Dialogues on the Left*, by Judith Butler, Ernesto Laclau, and Slavoj Žižek (London: Verso, 2000), 155.

Chapter 5

1	Amy Allen, *The Politics of Our Selves: Power, Autonomy, and Gender in Contemporary Critical Theory* (New York: Columbia University Press, 2008), 180. Hereafter cited in the text as *PS*.

2	For a strong example of this line of thinking, see Wendy Brown, *Regulating Aversion: Tolerance in the Age of Identity and Empire* (Princeton: Princeton University Press, 2006). Many of the queer theorists referred to in Chapters 3 and 4 also stage strong critiques of rights-based approaches.

3	Dominick LaCapra, *Writing History, Writing Trauma* (Baltimore: Johns Hopkins University Press, 2001), 154.

4	Allen provides an excellent overview of the matter in *The Politics of Our Selves*.

5	Judith Butler, "Restaging the Universal: Hegemony and the Limits of Formalism," *Contingency, Hegemony, Universality: Contemporary Dialogues on the Left*, by Judith Butler, Ernesto Laclau, and Slavoj Žižek (London, Verso, 2000), 15.

6	See, for instance, Seyla Benhabib, *Situating the Self: Gender, Community, and Postmodernism in Contemporary Ethics* (New York: Routledge, 1992).

7	Jamieson Webster, *The Life and Death of Psychoanalysis*, (London: Karnac Books, 2011) 112. Hereafter cited in the text as *LD*.

8	Michel Foucault, "Afterword: The Subject and Power," *Michel Foucault: Beyond Structuralism and Hermeneutics*, ed. Hubert Dreyfus and Paul Rabinow (Chicago: University of Chicago Press, 1983), 210.

9	Michel Foucault, *The Essential Works of Michel Foucault*, vol. 3, ed. James Faubion, trans. Robert Hurley et al. (New York: The New Press, 2000), 358.

10	Amy Allen, "Feminism, Foucault, and the Critique of Reason: Re-reading the *History of Madness*," *Foucault Studies*, #16 (September 2013).

11 Jürgen Habermas, *The Philosophical Discourse of Modernity: Twelve Lectures*, trans. Frederick Lawrence (Cambridge, MA: MIT Press, 1987), 322.

12 Seyla Benhabib, *Another Cosmopolitanism* (Oxford: Oxford University Press, 2006), 47. Hereafter cited in the text as *AC*.

13 Seyla Benhabib, *Dignity in Adversity: Human Rights in Troubled Times* (Cambridge, UK: Polity Press, 2011), 73. Hereafter cited in the text as *DA*.

14 Generally speaking, it is worth noting the parallels between Butler's attempts to derive a generalizable set of ethical principles from the Jewish heritage (discussed in Chapter 3) and Benhabib's argument about cultural translation (discussed above).

15 Nancy Fraser, *Scales of Justice: Reimagining Political Space in a Globalizing World* (New York: Columbia University Press, 2010), 21, 148. Hereafter cited in the text as *SJ*.

16 Seyla Benhabib, *The Claims of Culture: Equality and Diversity in the Global Era* (Princeton: Princeton University Press, 2002), 134.

17 Wendy Brown, *Edgework: Critical Essays on Knowledge and Politics* (Princeton: Princeton University Press, 2005), 51.

18 Judith Butler, *Parting Ways: Jewishness and the Critique of Zionism* (New York: Columbia University Press, 2012), 109–10. Hereafter cited in the text as *PW*.

19 Judith Butler, "Competing Universalities," *Contingency, Hegemony, Universality: Contemporary Dialogues on the Left*, by Judith Butler, Ernesto Laclau, and Slavoj Žižek (London: Verso, 2000), 150–1; emphasis added.

20 Slavoj Žižek, "Class Struggle or Postmodernism?," *Contingency, Hegemony, Universality: Contemporary Dialogues on the Left*, by Judith Butler, Ernesto Laclau, and Slavoj Žižek (London: Verso, 2000), 104–5.

21 As Benhabib writes:

> Particularly in the light of recent world political events, faith in international law and human rights has been shaken to its core: an illegal war was carried out against Iraq by the United States and its Allies; the US Patriot Act of 2001 gave the President unlimited and quasi-emergency powers to conduct the so-called "global war on terror"; the war on al-Qaeda in the territories of Pakistan and Afghanistan, originally justifiable according to UN Security Council Resolutions and NATO agreements, has morphed into a kind of nation-building with no clear goals or end in sight. And, adding insult to injury, the Guantanamo Camp in Cuba, Baghram Airbase in Afghanistan, and Abu Ghraib in Iraq have become new sites of the deepest violations of human rights law through the use of torture,

illegal interrogation techniques, and the general flouting of the Geneva Conventions. The cosmopolitan project appears in tatters. (*DA* 14)

22 Slavoj Žižek, "Da Capo senza Fine," *Contingency, Hegemony, Universality: Contemporary Dialogues on the Left*, by Judith Butler, Ernesto Laclau, and Slavoj Žižek (London: Verso, 2000), 218.

23 Judith Butler, "Is Judaism Zionism?," *The Power of Religion in the Public Sphere*, by Judith Butler, Jürgen Habermas, Charles Taylor, and Cornel West (New York: Columbia University Press, 2011), 76. Hereafter cited in the text as "*JZ.*"

24 Hannah Arendt, *The Origins of Totalitarianism* (New York: Harcourt Brace Jovanovich, 1951), 298.

25 Judith Butler, *Precarious Life: The Powers of Mourning and Violence* (New York: Verso, 2004), 89–90. Hereafter cited in the text as *PL.*

26 See, in particular, Chapter 3 of Kristeva's *Hatred and Forgiveness*, trans. Jeanine Herman (New York: Columbia University Press, 2010).

27 Hannah Arendt, *Eichmann in Jerusalem: A Report on the Banality of Evil* (New York: Penguin, 1994), 136.

28 Cornel West, "Prophetic Religion and the Future of Capitalist Civilization," *The Power of Religion in the Public Sphere*, by Judith Butler, Jürgen Habermas, Charles Taylor, and Cornel West (New York, Columbia University Press, 2011), 99.

29 Étienne Balibar, "Cosmopolitanism and Secularism: Controversial Legacies and Prospective Interrogations," *Grey Room* 44 (Summer 2011), 21.

30 Slavoj Žižek, *Less Than Nothing: Hegel and the Shadow of Dialectical Materialism* (New York: Verso, 2012), 1005. Hereafter cited in the text as *LN.*

31 Let me add the following texts to the ones already referenced in Chapter 4: Ann Cvetkovich, *Depression: A Public Feeling* (Durham: Duke University Press, 2012) and David Eng, *The Feeling of Kinship: Queer Liberalism and the Racialization of Intimacy* (Durham: Duke University Press, 2010).

32 David Held, *Cosmopolitanism: Ideals and Realities* (Cambridge, UK: Polity Press, 2010).

INDEX